DAEMNOS

JOSH BROOKES

THE
EVIL
BUNNY

This Edition published in 2018 by, The Evil Bunny
First published in 2015 by Javsco Books

Copyright © 2015 Joshua Braybrooke

Joshua Braybrooke asserts the moral right to be
identified as the author of this work

This is a work of fiction. All characters in this publication
are fictitious and any resemblance to real persons, living
or dead is purely coincidental

ISBN: 978-1-912663-00-2

eBook ISBN: 978-1-912663-01-9

Cover & layout design by Karen M. Dillon

1800223

ACKNOWLEDGEMENTS

This story originally existed as a thirteen episode script. During its unveiling, the series had one—I repeat—*one* dislike.

Thank you to all the people who liked the script back during its inception in 2010. Your unwavering love of the story and characters inspired me to re-imagine the concept into something far greater, and far more exciting.

Thanks to the people involved in the original version. Your hilarious voices made the characters what they were back in the day.

Special thanks to Karen, who, like she said about me in her book, is not getting paid despite all the help she put in.

Suck it.

And lastly, uber duper thanks to all the fans, old and new alike, who pick up this book and read it, furthering my goal of world domination.

You know who you are.

Mwuhaha!

Enjoy the story . . .

For Karen
For everything you do.

the DEMON SOULS series
BOOK ONE

DAEMNOS

PROLOGUE

(Four years in the future)

The agony of being thrown to the floor was far worse than TV shows would have you believe.

This was the thought of the tumbling warrior as he and his comrade were catapulted through the air by a powerful supernatural force.

They crashed to the floor violently, knocking over chairs and tables. With his head, the warrior's comrade even smashed apart the chest they'd never been able to unlock. Strange lights shot out as the lid cracked open; finally free from their prison, they escaped through the windows high up on the walls.

The warrior cried out in pain as his demonically crafted armour barely softened his crash landing, and choked as the air was knocked out of him.

His comrade, the elder of the two, was back on his feet in an instant, hardly dazed even after his head collision, his heavy armour making barely a sound as he dashed to the warrior's side.

"On your feet. This is where it ends."

"Yes," the warrior muttered in reply, as his helmet fell from his head, the joints that held it in place now smashed to pieces. "This is where *we* end it."

"Is it now?"

The warrior tensed at the sound of the voice; it was a dark, cruel voice, steeped in age, evil and unparalleled power.

And yet it was a young voice, an impressive voice. So it should have been: its owner was an impressive looking man.

Bold and strong. Powerful and dangerous.

Imposing.

He was practically emanating—like a field of energy—confidence and sovereignty.

The warrior stood straighter, facing the speaker head on as he converged on them, floating menacingly down from the ceiling like some kind of hostile apparition.

As he landed softly on the metal floor he pulled away his own helmet and threw it at his feet, revealing a face that would have looked handsome if not for the malicious gleam in its eyes.

The rest of the armour fell away, tumbling to the floor, to unveil a normal, human body draped in long black robes. It surprised the warrior to see this evil creature appearing so normal.

But neither he nor his comrade were fooled.

They knew this was no human.

The dangerous being grinned, revealing four razor sharp fangs, two on both rows of teeth, and continued, "This is where *you* end it? Your tenacity is admirable, but your grip on reality appears to have diminished."

"No!" the warrior shouted. "We *will* end it, demon! This is where you die!"

The demon laughed maniacally, throwing his head back in vicious glee.

The warrior glared furiously, hating the monster more now than ever before.

"I am the answer to every question you've had for the past four years," the demon cackled. "I am the cause of every evil you've ever had to face. I am the result of centuries of preparation." His grin widened, and the warrior saw the canines elongating further still. "What exactly do you think you can do to me? You don't have the power to hurt me."

"Not yet," the warrior smirked.

The demon sighed. "Humans are so . . . *strange*. I will never tire of studying you." One more sigh, and then the demon put a hand behind his back.

When it reappeared the warrior saw that it was now holding a gun. He tensed sharply, his eyes widening fearfully; it was a weapon they had designed themselves, so he knew it was extremely powerful.

If the demon fired that pistol . . .

"In a few short hours my demons and I will have what we came for. But before we go any further . . . you will both be dead."

Before the warrior could respond, the demon raised the pistol and fired.

chapter
ONE

(Present Day)

He couldn't help but scream.

This had happened so many times before.

Always the same

Never changing.

This time he could do nothing to stop the feelings of despair and fear that built within his chest. His stomach churned sickeningly, his body shaking with the terror of a damned soul entering the deepest, darkest circle of Hell.

His brain hurt from the strain pressing on his eyes, and though he tried to close them it was as though the lids were being torn open, forcing him to look.

The room was red.

An unnatural shade of crimson. As if someone had thrown a

filter over his eyes and now he could see nothing but red.

Who made it like this? And why?

He wanted to know *why!*

But Badrick Varner wasn't about to get an answer.

In his dreams, he never did.

All he could do was stare, taking in the sheer vastness of his surroundings; the walkways above him, the archways into unseen areas, the ramps to other rooms, and the huge window at one side, so high up on the wall that it was impossible to see through.

It was the biggest room Badrick had ever been in. It was larger than his damn house, plus the five next door.

But it wasn't the room that caused Badrick despair—he had been here many times now—nor was it the loneliness of being in such a vast place without another soul around; it was the *damn red!*

Badrick wasn't sure why he hated it so much. It just felt . . . unnatural, and it had assaulted his nightmares so often now that he could no longer stand it. He stomped around, throwing his body left and right, scratching at his scalp and trying to clench his eyes shut as tightly as he could. Anything to distract himself.

That was when the whispering started.

A horrid voice, speaking words Badrick could not understand. They echoed throughout the entire room, bouncing off the walls and overlapping. Badrick shivered in fear, his eyes darting left and right, his attempts at closing them long forgotten.

This happened every time.

Every dream was the same, following a strict series of events; Badrick would study the room, fret about the red, the whispering would start . . . and then . . .

Just like that, *he* was there.

Standing only a few feet away, his presence tainting the small display that adorned the middle of a decorative pond.

As though he was *supposed* to be there.

An armoured figure.

Badrick could not see his face, could not even see the head; his perception literally would not allow him.

It was as though a forcefield was blocking his eyes, and even his peripheral could not make out a single thing.

He knew the body, the hands and the feet, the details in the armour the figure wore, and the weapon he held. Badrick had seen it enough times that he knew it all like the back of his own hand. But he could never focus on anything higher than that.

He was sure that this unknown person was the source of the whispering. It had to be him; he was the only other person in the room—

An electric white light interrupted Badrick's thoughts and surrounded the figure. As this happened, it balled up a fist, raised it into the air, then brought it crashing down, splashing water everywhere, spreading cracks along the floor and causing the room to rumble.

At the same moment a horrific scream reverberated around the room, deafening Badrick. It sounded like young children shrieking in fear, like the soundtrack to a terrifying horror movie.

He slammed his hands over his ears as his heart jumped in terror, and he screamed along with them.

The scream escalated. Badrick could feel it in every fibre of his bod—

"Badrick!"

In a rush of images, Badrick snapped back to reality as the memory of the previous night's dream vanished.

He realised his eyes had blurred, and he shook his head dazedly to clear them.

"Eh?" he muttered groggily

As the room swam back into focus, he blinked in surprise, only now remembering where he actually was, and he gazed around, taking in the familiar, yet infuriating sights.

His therapist, Doctor Brian, sat opposite, his legs crossed and his pen tapping irritably as he stared at Badrick impatiently.

Oh bloody hell, Badrick thought, as he caught sight of that annoying look. *I forgot I was in this stupid therapy.*

He gazed up at the clock and sighed tiredly, still half in the land of memories, the sound of children screaming rattling around his head.

6:32 PM. Another half an hour to go.

"Are you back with me?" the therapist was asking him.

"What?" Badrick said in reply, his mouth feeling slightly numb.

Doctor Brian also sighed and lowered his clipboard. It had been balanced beneath his pen, which was now poised above the paper, interrupted from its frantic note taking.

"We were talking about your dreams, Badrick, remember? You were telling me about your recurring dream. About the man who talks backwards."

"I was?"

"Yes, you were, right before you faded out of reality and began to daydream."

Badrick ran a hand through his dark brown hair, messing it up but not caring in the slightest. "I'm sorry, Doctor Brian."

Which was a lie.

The doctor shuffled in his seat as he regarded Badrick with harsh, piercing eyes. "This is not the first time you've lost your grip on reality during one of our sessions, Badrick," he tutted. "It's happening more and more. Do you know why?"

Badrick shook his head.

"Well, that's why we're here, isn't it?" Brian rolled his pen between his fingers as he spoke. "To help you act the way you should be."

The way he should be. Badrick heard these words more often than he cared to admit. The very first time was during the worst day of his life; the day of his parent's funeral, all those years ago.

It was the first time he'd met his uncle. He could remember it clearer than anything, as if it happened only the day before. His uncle had just gained custody of him and started the next seven years with the hardest slap to the face Badrick ever received in his life.

"It's your fault!" his uncle had shouted. "If you weren't messing around your mother wouldn't have left the stove on. If you were as good children should be, they would still be alive!"

His face red and stinging, Badrick had only stared in horror.

A shuffling of papers reminded him that he was still in the therapist's office. In response to Brian's statement, he gave the doctor a strained smile and snarled, "Aha."

Doctor Brian nodded, as if his reply told him everything he wanted to know, and scribbled a note on his clipboard. The sound of the scratching pen angered Badrick immediately, a feeling of despair sitting painfully in his heart and making him want to cry out. The scratching continued, as if the noise was a substitute for actually trying to help him, like the doctor couldn't be bothered to do anything else.

Badrick watched him sadly, actually fighting back desperate tears for the first time in years. As the doctor continued to do nothing but write, he clenched his fists in barely contained fury and glanced back at the clock in an attempt to drown out the pen.

6:37 PM.

How the hell was that possible? Only five minutes since he'd looked at the thing last? It felt like hours.

Of course, time standing still was far better than what happened to him earlier.

It was like time had . . . jumped. On his way to Doctor Brian's office, he'd ended up an hour late.

Which made no sense, because he'd left right on time, had even checked his phone in sight of the entrance to ensure he wasn't tardy, and then he'd walked in.

An hour late.

He'd figured his clock was slow, or maybe he'd read it wrong, especially after the receptionist angrily shouted at him for arriving at six instead of five. Apparently, he'd held up their entire schedule.

Doctor Brian had still accepted him into their appointment . . . but still . . . Badrick could not fathom what had happened. If he hadn't known better, he'd have said he time travelled.

Which was stupid.

Either way, it unnerved him, to say the least.

Badrick jumped a little as Doctor Brian spoke once more. "Please continue with what you were saying. About the man who talks backwards."

Badrick tutted and sighed. "What else is there to say? He whispers at me . . . backwards."

"I've heard that you told your last therapist something different. Tell me . . . what did you say to him?"

"Oh for the love of . . . " Badrick rubbed his eyes anxiously. A stabbing fear was building in the pit of his stomach, a fear of what was to come.

It was all happening again. He could tell.

"Go on."

"*Fine!* The man says that psalm twenty three . . . erm . . . colon four or whatever it's called."

Doctor Brian stared at him for a moment, his eyebrow raised in confusion. "He does what?"

"*Though I walk through the valley of the shadow of death, I will fear no evil,*" Badrick recited perfectly. "That one. I never understand it in the dream. It's just noise. But when I wake up I know that's what he's saying. Well . . . backwards."

"You just . . . know?"

"Yes!" Badrick barked. He blinked, and tried to calm his voice. He was getting angry again, and he didn't like it. His rage had a habit of scaring him, as though he thought he was capable of . . . terrible things. Badrick did his best to unclench his fists. "But here's the weird part; I never knew about the thing before the dreams."

"By thing, you mean . . . "

"The psalm, Doctor Brian. Do try to keep up. I'd never heard it before. Not until the very first dream, and then I just woke up . . . knowing about it. After having heard it whispered backwards, that is."

The Doctor stared at him with disbelieving eyes, his mouth twitching as though he were holding back a smirk. "Aha." Another note was scribbled. "Let's talk about your home life."

Badrick sighed dramatically, not bothering to hide his frustration. Better to show *that*, than his fury. He'd known from the start this question was going to spring up. This was the reason he was here after all, even though no one ever said it outright.

It was too obvious. Badrick's last therapist refused to work with him any longer, citing his 'horrible lies about his uncle' to be the problem.

Because *apparently* that wasn't part of his job description. As if he wasn't supposed to deal with lying kids all the time, and help them past it all.

Useless.

Introducing Doctor Brian; he was here to scrutinise these so called 'lies' and see if he would have any luck at doing what the previous therapist failed to do.

The only problem was that the stories Badrick told these idiot shrinks weren't lies at all.

10

But not a single soul believed him. Not even the receptionists. It was ridiculous.

Was his uncle really so awful a person that he was an unbelievable character?

"It's not that good," Badrick muttered in response, treading carefully. He wanted to see how this would work out before he got brazen . . . which he worried was about to happen.

If the doctor pushed the wrong button . . . these days he didn't have a lot of self-control.

"Could you elaborate?"

That was all Brian said.

And, for reasons Badrick didn't truly understand, it sent him into a rage.

Maybe it was the nonchalant way the doctor had spoken. Maybe it was the smirk that told Badrick he would not be believed no matter what he said.

It could have been anything.

In the end it didn't matter.

The doctor knew *exactly* what the elaboration would be because he was here to scrutinise the 'lies'. Badrick's head buzzed with anger, fuelled by an overwhelming feeling of loneliness—there truly was no one who would help him—and he couldn't help but bare his teeth at Doctor Brian.

Losing control, he kicked his glass of water from the table. It smashed on the wooden floor, spilling the liquid all over the place. The doctor jumped in surprise, his pen flying out of his hand and landing, almost comically, straight into the waste paper basket beside his chair.

Badrick sat forward and treated him to his most furious glare. "What about this then?" he snarled, his hands shaking as he fought back tears. "This morning I woke up from my nightmare *again*, so I went down to get an early breakfast. Before I'd even gotten downstairs my uncle appeared, yelling at me, holding a vodka bottle, and punched me in the face. Right on my right eye."

Doctor Brian said nothing, only continued to watch him.

So Badrick continued, "I've lived in fear, been kicked, punched, had things thrown at me, starved, grounded for months on end for no reason, made to feel scared and alone . . . for seven years, doctor. *Seven!*"

"What do you mean 'made to feel scared and alone'?"

"My uncle plays the psychological game well. He slams doors just so I can hear them, just so I know to fear him, just so I can hear his anger once he's forced me upstairs without any dinner. I mean having my school work thrown at me, told it was garbage and trash and . . . words you don't even want me to repeat.

"I get punished for non-important things. Stuff so inconsequential you'd make fun of me if it upset *me*. One time, right, a film about Jesus was on TV—"

"Whoa there, Badrick. I am not here to listen to your religious—"

"This has nothing to do with my religious views, you idiot. I'm not bashing Jesus, so would you be quiet and let me talk?"

The doctor nodded slowly. "Alright, continue."

"A film about Jesus was on the television. It was just some stupid movie about his life and crap like that, right? At one point there was a part with some guy I don't even know . . . I'm not even certain he was that important. Could have been *anyone* for all I know, maybe Judas or someone else from his super hero gang. Who knows?

"Anyway, this guy says something random at one point. Not even anything intellectual. If I remember the line was, 'He is disheartened about the choices the people have made'. Something utterly random. Something not in the freakin' bible.

"And to make conversation, I turned to my uncle and said, 'I didn't know he said that'."

The doctor frowned in confusion. Badrick wasn't surprised; he was rambling now, barely coherent with his words. "What do you—"

"I mean I was trying to sound a little smart to impress him. I don't freakin' know, alright? I was, like, nine. Nine year olds just say stuff. Any old stuff. And you nod along and smile and laugh at how they try to be like you. I just wanted to say something so I said the first thing that popped into my head. I can't explain the logic behind a nine year old's thoughts!"

Badrick took a deep breath and glanced at the clock one more time. Their hour was almost up, thankfully. Maybe this would be the last thing they talked about today. He took a few more breaths, and then continued.

"So picture this; a character in a film says something about Jesus. I want to try and talk to my uncle normally. I think I believed that it was a bible quote. I know better now, of course. I say the first thing I can think of to my uncle, that I never knew *this* character said that in the story of Jesus."

"And what was the result, Badrick?"

The doctor jumped in his chair again as Badrick slammed his fists upon the table, this time his clipboard flying across the room and crashing to a stop in the corner. "I was screamed at for not knowing that line from the story. I was punished with no dinner, and he threw the entire contents of my school bag at me whilst screaming how worthless I was. Ever had the stuff from a maths set lobbed at you? There's some sharp stuff in those metal boxes." Badrick leaned in even closer. "It was a bloody dramatisation, Doctor Brian. Do you understand? A freakin' TV movie. It was a made-up line for the film, it wasn't important whatsoever, and it was *not* in the goddamn bible!

"Either way, expecting a nine year old to have the whole damn book memorised is bloody ridiculous, and punishing them for it is not just moronic, it's *evil*.

"But let me tell you, doctor, my uncle is a drunk. Not only that, but even if this line had been the most important quote from the bible, my uncle would have had no clue either. That didn't matter. It wasn't important. He simply saw a chance to enforce his power over me."

Doctor Brian's eyes were somewhat wide now, and it amused Badrick to imagine the cogs clunking pitifully in the psychiatrist's mind. This man wasn't going to help him. Judging by the expression he wore it appeared as though he was going to tread the same path of mocking disbelief everyone took.

So Badrick couldn't help but take what he could get; if he couldn't get help he would draw amusement from the man's discomfort, using the doctor's unease to calm himself. He wasn't sure what he was thinking, but at least Badrick managed to shock him.

"Do you have any kids, Doctor Brian?" he asked, interrupting the tense silence that had ensued after he'd finished his story.

A proud smile lifted the man's features, and Brian nodded, saying, "I have two sons."

Badrick didn't let him smile for long. "Would you ever take one of your son's school books and smack him on his thigh as hard as your arm muscles would allow because you apparently felt 'threatened'?"

The doctor looked horrified at the question, and he scowled at Badrick as if he'd actually been accused of doing such a thing. "Of course not. That's atrocious."

"I was eight, Doctor Brian. My uncle was shouting at me, told me to get my maths book, and when I came back I was so agitated that I slapped it against my leg with *attitude*. To show him I was getting impatient with his abuse. He brought me over, snatched it from my hands, and smacked with it. Just like I said.

"*Eight!* Do you honestly believe that a forty year old feels 'threatened' by an eight year old in any circumstance? Especially one who showed childish attitude. You'd laugh, if anything. Saying he felt threatened was a lie to defend his actions and give him an excuse to hit me."

Badrick fell back into his chair; he actually felt out of breath now. He'd been talking for what felt like hours, and so he simply sat back, allowing the impact of his words to sink in as he finally drifted into silence.

There was no way to know what would follow, but Badrick could never do anything but tell the truth. Any lies would make things harder.

It was up to *them* to distinguish the truth from the lies.

Something they had so far failed to do.

Brian gently twirled a second pen—which he'd retrieved from his pocket—between his fingers for a long time, chewing his lip and watching Badrick, as if waiting for more. When Badrick continued to stay silent, the doctor cleared his throat and slowly said, "You say your uncle punched you in the face this morning."

"You don't believe me," Badrick scoffed and tapped his hand on the arm of his chair in resignation. The feeling of despair returned to the pit of his stomach. It was unbelievably unbearable.

He wasn't sure how much longer he could do this.

"I believe you believe it."

"Well, *you* believe it instead. That'd be much more helpful."

Doctor Brian appeared to temporarily lose his cool, and he sat forward to say, "Badrick! If your uncle had hit you this morning, don't you think you'd have a broken nose? Or a black eye? Or the slightest cut to show for it?"

Badrick felt the muscles in his arms tense with anger as he watched Brian place his various pens onto the table, and start to tidy up the desk. It appeared their meeting was ending soon, and Brian was planning on finishing it with this final, horrible dismissal.

But Badrick could not deny the doctor's logic.

Because it was true. He should've been black and blue as a blackcurrant. And this morning, when he'd left for school, a small cut and an almighty bruised eye marked his encounter with his uncle's fist.

It had been such a terrible wound that this time—*this time*—Badrick had hoped it was enough to stay. This time he might have gotten lucky and finally have proof.

But by the time he'd reached the school gates his face had completely healed. There wasn't even a trace left.

Per the usual.

As always, what he'd gathered to be an enhanced healing of some kind, maybe a disease that no one managed to identify at his birth—and not a soul believed to be real—left him with nothing but hopelessness.

Because how was he supposed to prove the abuse if he had no injuries to help him do it?

Then again, why did everyone so easily dismiss his claims? Not a single person ever believed him, all the way from other kids to teachers, therapists and even people on the street.

No matter who he turned to . . . *no one*.

Surely there was someone out there who thought there might be something honest to a small child crying on the road, pleading with strangers to help him.

"I'll tell you what I think," Doctor Brian continued, sitting up in his chair. "I think the horror of losing your parents in such a violent manner has left you traumatised. You feel the need to create fantasies because it's better than living in the real world with how you really feel. I think you still haven't accepted your parents' deaths yet, not properly, and therefore try to retreat from your pain."

Badrick didn't say anything. He only stared at the doctor in complete, and utter disbelief.

How, in the name of holy hell, had he come to *that* conclusion!?!

"I'm not lying," Badrick whispered. "I promise you . . . I'm not."

"I believe you believe you're not lying," the doctor said.

The words ringed in Badrick's ears. His mind flared with indignation.

And then everything went fuzzy.

A white hot pulse raged within Badrick; hotter than he'd ever experienced before, his every sense fogged. The fury escalating within him in that moment was so intense he could feel pain in his chest; it was unnatural, vicious, capable of terrible things.

Beneath the monster rising within, Badrick felt a terror at the cruelty behind the anger, actually fearing himself.

But it was not enough to quell him.

And before he even knew what he was doing he was reaching for the pens on the table with the intent on driving one through Doctor Brian's eye.

He had barely moved when he heard a third voice in the room. One that hadn't been there before.

"*Hello, boy!*"

chapter
TWO

Ⓐ Ψ Ⓜ

Badrick jumped to his feet in fright and swivelled, looking for the source of the voice. His eyes were wide with an indescribable sense of fear—why was he scared?—and he thought he was about to start sweating. A sense of pressure was hurting his mind, and a pain stabbed at his chest, deep inside, as if inside his soul, ripping it agonisingly.

And then he saw it.

In the corner of the room.

The source of the voice.

Him.

The same figure from his dream . . .

The armour, blood red, the black leathery under-suit, the huge gun in the man's hands . . . *everything* was the same.

Including Badrick's inability to look at the man's head.

He opened his mouth to cry out in alarm, but before he could the figure spread his hands, the weapon still gripped in one of them, and laughed. It echoed throughout the room, reverberating from the walls and hitting Badrick's ears like an explosion.

It was so loud that Badrick slammed his hands over them and clenched his eyes shut against the din.

He stayed like that for quite a while, until he was sure the noise had ended. He tried to open his eyes slowly, fearful of seeing the figure still standing there.

It was only when he noticed the decorative pond that he flung them open completely, his mouth dropping open in horror.

The therapist's room was gone.

Badrick whipped around, turning left and right, swivelling on the balls of his feet as he stared around in shock and disbelief.

It couldn't be. It was *impossible*.

He was in *the* room.

The huge hall, with the walkways above his head, the archways into rooms on either side . . . and the window, high up near the ceiling.

But this time his vision wasn't tinted red.

This time everything was normal. He could see it all now. Clear as day.

The walls had a blue-gray tinge to them, and appeared to be made of a kind of metal, or maybe concrete, or some other kind of building material. The decorative pond didn't look like blood, as it so often had, and the glass in the window was now clear, no longer stained with colour.

Badrick was frantic, his mind trying, and failing, to get over the impossibility of him being here, a place from his dreams, when he had been somewhere else, somewhere real, not two seconds ago.

"How are things?"

The voice interrupted his panic, and Badrick lowered his gaze to see the figure still there, standing in the pond where he always was. With a moan of frustration, Badrick struggled to get even a glimpse of the man's head, but ultimately failed.

Was it armoured like the rest of him?

Or was his face exposed?

"What . . . the . . . " was all he could mutter.

"Your anger isn't building up again, is it? You should be more careful."

Badrick wasn't listening; he was desperately trying to look this man in the eye. But even in his peripheral, it was impossible. It was as if the same forcefield from the dreams protected him.

It was like he just . . . *ended*, but Badrick knew he must have a head. How else would he be speaking?

Somehow, despite his panic and fear, Badrick succeeded in getting his tongue to obey his barely rational mind and managed to shout a simple, "What the hell is this!?!" The only response he received was another cackle. "Who are you?"

"You should know that by now, Badrick." The figure spoke slowly, with a voice that was cruel, laced with malice, not to mention uneven tones and decibels, suggesting a hefty element of insanity. "I have always been here. You have always felt me."

A terrified chill ran down Badrick's spine. He shivered fearfully.

But then a soft chuckle came from the figure, and incredibly this seemed to help Badrick compose himself. He didn't like being mocked, no matter who it was, and that chuckle had been extremely derisive.

It helped him overcome his fear and get his anger back. Terror was useless to him; rage he could substitute for bravery. It was just sufficient for him to look this man in the face (or close enough) and shout, "That doesn't answer my question!"

"Doesn't it!?!"

"No!" Badrick roared. "Who are you? What is this place? What's going on? Stop playing games and just answer me."

"Your anger needs controlling, Badrick," the red figure taunted him. "Look at you. You're fearful of me, yet you're directing that fear into anger. That's good, but if you could control that utterly, then you'd have power beyond imagining."

The figure dropped his weapon, which splashed into the water, and raised his arms. As Badrick stared in horror both of his hands burst into flames.

"Mr Varner?"

Badrick started as he became aware of another presence in the hall. A small memory of some kind of doctor crept into the forefront of his mind.

"Looks like someone wants you," the figure crooned, the fire in his hands spreading down his arms. "Put the pen down, Badrick, and I'll be seeing you soon."

"Badrick!"

This angered shout infuriated him so much that he turned to confront whoever was yelling at him. He opened his mouth to swear furiously . . .

When everything changed again.

He was back in the psychiatrist's office. Doctor Brian was standing, one hand still half on the arm of his chair and his eyes regarding Badrick, not with concern, but wariness.

The hall was gone.

"Eh . . . " was all Badrick managed to say.

"What the hell just happened?" Doctor Brian demanded loudly, completely failing to remain professional.

"What . . . um . . . what?"

Badrick was swaying on his feet now, a feeling of dizziness overriding his senses, so he gingerly reached for his chair. He fell into its cushions with a heavy thump, bouncing off one of the arms, moaning painfully as the world lurched upon his descent.

What had just happened?

The last thing he could remember . . . he was about to . . . he was angry . . . hadn't he been angry about something?

Badrick blinked his eyes, still ignoring the blustering doctor. Now that he was sitting down calm and steady, images were flooding back to him; the hall, the armoured figure.

He'd had some kind of delusion, one so powerful that it literally made him groggy. His original idea that he'd been transported, he could now see, was ridiculous. He had been standing in this room the entire time, while Doctor Brian watched him converse with phantoms.

Great. Like that doesn't make me look crazy.

Though it wasn't like he could prove he wasn't . . .

"Are you back with me?" Doctor Brian was asking, his voice only just puncturing the haze in Badrick's head.

" . . . Yeah."

The doctor nodded. "Good . . . because I think we're done here."

Badrick's ears practically pricked as he detected something in the man's voice. He looked up at his psychiatrist warily. "For today?" he asked, already guessing the answer.

That was quick.

"These sessions aren't helping, are they? I can tell they're not, and frankly I believe you being transferred to me was a bad idea. It's confused you. You don't know who you're talking to anymore."

The doctor reached for his briefcase and opened it, retrieving a jet black laptop. He opened it and booted it, tapping impatiently on his armchair as he waited for the computer to load.

Badrick frowned confusedly when he heard the doctor mutter,

"Damn executive orders." But otherwise he did not comment, only waited, worried about what was going on.

"Done," said the doctor after a moment. He reached into his briefcase once more, and produced a small business card, handing it to Badrick.

Badrick took it, but utterly failed to study it, unable to do anything but stare at the doctor. Was this actually happening already? Brian was done with him?

"I'm referring you to a specialist."

"You're what?" Badrick snapped out of his daze and sat up straighter, his eyes darting to the card. Upon it, written in fancy ink, was an address. "A *specialist?* So your diagnosis is I'm confused about who I'm talking to, and to fix that you're sending me to another total stranger?"

"Yes. Someone who is better trained to deal with this sort of thing. Violence, I can handle, but what just happened here is way out of my league."

Badrick twirled the card between his fingers, his eyes boring into Brian's face. "You're supposed to be trained to deal with anything."

"Says who?"

"*You!* When we first met. You idiot!"

Brian's nostrils flared angrily, but he otherwise ignored the insult. "I want you to go to the address written on the card right now. I will call ahead and tell them to expect you."

"Right now?" Badrick retorted disbelievingly. "It's past seven at night. And I don't have an appointment. Why don't you book one?"

"I can't do that, Mr Varner. As your psychologist I am instructing you to go to this address immediately. If you do not, I will be ringing your uncle."

Doctor Brian cried out in pain as the pointed edge of the card found his cheek, and opened a small cut on his face. Satisfied that his aim was good, Badrick lowered his throwing arm.

"Fine!" he roared lividly. Badrick said no more. Picking up his bag, he stormed out of the room.

The receptionist jumped back and eyed him warily as he barged through the reception and kicked open the front doors, almost as though she expected him to attack her at any moment.

Badrick stood at the top of the steps for a moment, breathing heavily through his rage. He thought about what the doctor had said about the specialist, and immediately felt the need to disobey him, simply because of the threat attached.

But it was because of that threat that Badrick succumbed to resignation, closed his eyes tiredly, hefted his school bag and made his way out of the car park.

He couldn't go home.

He couldn't go back to that . . . not yet.

Badrick had memorised the address before he threw the card at Brian. Luckily too, because he never got it back.

He allowed two fire engines, which were hurtling down the road at incredible speeds, their panicked sirens startling every motorist nearby, to pass him before he crossed the road and walked back into town.

Apart from that disturbance, the evening was quiet. Hardly anyone seemed to be around, aside from the odd car. Everything was still, and not even the usually rowdy gangs that hung around the *Odd Monument* ruined the calm.

Badrick took a moment to study the monument as he passed it. It wasn't really a monument exactly, and no one in the town actually knew what it was. It was the size of a car, purple in colour, shaped like a tear drop, and appeared to have fallen on its side at some point.

In a gap that ran through it Badrick could see a glowing, blue light, whose source he could not determine. It was like it just shone from nowhere inside, and he didn't understand how in the slightest.

No one in the town did.

No one alive could even remember where it had come from.

It was just *there*. An old memory in an old forgotten town in the middle of old England.

Badrick smiled slightly—he'd always liked the design of this thing—and ran a hand across the aptly named *Odd Monument* before he turned away and continued on to the address he was looking for.

He immediately jumped back, pressing against the monument as a motorbike zipped past, its driver and backseat rider whooping with glee, almost running him down and killing him on the spot.

They barely missed, and as they vanished down the road Badrick couldn't help but scream, "Watch it, you idiots!"

Of course they didn't hear him. There was no way they could have, but it always felt better to shout at bad drivers than it did not to.

With a sigh, he let go of his annoyance, and hurried down the road, weaving through the streets expertly. He'd never been to this address before, but he knew the town, and if he didn't recognise an address then it had to be one of the only two areas he'd never visited.

Luckily for him, it turned out to be his first choice. It was tucked away behind a long stretch of bushes along the main road, the entrance haphazardly cut into them, but the address was clearly written on a signpost outside. He quickly pushed open the gate with relief; it was getting dark now and he wanted to get inside somewhere brightly lit. He wasn't too fond of being outside at this time of the evening.

His relief vanished however when he realised he'd stumbled

upon a church.

His eyes darted between the various displays of gothic architecture as a growing sense of unease brewed in his stomach, and he felt a stinging of fear at the ominous way the building seemed to loom over him across the darkening sky.

However, it wasn't enough to drown out his incredulous reaction to the fact that it was, above all, a *church*.

"Are you kidding me?" he muttered aloud. "A church? What does he think I am? Satan?" He tapped his fingers on the gate, wondering what the point of this was and whether or not it was worth it.

Maybe he *should* just go home.

This wasn't where he wanted to be.

Badrick was about to leave; about to turn around and stride away without a second glance.

But something made him stay. Something deep inside, something he couldn't quite pinpoint. Call it curiosity or stupidity; Badrick wasn't sure which he boasted. In the end it didn't matter; the next thing he knew he was pushing open the huge ornate doors and stepping over the threshold.

Inside was pretty dapper, as churches went. He hadn't been to many, but none he'd ever stepped foot in had been this glamorous in their decor.

There was gold everywhere, or at the very least bronze—the dying light coming through the windows made it hard to tell. Either way, there was positively tons of it, and Badrick figured that if he made off with even one percent of it he'd be far richer by tomorrow.

It was the most blingin' church ever.

He never got the chance to steal anything however—not that he was *seriously* considering it—because at that very moment the creaking of an opening door sounded on the other side of the hall and a figure stepped into view.

It was a man; a priest, walking from some kind of back room over to an ornate altar that rested right in the middle of . . . was it a stage?

Badrick didn't know.

The priest stopped sharply when he spotted Badrick standing there. Their eyes met for a moment, blue meeting green, and an awkward silence ensued.

But then he cleared his throat and said, "Mr Varner, I presume."

"That's me."

"Good." The priest nodded sharply and beckoned him over with a rapid hand gesture. "My name is Hans. Please come over. I've had a hell of a day and I'd like to get this done as fast as possible. So we're just going to get it done, no small talk."

Father Hans certainly didn't talk like a priest, which gave Badrick some serious concerns about the wisdom of his choice to walk through that door. His hesitation stopped him from moving, something which seemed to irritate Hans immensely.

"Come on, boy, it's perfectly safe. Get over here and let's get this done."

Once more, Badrick wondered whether he was curious or stupid as he foolishly opened his mouth and asked, "Get what done?"

"Sit on the altar, please."

"What are you—"

"Mr Varner, for the love of God, *please*!"

He didn't know whether to laugh at Hans' agitation or run from it. But seeing as he was definitely far more curious than he was afraid, Badrick shrugged and walked over to the aforementioned altar, dropping his schoolbag along the way and jumping atop it.

He had hardly a second to look around before the priest yanked at his sleeve to reveal what looked like an enlarged iPod strapped to his arm. Hans tapped on it rapidly, beeping sounds echoing through the silence of the empty church.

"What is—" Badrick was interrupted by the sudden loss of surface beneath his hands. He yanked them away from their places on the altar and stared, eyes wide as two . . . *things* emerged from inside.

They rose to head height before stopping; things that Badrick likened to two solar panels, one on either side. The panels faced him, and started to glow.

"Er . . . "

"Quiet, please."

"No, screw you." Badrick decided he'd had enough. He tried to jump from the altar, but as he attempted to do so Hans pushed him back, pinning him down. "Get off me!"

"Jesus!" Hans sighed, frustrated. "I'm scanning you to see if you have what I'm looking for. You *are* the mental kid who was referred to me, right?"

"I'm—*hey!*"

"Just hold still, I'm not going to hurt you."

Badrick settled down, though he kept his eye on Hans. He didn't have a clue as to what was going on, but it at least *did* seem like he wasn't in danger. He would get out of here as soon as he could, though. This was too weird and Badrick didn't like it.

But right at that moment what choice did he have but to do what Hans told him?

On either side, the solar panel things made whirring sounds, giving Badrick the impression that he was literally being x-rayed. After a few uncomfortable moments, during which neither of them spoke, they made a series of clunking sounds . . . then finally nothing.

The solar panels stopped glowing and all went quiet once more.

"Can I go now?" Badrick asked, a little too quickly.

Hans didn't say anything at first; he only stared at his iPod.

But then, "Oh . . . "

"Oh? *What's oh!?!*"

Hans hesitated for a moment. He glanced up at Badrick with an expression that made him extremely uncomfortable and for a few seconds Badrick thought he saw anger in Hans' eyes.

But then he seemed to recover and, as if he'd never been anything but, adopted a happy smile. "Just as I thought," he said cheerfully, though Badrick had the distinct impression that he was lying. "Please, Mr Varner, follow me. I will now explain everything to you. I think you're due that much."

He indicated to the back room he'd emerged from. Badrick hopped down from the altar, giving Hans a questioning glance, but the priest only smiled and pointed more forcefully.

Sighing resignedly, Badrick wandered over and pushed the door open. Light shone out through the gap, and he squinted against the glare.

When his eyes had adjusted to the brightness he opened them once more, only to see that he'd walked into a tiny, completely empty room. It was horribly confining; the walls were made of brick with a sickly yellow paint slapped over them, and the floor was nothing but rocky stone.

"What . . . Is this it?" he managed to say. "Why—"

He got no further. A powerful blow connected with the back of his head, and Badrick fell to the floor, unconscious.

chapter
THREE

Badrick's screams reverberated throughout the room as he wrestled against the straps that bound him, his body writhing violently on the metal table. His wrists were now raw after what had to have been hours of torment. Badrick didn't really know how long he'd been here; the agony was destroying his coherency.

However, between his shrieks and fits, he *was* able to determine two things.

One; there were two other people in the room.

Two; they were jabbing him with metal poles that sent arcs of electricity flowing through his convulsing body.

That was the source of the pain.

Every now and then, as he thrashed and roared, Badrick would catch snippets of hurried conversation between his two torturers.

"His demon is retreating."

"We have to go deeper."

"We could damage his soul."

"If the energy spike was him, then we have to risk it."

"But it's not—"

The man was cut off as Badrick's foot broke free of its restraints and kicked him in the face. He recoiled and fell back into a surgical table laden with strange looking instruments.

"Alaric!"

"I'm alright. My demon will fix the break."

Badrick's victim reappeared, blood streaming down his face, and grabbed hold of his flailing leg, strapping it back down. "Do it. Go deeper."

Badrick's fresh screams were louder than ever before.

*

The scent of stale air assailed Badrick's senses, and his eyes flung open. Bright light blinded him and he squinted against the glare. Eventually the light became bearable and he let his lids open, although he did so slowly.

He found himself staring at a perfectly plain ceiling. It looked to be made out of metal, though Badrick could not be sure.

Deciding he wanted a better view, he attempted to sit up, only to realise that his entire body felt like it had been steamrolled. He moaned with the numerous aches and pains as he forced himself to sit up. A softness stroked his palms and he realised he was sitting on a single bed, covered with clean white sheets.

After he had managed to sit up straight, Badrick took the time to study the rest of his surroundings.

He was in a small room, the walls and floor the exact same blue-gray colour as the ceiling. There was nothing except the bed and a small light above him. Not even a window.

Using his hand to shield his eyes from the light, Badrick gently moved his legs off the bed and cradled his head.

He felt very strange . . . sort of light headed and oddly separate from the world. Like he wasn't really there, his body nothing more than an apparition.

Badrick could barely focus, everything was slightly blurred, and it wasn't until he'd struggled to his feet that he noticed the biggest oddity in his prison cell (because what else could this room have been?).

Three of the walls were perfectly normal. But the fourth wasn't even a wall at all.

It was somewhat transparent, and shimmering as if it was entirely made out of light or energy or something. Badrick stared at it in stunned silence, unsure of what to make of this new development. Surely his eyes were tricking him . . . right?

But no, that was impossible. This thing was real. It was definitely there. He could hear it buzzing slightly, humming, as though powered by electricity; a shimmering mass of energy with a strange colourful hue to it, as though blue and purple light were swirling in this one point in space.

He watched with wary fascination as it rippled, and reached a careful hand towards it.

Was it solid? Or could he go through it?

Badrick felt elation as his fingers began to pass through the energy, only to have his hopes immediately dashed when he felt resistance and could push no more.

He took his hand away and chewed his lip in thought. It appeared as though the strange light was keeping him in. There was no wall on this side, only the light. Beyond it, Badrick could see a hallway.

A means of escape perhaps?

If he could just get through the light . . .

Determined to prove he could break this . . . *forcefield*, Badrick placed both his hands against the energy wall and pushed as hard as he could. His arms strained with the effort, but he grinned as his palms began to sink through and the light began to bend under the pressure.

It was working.

Just a little more and he might be able to—

He cried out in alarm and pain as a jolt of electricity stung his hands and threw him backwards. He fell to the floor, hard, banging around his already aching muscles.

With his fingers jerking from the volts and his tailbone hurting from the fall, he sat up painfully and regarded the energy with angry eyes, cursing everything from crap therapists to ninjas disguised as priests.

That was the last thing he could remember; Father Hans falcon punching him from behind. Then he woke up here.

No . . . wait. That wasn't true . . . there was something else . . .

With a jolt of horror the memories of the torture he'd endured flashed into Badrick's mind; he remembered their aggression and the electrified metal poles they jabbed him with. Gasping from the recollections, Badrick raised his hands and pulled back his sleeves, studying with sadness the red marks on his wrists, cuts and bruises marring the Caucasian white.

His ankles had suffered similar abuse.

And upon closer inspection he found that his ribs and chest were a deep shade of purple.

His clothes were in a similar state; they were half ripped to shreds and appeared to have burn holes in them.

Possibly from the electric poles.

Badrick gulped, trying to control his panic. He forced himself to focus and studied his cell one last time, thinking hard.

He'd been kidnapped, tortured and imprisoned.

But why?

And by who?

Had Doctor Brian known this would happen when he'd sent him to Hans?

Surely.

Right?

The creepy bastard was going to murder him.

Or maybe it was something more sinister.

Whatever conclusion Badrick may have eventually arrived at, he never got the chance to find out what it would be; a large clanging interrupted him and with a start he became aware of someone walking into view on the opposite side of the forcefield.

"Ah, awake are we? I thought I heard sounds." It was a man, with brown hair a shade similar to Badrick's and a smile that seemed genuinely kind. He lifted a finger to the forcefield, watching as Badrick instinctively shuffled away. With an amused chuckle the man tapped the wall of energy . . .

And it vanished, dissipating in an instant.

Badrick blinked in surprise. "How did you do that?" he found himself asking. "Who are you?"

The man clapped his hands and smiled once again. "Well, that's what you're going to find out. Come on . . . we're going to tell you everything."

He turned away and disappeared down the hall, returning moments later when he realised Badrick hadn't followed.

"You comin'?"

Badrick gulped, and muttered, "The last time someone said that to me, I got kidnapped and tortured."

The man grimaced and stepped into the cell, hunching down so he was at Badrick's level. "Yeah . . . erm . . . sorry about that. This probably doesn't help, but I promise you it was necessary.

For your own good, actually. We wouldn't have done it if it wasn't."

"I'm supposed to believe that?"

It was a fair question, which the man seemed to realise. He held his hands out, palms upwards. "Look, I'm not very good at explaining all this. But no tricks this time, I promise. You can knock me out and run that way if I pull any dodgy crap." He pointed haphazardly over his shoulder.

Badrick hesitated for a long time. Too much had happened to him in the last . . . however long it had been for him to truly trust anyone right then.

Clocks lying to him, horrible nightmares, mental hallucinations, karate priests . . . torture . . .

But something about this man, and the kind, reassuring smile on his face . . . it calmed Badrick, and for the first time in as long as he could remember he felt genuinely safe.

Which was utterly stupid, because surely this guy had been part of the torturing.

Nevertheless, Badrick stumbled to his feet, with the help of the guy, and slowly followed him out of the cell. It wasn't like he had anywhere else to go, after all. He just had to hope it would get better than this from now on.

They passed more prison cells as they shuffled down the hallway, each with their own forcefield door. Many had people inside, most simply sitting on their beds, heads in their hands, though others were punching at the energy blocking them in.

It felt so wrong, seeing them in their captivity, walking past them as though it were normal, and Badrick was already reconsidering his notion of safety.

But it wasn't until they passed cell forty two that his feelings of security vanished from his head completely.

As they drew up beside it, something smashed against the

forcefield so violently that Badrick automatically turned to look.

What he saw made his heart stop.

He fell back, screaming in terror, his vocal chords ripping to pieces as he tried to back away, but was stopped by the hallway wall, causing him to stumble.

It was a monster.

A bloody *monster*.

Its skin was brown, and it was muscular, with rippling arms and legs. Horns and ebony spikes protruded from half its body, and its face was elongated into a reptilian snout, like some kind of mutant dinosaur.

The creature's mouth was full of razor sharp teeth, many of them extending past the mouth.

The monster smacked the forcefield and roared viciously, saliva flying everywhere.

"Oops, sorry," said the man, with the air of someone apologising for uttering a minor swear word. "Forgot he was down here." He helped Badrick to his feet. "Don't mind him, he's just grumpy 'cause we ain't fed him yet today."

Badrick wanted to shout. Demand to know what he was looking at. Use the words he'd been gifted with in all his years of privileged education.

But he was in so much shock that all that came out was, "*Wha' irra'?*"

The man frowned. "Excuse me?"

Badrick coughed, clearing his throat, and tried again. Slowly.

"What . . . is . . . that?"

"Kalik demon," the man smiled. "Stupid creatures, the lot of them. Pointless things, if you ask me. Come on, we'll be late."

And he walked away. As if this did not demand further discussion. Unable to believe what was going on, Badrick ripped his eyes away from the thrashing monster, knowing from experience it was safely contained, and chased after his departing escort.

"What the hell does that mean?" he demanded as they continued down the never ending corridor. "Who are you? Where am I?"

"It's not really my place to tell you that, I'm afraid. Though I can say my name is Malcolm. I'm the jailor here." Malcolm turned his head to smile in his direction. "Nice to meet you."

"Nice to meet you," Badrick muttered, not knowing what else to say.

The roars and pounding of the monster followed them all the way down, until they finally reached yet another of the forcefields.

Malcolm tapped it with his finger and it immediately disappeared, allowing them to pass.

"How do you do that?"

Malcolm grinned happily and wiggled his fingers. "It's my power. I make shields of energy."

Badrick almost laughed, and repeated, "*You make shields of energy?*"

"That's me." The jailor pushed open a wide door and invited Badrick through. "Come on. We'll be late."

Before he passed over that threshold, Badrick believed he couldn't have seen anything weirder, and that the biggest shocks of the day were behind him.

He was wrong.

He immediately lost the strength in his legs and stumbled back against a wall for the second time, staring up at his new surroundings, his mouth hanging limp and his eyes wide.

It was *the* room.

That massive hall that had haunted him for well over a decade, with the blue-gray walls and walkways spreading above him, connecting either side of the room on various different floors. The decorative pond was in the centre, set into the floor, the water shallow and clear, complete with the small island as well as a strange, swirly sculpture smack in the middle.

And the bloody window was up there too!

"Am I . . . hallucinating again?" he asked shakily. "Do you see this too?"

Malcolm raised an eyebrow questioningly, and looked up in the direction Badrick was facing. "No . . . all I see are pathways."

"I've had dreams about this place. Hallucinations."

"Have you?" Malcolm's other eyebrow joined its companion in surprise. "That's new."

"Is it?"

"Come on," he urged him. "The sooner we get you to the boss, the better. You need to be debriefed as soon as possible."

"Debriefed?"

Malcolm offered no further explanations. He hurried away, gesturing frantically, leading Badrick across the length of the hall. As they traversed it, Badrick craned his neck to look up at the ceiling.

It was so *very* high up.

Badrick actually got dizzy looking at it.

It was only now, free of the red filter and the presence of a terrifying armoured figure, that Badrick was able to appreciate the design structure, and noticed that the walkways were primarily made out of glass, with metal supporting them.

People were hurrying across them, back and forth as though extremely busy. Though Badrick couldn't see clearly from this distance and angle, they seemed to be wearing some kind of weird clothes.

He didn't get to examine further; Malcolm had now abandoned gestures and was proceeding to push him along.

He followed the jailor through an archway that led into a room filled to the brim with computers that looked like they had been designed in a sci-fi movie. Most of the walls were adorned with massive television screens, which showed a variety of different images.

If Badrick had thought the rest of the place had been overly blue, then he had been sorely misled. This room was *insanely* blue, so much that even the light bulbs emitted blue light.

"What the hell?" Badrick grumbled. "What's with the colour?"

"You think that's bad? You should see the RCR. Red everywhere."

"RC . . . what?"

Again, and much to his growing irritation, his questions went unanswered. None of the people in the room paid attention to the newcomers, and Malcolm ushered him through it so fast that Badrick couldn't get a good look at them.

Once they were out of the room, he took Badrick up a flight of stairs and around the corner, right over one of the walkways, to the opposite side. From there, it didn't take Malcolm long to bring him to a perfectly square door, where they immediately stopped.

"We're here," he said proudly. "Knock, and you'll be let in." He held out his hand. "Good luck, mate."

"Er . . . thanks." Badrick took the hand, and Malcolm gave it a firm shake. He then saluted him, before turning on his heel and hurrying away so fast Badrick barely saw him leave. "But wait . . . what . . . "

With a resigned sigh, Badrick faced the door. He studied it for a moment, completely and utterly distrusting of what may lie behind. Still, he raised his hand and gave it a firm, but hesitant, knock.

"Come in."

"How?" Badrick muttered, only now noticing the lack of any kind of opening mechanism.

Like a door handle.

There was a muffled irritated tut from the other side, and Badrick jumped back in surprise as the door flew open, like an automatic door at Tesco's.

Except it went up instead of sideways.

Badrick took a tentative step inside and looked around. The room beyond the door was small, and pretty empty except for a single desk, one lonely bookcase, a stack of shelves with an assortment of junk littering it, as well as two chairs.

Not to mention the man sitting behind the desk, who was watching Badrick intently as he gingerly walked inside.

He was serious looking, with a mop of brown hair lighter than Badrick's, and a handsome, chiselled face.

He was also wearing a uniform that looked like it had been stolen from the navy, except it was bright red instead of white.

"Master Varner." Badrick was gestured inside. Though he was feeling a little irate from all the hand signals being made at him today, he nevertheless sat down opposite the desk. "Welcome, Master Varner," said this new person, "to the Daemonium."

"The what?" Badrick almost snapped back.

"The Daemonium."

"And what, pray tell, is the Daemonium?"

The man behind the desk laughed and offered his hand. Badrick took it reluctantly.

"Brazen," the man said. "Good."

"I've had a hell of a day," Badrick replied honestly. "I just want to know what's going on."

"Well, let's not waste time, then. My name is Sergeant Daniel Reynolds. This is my office. And you are in the HQ of the Daemonium."

"How did I get here?"

"That's not easy to explain without you knowing certain other facts first."

Badrick sighed and rubbed his eyes impatiently, his irritation getting the better of him. "OK. Like I said, what's—"

Reynolds cut him off with a wave of the hand. His face was solemn now, and he was watching Badrick carefully. "I have to warn you, Mr Varner—"

"Badrick."

"I have to warn you, Badrick, that what I am about to tell you is of a very sensitive nature. A lot of it will seem ridiculous to you. You may even be inclined to call me a liar. But what I will tell you today is the truth." He stopped to allow Badrick to reply, but he simply sat and stared, waiting.

"Well, there's really no use beating about the bush. Badrick, demons are real. And I mean vicious, terrifying monsters that will kill you and devour your soul to become more powerful. Such creatures from places mankind would never tread. Monsters that even gods would cower from. I tell you this not to scare you, but to prepare you for what I must tell you next."

He took a moment to apparently gauge Badrick's reaction.

He didn't get one though; all Badrick could do was stare, stunned at being told such a ridiculous thing.

It was impossible. Obviously a lie.

Who did this Reynolds guy think he was?

Then again . . . that thing downstairs . . .

Reynolds reached under his desk and removed a folder, which he dropped onto its surface. He opened it, pulling out sheets of paper and studying them.

"Badrick Varner," he read, "aged seventeen, Caucasian, lives with his uncle, parents deceased, has a history of . . . I don't even know what that means."

"It means I'm *mentally unstable*," Badrick muttered, knowing *exactly* what was in that folder. Though that didn't make him feel better about it; he still couldn't believe his therapists had put *that* down as his 'condition'.

He was glaring at his own knees now, dreading what might be coming next.

Was he in an asylum?

He had to be.

It had all the hallmarks.

Testing.

Torture.

Mean orderlies.

"Why would they call you that?" Reynolds inquired slowly, as if he already knew the answer and just wanted to gauge Badrick's response.

"I don't know," Badrick whispered, unwilling to engage with this man.

"Well, good thing I do, then."

Badrick's ears pricked immediately and he raised his head to gaze at Reynolds. The so-called sergeant smiled, confident he had his visitor's attention, and moved his hand under the table again.

Something clicked. A whirring sound started.

And an image flashed into existence on the table.

Badrick stared it, unable to believe his eyes.

He was looking at a hologram.

A true, honest to God hologram.

"Cool, isn't it?" Reynolds grinned. "We're very advanced here. Courtesy of one of our men."

Badrick was hardly listening; he was staring at the image with wide, fearful eyes.

This was because it was *the man*. As always he was clad entirely in dark red armour, with a black leathery under-suit beneath.

Badrick obviously recognised him immediately.

And this time he could see his face.

Though, not properly, as it was obscured by a huge futuristic helmet, as red as the armour. It didn't look right at all; it was more cube shaped than it was round, like a normal helmet would have been.

But what was worse was the visor; gold coloured, reflective, and it reminded Badrick of a pair of sunglasses, set into the helmet, giving it a very threatening appearance.

It was horrible looking into those emotionless visor-eyes, as if there was nothing behind them. No emotion. No kindness.

Just evil.

"For thousands of years now, Badrick," Reynolds continued, "demons have been found in humans. No one knows why. Not even the demons understand why it keeps happening. Sometimes when a person is born a demon is sucked right out of Hell and trapped within the soul of that baby."

"What does that mean?" Badrick croaked, his eyes still transfixed on the hologram. He could not drag them away from the visor . . . it was entrapping . . . terrifying . . .

"It means chaos," Reynolds sighed heavily. "For one, it grants the human the powers of that demon. We call these people Enthrallers, and let me tell you they are *extremely* dangerous. This place, the Daemonium, is a beyond top-secret organisation, beyond the police, more powerful than the Government, estranged from the world, dedicated only to dealing with these people."

Reynolds last sentence punctured Badrick's bubble of numbness and he glanced over warily, his muscles tensing even further than they had been. "*Deal?*" he repeated. "Deal with them, *how?*"

"First; we find them. Second; we identify their demon. Third; we offer them a place in the Daemonium."

Badrick had never credited himself with smarts. He'd never felt confident that he was an intelligent guy. But he *was* clever enough to piece the puzzle together, and he actually felt like he was going to throw up as he whispered, "And you think I'm one of these . . . Enthrallers?"

Reynolds didn't answer that question. Instead he lifted his hand—Badrick actually flinched as he did so—and pointed at the hologram. "*This* is *your* demon. We identified him only a few hours ago. I apologise for the excruciating torture we put you through. In fairness, it shouldn't have hurt you that much. But . . . this demon really *did not* want us to identify him."

Badrick blinked and stared at the sergeant, unable to believe his ears. This man had just admitted to torturing him, and his only justification was that it shouldn't have hurt that much?

Are you kidding me?

"Why the hell did you push so hard, then!?" he found himself shouting, the memory of the agony all too fresh.

"We have to, Mr Varner," Reynolds told him sincerely. "Do you know how dangerous an unchecked Enthraller is? We had no idea what demon you had inside you. For all we knew you could have been harbouring the next Satan, and let me tell you something, I fought the Devil, and I have no desire to do it again."

Badrick blinked. "You fou—"

"Your demon is called Vulrick," Reynolds interrupted him. "Relatively low-level, thank God, though he does appear to be a Singularis."

"*A what?*"

"More than half the demons out there all have a set of basic powers. Energy ball throwing, super jump, etcetra etcetra. They are known as the Ordinarius. But there *are* demons out there who have . . . *specialised* powers. We call them the Singularis. They are unique, and your demon, as far as we can deduce, appears to be a pyrokinetic, meaning he can throw fire." Reynolds chuckled, and added, "Ridiculous though it may sound, but among demons that's actually quite rare."

He was quiet for a while after that. His eyes scanned the contents of Badrick's folder, his hands shuffling through the pages.

Badrick didn't know what to say anymore. Back at the cell he'd had a focus; find out where he was and what he was doing here.

Now he knew the answers to both those questions, and everything had become so much worse.

Answers were supposed to bring clarity to confusing situations. Help you move through bewilderment. But the ones he'd gotten . . . everything Reynolds had told him, what he'd seen since waking up . . . it just made him numb.

How could he possibly believe any of it? It was silly . . .

No, it was outrageous.

It sounded like something out of a ridiculously bad Hollywood movie.

He couldn't even move. He should have been trying to figure out how to get away, to escape, or to at least fight back.

Something!

These people had tortured him.

But after everything he just couldn't work up the energy.

Reynolds was looking expectantly at him now, the folder closed beside him on the desk.

Badrick stared back, his eyes wide, his mind buzzing.

Eventually, he managed to lick his lips and say the first thing that came to mind. "How can you tell?"

Reynolds lifted an eyebrow. "How can I tell, what?"

"Pyrokinetic," he croaked back.

Reynolds didn't answer for a moment. He drummed his fingers against the desk and chewed his lip thoughtfully.

But then he sighed, rubbed his eyes, and began, "It appears

Vulrick has spent a great deal of energy trying to get you here. He really, really, *really* didn't want us to identify him, but when we did, he was happy enough to tell us a few things. Things like your dreams about this place, and apparently, through some kind of hypnotic suggestion, he has been altering the behaviour of everyone around you. He told us that he did this to your many psychiatrists."

Reynolds fell silent, allowing his words to hit home.

On his part, Badrick couldn't believe what he was hearing. This *Vulrick* person had done *what?*

What a stupid thing to say.

Nobody could do that. Especially not to so many people.

Badrick should have dismissed it all as folly.

And yet . . . he couldn't.

Why would everybody, from professionals to people on the street, ignore the screaming pleas for help from a small child? It didn't make any sense.

It never had.

And what was that word?

Pyrokinetic?

Fire throwing.

Surely that was too convenient to be coincidence. Badrick had never truly believed the stove had been the perpetrator . . .

But no, he couldn't have.

Almost as if Reynolds was reading his mind, he continued, "We also have to give you some bad news. I'm afraid your uncle is dead."

Badrick almost jumped from his seat. "What!?"

"Vulrick. He burned down your house. He murdered your uncle because of how he treated you. He told us that was the one person he never manipulated, and the man's crimes against his Enthraller were punishable by death."

The world seemed to roll upside down. The chair didn't feel solid anymore. What Badrick was hearing made him feel like he was about to fall through it, everything was . . . dizzying. His eyes darted back to the hologram of the demon that was supposedly inside him . . . inside his *soul*.

"Vulrick also wanted us to convey a message to you." Reynolds hesitated for a moment. "He said he's very sorry about your parents. As you always worried, deep down, as you've always instinctively known, it wasn't the stove. It was never him who killed them, but a child cannot always handle the power a demon provides. It's why he spent so much energy getting you to us."

There was silence for a moment. Neither of them spoke, both just sitting on their separate seats.

Badrick continued to watch the hologram, studying the dark red features.

Why?

Why had everything Reynolds said made sense?

It was a story.

A lie.

He was in an asylum.

They were testing him for his reactions.

That was the truth.

But deep down Badrick knew it wasn't. Reynolds was giving it to him the way it was. Everything happening here was real.

"It's not your fault, you know," Reynolds spoke, breaking the silence, "if what Vulrick says is true. You don't punish a child for being unable to drive a car; you can't punish one for this. It was entirely out of your control."

"How . . . " Badrick began, almost cutting him off—he'd barely been listening. "How did . . . *Vulrick* burn down my uncle's house? When did this supposedly happen?"

"About an hour before you visited the therapist," Reynolds

informed him, glancing back into the folder.

"And how is that possible? If he's inside me, how did he burn down my house without me knowing about it?"

Reynolds' confident smile reappeared and he slid the folder across the desk. Badrick stopped it from falling and opened it shakily, a feeling of dread in his stomach at the thought of what he might find inside.

"Fourth page," Reynolds announced.

Upon locating it, Badrick found what appeared to be some kind of diagram. It looked like a hospital heart-rate monitor.

The line was drawn in an even zigzag pattern, as if someone's heart was having a breakdown. But at the right hand side of the page, the line shot up, higher than the rest, right off the paper.

"Our sensors don't have a measurement for how high it went up," said Reynolds.

"What is this?" Badrick enquired.

"Power levels. Demonic power levels. The demonic levels in your town, to be more specific."

The folder actually shook in Badrick's trembling hands and he had to fight to calm them. He took a few deep breaths before saying, "My town?"

"Yesterday, on the way to your therapist, you might remember some missing time. Or maybe you don't, you probably forgot. I suppose that's why they call it 'missing time'."

"What are you talking about?"

"Some demons, Badrick, the exceptionally powerful ones, can take over their host's body. For a limited time only, of course. Manifesting on this plane of existence isn't easy for a being that is stuck as metaphysical energy.

"Now, being as low-level as he is, Vulrick shouldn't be able to do that. But as you can see our scans detected a massive burst of demonic energy in your quaint little town. Incidentally, this burst happened a mere half an hour before your house fire.

"It took us a while to figure it all out after our computers exploded, but after you visited one of our safe houses, the church, our agent detected that this spike originated from you. It is our understanding that Vulrick utilised this power to take over, push your mind and body inside the recesses of your soul, and manifest into this world as a physical being. He used the time granted to him to kill your uncle.

"When he was done, and the power subsided, you took back the reigns, completely unaware of what had just occurred."

Reynolds tapped the desk and studied Badrick through piercing eyes, seemingly waiting for him to respond.

But Badrick had stopped listening quite a while ago.

He hadn't cared for much of what Reynolds just told him.

The only thing that mattered was that little bit about lost time.

Because he *had* lost time.

On his way to Doctor Brian's office ... that weird moment when all the clocks had told him he was an hour late, even though he should have been right on time.

He'd chalked it up to either his phone being set incorrectly, or his own incompetence with time-keeping.

And though it sounded so *stupid* ... Reynolds' explanation actually made more sense to him.

Now that he was really thinking hard, *really* focusing on the phenomenon, he could remember feeling a little nauseous as he'd entered the office. He'd believed it to be anxiety. He thought he was nervous.

But Badrick had no reason to be; he'd had many psychiatrists and he'd never cared for the sessions. All he'd ever felt before was irritation, so why would he have been nervous then?

Answer; he hadn't been.

He'd been feeling sick because a demon had taken over his

body.

"Oh . . . my . . . " He never finished the sentence.

In that moment, everything Reynolds was telling him, he believed.

Why *this* particular part of the story was enough to convince him, he had no idea.

It just felt right.

"Badrick . . . are you alright?"

Shaking his head, Badrick realised he'd been in his own thoughts for quite a while. He looked up at Reynolds, his brain whirring with questions. But for starters, he began with a simple, "So what happens now?"

Reynolds' head bounced, giving the impression of a bobble-head. "Well, there's only three options available to you."

"And what are they?" Badrick asked quickly.

"One; you join up. Become part of the Daemonium, join us in our operations, and learn how to control your demon, living a life of servitude to this world, fighting monsters.

"Two; we imprison you.

"Three; we use an exceptionally agonising procedure to extract your demon from your soul and cast his good for nothingness back into Hell. You won't survive the process, and neither will the three agents required to perform the procedure."

There was nothing else to do, except stare at Reynolds in disbelief.

"Are you kidding me?" Badrick called. "I have to choose from those? I can never leave?"

Reynolds fist hit the table in a sudden display of impatience. "Do you not understand what we are facing here? Enthrallers are dangerous people. You have a *demon* in your soul, Badrick, a force of *pure evil*. If you do not learn how to control him he *will* run amok.

"Vulrick is one of the most unstable demons I have ever encountered. He appears to genuinely care for you, a trait I have seen in only *one* other demon, yet he is far too willing to commit brutal murder.

"Now . . . we're going to let the murder of your uncle pass. The whole thing is totally screwed up. A jury would see you go to jail immediately. But we're different. For the better, I hope. There's no point blaming those who had no idea of what danger they posed. It wasn't a random butchering, fuelled by nothing but anger and/or cruelty, as we most often have to deal with. You have no idea how many of our agents have that on their conscience, and yet still have to live with the monster that made them do it.

"But if we let you go free you *will* kill again. That is inevitable. We are fighting an enemy that is also our ally. It is the most dangerous and frustratingly complicated war on this here planet. Human ideologies of justice no longer apply.

"And that is the only, final choice you have."

Reynolds sat back in his seat, his eyes boring into Badrick's.

"You either join us, or we stop you."

chapter
FOUR

You either join us, or we stop you.

It didn't seem like Badrick had much of a choice, and as he studied the sergeant tapping furiously on the familiar, enlarged iPod-looking thing strapped to his arm, he couldn't help but wonder how he'd gotten into this mess.

It was that bloody ninja priest. If only he'd gone back home instead of going to the church.

But then again it wouldn't have mattered; his house had already burned down. Vulrick had struck. He had no home to go to.

The Daemonium would have found him eventually.

"I'm just a kid," he finally muttered.

"You're seventeen," Reynolds scoffed. "Old enough to start a life on your own."

"But . . . I'm just a . . . "

"Badrick, let's not play games. Stop trying to undersell yourself. We're all angry. Every single one of us. You think I happily entered this life? You think I was happy when I accidentally used my powers in the biggest boxing match of my early career? That kid will never breathe God's air again, and I can never take back what happened. But I do what I can to make up for it. And that mission rests here, in the Daemonium."

Badrick didn't know what to say; his brain had gone to mush.

Thankfully, he was saved the pain of commenting by a vigorous and tuneful knock on the door behind him.

"Come in," Reynolds called.

The door slid open, and Badrick automatically turned in his chair to see who was there.

The most intriguing person sauntered in.

The first thing Badrick noticed was the darker than black uniform, exactly the same as the sergeant's in every aspect but the colour.

But the strange clothes were thrown from Badrick's head when he looked up at the guy's face.

Whoever this guy was he appeared beyond human. His eyes were an electric blue, and not just in shade; they literally shone, unnatural in their colouration, as if intense voltage powered the orbs. His face was annoyingly good looking, and yet he looked fair, not bulky and strong like one would have attributed to such an appearance.

Badrick guessed his age to be around nineteen or twenty, thought he wasn't quite sure.

Because he didn't walk like he was twenty.

Or male.

He moved with the kind of . . . ethereal grace that Badrick would have attributed to an angel.

Or a Tolkien elf.

As though he was more than mortal.

And the hair. It was *ridiculous!*

It was brightly blonde, longish and thick, the front tickling his eyebrows and the back and sides long enough to cover his ears and neck.

And it flowed. Like the *freakin'* leaves on a tree, it flowed as he walked, as if the guy were an ad for women's shampoo.

Badrick couldn't help but gape, and actually felt like laughing when Reynolds caught him staring and remarked tiredly, "You'll get used to it."

The sergeant stood and shook hands with the newcomer. With them standing next to each other, Badrick was able to study the pair of them together.

Now he'd gotten over the initial shock of the new guy's appearance, and he could finally see them both in full profile, his focus went back to the odd uniforms. Reynolds' was indeed bright red, except for the trousers, which were black.

The newcomer's uniform was nothing but, and Badrick had the distinct feeling that it meant he was something special.

"Badrick," said Reynolds, "meet Zale Hood. Zale, meet our newest member . . . er . . . maybe."

"Oh?" the man called Zale chuckled. "It's not definitive yet?"

"I don't think so, no. Maybe you can show him around, convince him otherwise."

"I'll be honest, Reynolds, if he hasn't already decided to live, I don't think I can change his mind."

"It's not as simple as that, you arse!" Badrick recoiled as the words escaped his lips; he hadn't meant to snap at the newcomer.

Zale laughed loudly. "Interesting. I'm guessing this one has already tried to kill someone?"

"Well deduced. His therapist, actually. With a—" Reynolds

double checked the folder "—*pen*. And his demon has already taken a life."

"*A pen!*" Zale cackled.

"Though, I hear it was the demon who stopped the act from occurring. Conflicted, this demon is. He has a lot of influence on the kid."

Badrick was fuming now, furious at being talked about as if he weren't there.

"Well, we're sure as hell going to fix that." Zale gave a menacing grin.

"Oh for the love of . . . " Reynolds sighed dramatically. "Ignore him, Varner. He's being mean on purpose. He's just cranky that I'm assigning you as his partner upon your joining."

"I haven't joined you," Badrick snapped. "I don't *want* to."

"Well, the other choices aren't exactly inviting," the black uniformed man laughed. He snapped to attention and offered his hand to Badrick. "It's nice to meet you, though."

Badrick glared at the hand for a while, giving it a wide berth. Eventually he decided there was no point in being rude, and he took it, shaking it firmly, looking Zale in the eye.

He gasped in pain as Zale's hand suddenly tightened, and the man's mouth opened slightly, as though he'd just had a shock.

"Ow . . . " Badrick managed to utter through gasps of pain.

"Sorry!" Zale released him quickly and took a step back. There was an awkward silence, during which Zale stared at him.

Then he turned to Reynolds, treating him to an expression that appeared to be a cross between anger and relief. "So . . . he's finally here."

"What?" Badrick immediately said.

"Nothing," Reynolds muttered, glaring at Zale. "It's just Vulrick. We heard tale of his ascension to Earth a while back, so . . . well, we found him obviously."

Badrick glanced between Reynolds and Zale, trying to deduce what they were silently communicating.

He failed epically, and lost his chance when Zale snapped back to attention, gave Reynolds a sharp salute, and turned on his heel. "Come on, man," he said. "Let's get out of this crappy office."

"Watch it, Hood!"

"Ah, you love me!"

At an exhausted nod from Reynolds, Badrick jumped up and followed Zale out of the office. He was led further up, continuing to climb endless flights of stairs before finally reappearing into the hall Badrick had dreamed of for years, stopping in the middle of one of the bridges, much to the irritation of a group of women.

When it proved impossible to work a way through all three jumped over the side, landing gracefully on the ground floor without a single broken leg.

Badrick stared after them, his mouth hanging open.

As for Zale, he was spreading his arms wide, and turning on the spot, a proud grin on his face. "*This* is the HQ of the Daemonium," he announced, apparently skipping the small talk. "This is where the operations of the place all take ... erm ... place. We're currently standing in the Main Hall, the blue room you would have passed through earlier is the Agent Control Room. We call it the BCR."

Badrick nodded, only half listening. From this height he could finally see out of the window that had eluded him for so many years in his nightmares, and was able to get a grasp on his location.

It was green outside, nothing but fields and trees for miles, so he guessed it was still somewhere in the UK, but he couldn't be sure. In his time walking through the building he'd heard a variety of different accents and hadn't found the time to pinpoint the most prominent. It could have been English, but . . .

In the distance was a huge wall that stretched from either side of the window, and probably further. Did it surround the entire area?

"There's another room," Zale continued, apparently refusing to accept that Badrick was preoccupied and trying to think. "Lit up with red. The Army Control Centre, though we call it the RCR."

Now Badrick turned his full attention to Zale, and incredulously asked, "Army?"

Zale nodded vigorously. "Aha."

"You have your own army?"

"The Daemonium is split into three divisions; agents, army and special operations. Our agents act out singular missions, recon and the like, alone or in teams. The army defends this base, and any outposts we have out there."

"Oh, OK," Badrick responded sarcastically. "Of course they do. And what are special operations?"

"SpecOps do both. The most dangerous missions, and the elite units in battle. We're very special."

"*We?*"

"Yes, 'we'. I am part of the special operations division."

"How'd you swing that?"

"I'm just awesome."

Despite himself and everything he'd been put through, Badrick actually laughed.

His logical brain was fighting his emotions now. He couldn't forget everything that had happened, or his fear of everyone in the vicinity, but he couldn't help but grow more curious with each passing second. There was something about Zale that the sergeant had lacked. A sense of security.

Fun.

He made it all sound interesting.

And so Badrick found himself asking, "Anything else?"

Zale's eyes brightened—even more—evidently pleased that Badrick was partaking. He flicked his hand, indicating the area around him. "The HQ also includes the generator chamber, the armoury, etcetera. There are other sections to this place though, including the Quarters Towers, which is where all the bedrooms and hygiene facilities are.

"There's the Gate, which speaks for itself, though that whole section's where most of the training areas are, as well as the duelling arena.

"There's also the prison . . . we've all been there.

"And finally, the grounds, which includes our vehicle depot."

"And what is that?" Badrick asked, pointing out the window.

"A wall . . . *obviously.*"

"Yeah, *thanks.* I mean what's it for?"

"It's a defence, numbskull. The wall is a giant circle, surrounding this building, which is freakishly immense, by the way." Zale lifted his arm and pulled back his black sleeve, revealing the same arm-computer Reynolds and Hans sported.

He tapped upon it for a moment, and then aimed it out into the hall.

Badrick jumped in surprise as the device poured out light. His jaw dropped once more as a *humungous* hologram flashed into existence, filling up half the hall, but low enough that Badrick could look at it from above.

It was incredible. Utterly *amazing.*

"This is the Daemonium facility," Zale announced. "Presented to you in 3D."

Zale was right; the wall did surround the place in a perfect protective circle, spread out far enough that there was quite a sizable grounds.

The building itself, even without the wall, was impressive.

It was *immensely* tall, spiked towers stretching up and above like some kind of half closed lotus flower.

That was the only way Badrick could describe it.

In the middle was the tallest tower, looming high above the rest.

"That middle one is the Quarters Tower," Zale informed him. "It's amazing in there, I'll have to show you later."

"How have I not heard of this place?" Badrick asked. "Where are we? What country?"

"We're in England," Zale said. "And in answer to your question, you've never heard of us because we're protected. This is a no fly zone, no satellites but our own allowed, such a restricted area that the birds don't dare come in, and no outside contact whatsoever, except in an official capacity. Just looking at this place without permission is bound to get you arrested for life, though my personal favourite bit is that the police wouldn't even understand why they were arresting the perp. They don't know about this place either."

"How is this afforded for?" Badrick gaped. "How do you stop people stumbling on it? Just . . . how!?"

"Let me put it to you this way." Zale tapped on his pad and the giant image vanished into thin air. "Money. Power. And a whole lot of persuasion. Money, especially, is power in this decaying, stupid world. We get whatever we want, whenever we want. Except this job being done successfully . . . that tends to elude us more often than not.

"We also have demons, remember? Didn't I hear rumour that Vulrick performed hypnotic suggestion on people around you?"

Badrick nodded slowly, the thought of that still making him sick. He wasn't sure how he felt about it yet.

"Well, it's the same thing, except done by Singularis and Enthrallers that have a lot more power than your low-level Vulrick.

"It's also how we find potential recruits, the ones we don't locate through scans or end up fighting. There are executive orders in every government organisation, every administration. That's how we found you, I heard. Every therapist in the world is under orders, that upon witnessing certain . . . *attributes* from their clients, they are to send them to the closest 'expert', meaning our safe houses, which is where you were sent.

"The people are then scanned to see if there's anything to them. If not, their memories are wiped and they are sent on their way. If yes . . . well, here you are."

Nodding was all Badrick could do again; the numbness was back. Every time he thought he had gotten past the magnitude of what he'd been told, he was informed of something new, something even more impossible than before.

"You're higher than the governments?" he whispered

"The governments fear us. Well, they would if they knew about us. All they know is there's someone out there more powerful and more deadly than anything they can imagine. They do whatever we say when we need to make them."

Badrick felt even sicker at this, he couldn't believe it. "No one should have that much power."

Zale simply shrugged. "We deal with very serious threats. Imagine if the human world got in the way. Chaos. Sometimes fear is the only thing that can keep you safe. Sometimes respect just isn't enough."

Badrick didn't agree. His moral compass wouldn't allow him.

It wasn't *right*.

Zale didn't let him argue the point again; he gestured for him to follow across the bridge.

For the first time in a few minutes, Badrick considered trying to run. This place, this *Daemonium*, scared him.

There was enough space between them, as Zale stepped

through an archway, for him to leg it in the other direction.

He might be able to get somewhere.

In the end, two things stopped him.

One; there were loads of these Daemonium people everywhere, below him on other walkways and on the ground floor. He would never get past them all.

Two; where else could he go?

In the end, all he could do was trudge after the expectant Zale, who waited for him at the archway.

The young SpecOps operative led him out of the HQ, through a much larger arch, decorated with the word 'GATE' in large neon letters.

The Gate turned out to be more than that. It was an entire section of the base, one floor only, with entire rooms dedicated to physical training. Badrick saw sparring rings and obstacle courses, not to mention a great deal of people using the facilities to the best of their ability.

The actual gate itself that led out of the building and into the grounds was an enormous, metal, automatic blast door, with reinforced . . . *everything*.

Finally, Zale ended the tour at his self-proclaimed favourite place.

"Alas, the firing ranges," he grinned. "Best place in the world."

Badrick was dubious. It was nothing but a long, tall room, with circular discs set into the floor in a line near where they'd entered.

But that was it.

"Where are the targets?" Badrick asked, an eyebrow raised.

Zale sauntered to the corner of the room and yanked a lever Badrick hadn't noticed before, the kind that looked like the sort of thing that would be used to turn on a generator. As it reached the end of its arc there was a deafening zap, and Badrick jumped in alarm.

At the end of the room, far from them, something had appeared, and when Badrick focused he realised that it was a row of large, glowing, self levitating orbs of energy,

They'd appeared as if from nothing.

And they were floating.

Floating.

"What the . . . " Badrick started.

"Cool, isn't it?" Zale grinned, parroting Reynolds from earlier.

"How do you do this stuff? The holograms, the energy walls, these things . . . "

"They're all generated from the powers of other Enthrallers," Zale told him. "I'm . . . I suppose I'm what you'd call smart. I'm very good at combining technology with the powers of others. The holograms were a power owned by an agent who died a year ago, but before he did I was able to take his power and replicate it on our computer systems, to put it into simple terms. Now we can not only generate them ourselves, we can make an image of anything we want. Naked women, even."

"How do you do it?" Badrick asked, ignoring the last comment.

"Oh, it's all very long and complicated and boring." Zale came back to stand next to him. "But it works. These things you see before you belong to the guy who runs this firing range. He doesn't do much anymore, but he still runs the range and issues out testing weapons. But otherwise I sort of made him redundant by replicating his power and making these orb things. He doesn't mind though; less work for him to do.

Badrick smiled at that, and asked, "Where are the guns?"

A crafty grin appeared on Zale's smooth features. "Oh, we don't use guns in *this* room."

"What do you use?"

Zale didn't reply. Instead he stood upon one of the discs,

raised his hand, twirled it in the air and threw it towards the orb opposite.

Badrick didn't have enough time to wonder what he was doing. The moment his arm reached its full extent, a startling bright light shot from Zale's hand and struck the target violently, causing it to explode.

Seconds later, after Badrick had the time to process what he'd just witnessed, he realised that Zale had thrown a huge surge of electricity.

Straight from his hand.

"What the hell was that!?" he immediately cried, jumping back, unsure of whether to run or gawp.

"That was my power," Zale winked. "By my demon Horas. He's a powerful Singularis, an electrokinetic. Well . . . sort of."

Badrick was still too stunned to reply. Until that moment he had yet to witness one of these so called Enthrallers use the powers they claimed to have—he'd never believed the jailor had a power, and the three women could just have easily used rappelling equipment he hadn't noticed.

But there was no disputing this. Zale wasn't wearing anything but his pure black uniform. He didn't have anything that might have generated some kind of electrical surge for him to throw.

It was real. Zale had a power. So did all the others.

Badrick gulped, hard, and muttered, "What do you mean, 'sort of'?"

"A true electrokinetic can manipulate electric currents and magnetism and absorb electricity, etcetra, etcetra. We've never seen a demon like that. What *I* can do is generate electricity myself. I can use it to enhance my body, or I can throw it in an attack."

He turned to the targets, gazing at the orb opposite, which had just sparked back into existence.

"Whoa," was all Badrick could say.

"Speaking of enhancing bodies, you need a bloody shower." Zale laughed. "I can smell you from here."

"That would be singed clothing, thanks," Badrick grumbled. Eager to change the subject, he added, "So you can do that all the time?"

"Don't ask me to do *that* again," was the reply. "I'm not very good at huge, sustained bursts, and I feel weak after. I only did it then to give you a proper example. Newcomers react well to a *proper* example."

He was right about that at least. "Duly appreciated," Badrick gasped, clutching at his chest.

"Something wrong?"

"Just . . . " Badrick twirled his hand in the air, " . . . a lot to take in."

"Just breathe." Zale whacked him hard on the back, making Badrick cough and not helping in the slightest.

"This is insane," he wheezed. "This *can't* be real. It's . . . too horrible to be."

"How is it?"

"Demons and Hell! It's all real. And we have these monsters inside us? We're damned. We're all damned—"

He stopped when Zale grabbed him by the shoulders and shook him so hard Badrick was sure his neck almost snapped clean off.

"Feeling better?" he was asked after. Badrick gave him a half glare/half nod. Zale exhaled and rubbed the back of his own neck, his fingers getting entangled in the blonde locks. "Look, Badrick, this life isn't great. We all know that. But the problem we all face is an identity crisis. Who are we? What are we? How can we truly be someone in this world with a bloody evil bastard lurking in our souls?

"This place, man, it really helps. It's brutal here, yes, but it has to be, and it *really* helps. People like you and I often have trouble aspiring to anything. We're hunkered down by these powers we can't control and this evil we fear is our own.

"But the Daemonium gave me a purpose. It gave us all purpose in a world that would persecute and *execute* us if it ever discovered the source of these, I'll say it, fantastic powers."

Zale stepped back, and held his hand out to Badrick. "How about it, Badrick. Are you ready to be someone?"

It was a blunt offer. Zale didn't waste time.

Badrick stared at the hand for a long while, a million different thoughts going through his head, an argument as loud as can be raging in his mind.

This monster inside me wanted me here. That sounds bad. It's evil. I should do the opposite of what it wants.

But he killed my uncle. He did it for me. He saved me.

How can I justify that? No matter what my uncle did, I cannot condone murder.

But what would I have done eventually? I almost murdered my therapist, if not for Vulrick stopping me.

That's because of the demon inside me, though. It killed someone. It killed my parents!

But that was me. A total accident, but it was me.

Again, because of the demon inside me. It would never have happened if the demon hadn't latched onto my soul.

But . . . was that its doing at all? Reynolds said the demons don't know why it's happening.

Fine, forget all that, this place is still wrong! *You heard what Zale said.*

I also heard what he said about the persecution . . . he's right . . .

Maybe they deserve it.

Do they? Really?

This argument raged for so long, Zale looked to be getting

quite impatient with him. Or maybe that was simply because his arm was getting tired.

It felt like they were standing there for weeks, but in the end, Badrick settled on one single, final conclusion.

Where else can I go now?

"Alright." He took the hand and gave it a strong shake. "I'm in. Just, for the love of God, help me."

Zale smiled and spread his arms. "I'm Zale Hood, mate. I won't let you down."

chapter
FIVE

It was quiet where he was. He wasn't used to it. Where he'd positioned himself, the people he had to endure as he hid amongst them were always so very . . . noisy.

It was infuriating.

The demon savoured the quiet, with only the odd birdcall to disturb it.

He'd kill it if he figured out where the bird was. He could use some fun.

"Well?"

The demon ground his teeth with irritation, but turned back to his fellows nonetheless. He regarded them from underneath his skull-inspired helmet, wondering why he had entrusted these two pathetic Ordinarius as spies.

They were so ungrateful. They wouldn't have even been able to manifest on Earth without his help. The first Ordinarius to walk the earth in their own forms, and all they did was moan and bitch and hide, too scared to attract the attention of those who would, and could, kill them.

"It will happen soon," the demon snarled, his voice cruel and gravelly. "Have no doubts."

"How can you be sure?"

He reached out and ran his hand across the rock of the cave mouth where he'd met the Ordinarius.

It was pitiful, to say the least. In Hell he'd had a huge chamber, filled to the brim with glorious death and decay.

Nothing could come close, especially not this dank cave.

"Daemnos is a powerful demon," he told them, putting aside his memories of home. "He won't be able to resist coming to this realm again."

The second Ordinarius, the one who had yet to speak, scowled and scoffed, "If he is as powerful as you claim, how do you know you will be successful?"

"Daemnos may be powerful, but *I* am stronger. I am far—"

"And if he infiltrates the Daemonium? How will you get to him then?"

The demon couldn't help but laugh. Could these two figure nothing out for themselves? Ordinarius were so pointless. "I'm counting on that happening. In fact, I plan on doing nothing until he has done just that."

"Your plan will—"

"My plan will not take effect for several more years. Ten, at the most. That is when—"

"That is '*soon*' to you?"

The demon's eyes flashed with fury, but, with effort, he chose to ignore the disrespect and allow it to go unpunished. He could kill these two later if he so desired.

When they were no longer necessary.

"That is when Daemnos will most likely manifest and seek out the Daemonium. My plan is set to take effect the moment that occurs. It is *that* efficient."

The less argumentative one, the Ordinarius who had spoken first, spat in disgust. "The Daemonium," he snarled.

"Speaking of which," the demon chuckled, grinning maliciously, "the Apostaticus plans on attacking them in three days. Sport, if nothing else."

Much to his amusement, both Ordinarius shivered with fury. "Those pathetic creatures," the second hissed. "What a ridiculous title. And they think it has some important meaning?"

The first remained more composed, and uttered a more intelligent sentence. "And if the Apostaticus destroys the Daemonium? Your plan will be rendered useless if that occurs."

"Let them have their fun." The demon openly laughed dubiously. "They're nothing but mad dogs. They can't do much."

The Ordinarius looked at each other, communicating through expressions their lack of faith in the demon.

He did not care.

"Of Daemnos," one of them said, "what is it you plan on doing with him?"

The demon grinned ever wider, taking a step forward and bringing himself closer to the shaking Ordinarius.

They truly were pathetic, terrified of his very presence.

"You'll see."

And he laughed.

*

It took three days for the Daemonium to get Badrick settled in. First they had to organise his old life, with the aim that no one would go looking for him. If there was a police report about his disappearance everything would get complicated.

It was harder than usual because of the unfortunate circumstances involving Badrick's arrival to the facility. The police had already been to his house because of the fire, and therefore tried to find him, already figuring out he was missing.

But the Daemonium was nothing if not good at what they did, and though Badrick didn't entirely understand the procedure utilised, the agents in the BCR did some inspired hacking work.

This included wiping his details from the country records, as well as some clever work confusing the police and his school as to his whereabouts.

"Seventeen . . . and still in school?" an amused Zale asked him.

"I was held back," Badrick told him softly, the thought of it tying a knot in his stomach. "I don't want to talk about it."

"Sorry, man." Zale said no more about it.

That was the first day, aside from cleaning him up and finding him some new clothes. The second involved locating a room for him in the Quarters Tower, which proved much harder than anyone expected.

"Six thousand plus bedrooms in this bloody place, and we can't find a single one!" Zale could be heard ranting for half the day. "Whose bright idea was it to use the top five floors as temporary storage? It's gonna take weeks to get all that crap out."

For the first night Badrick slept in Zale's room, as the SpecOps agent was too busy dealing with him to need it.

After the second day, it was eventually sorted, and Badrick had his own room in the extravagant Quarters Tower.

It was *amazing*. Every floor had a lobby, with winding corridors and rooms attached. It wasn't like the dull blue-grey climate downstairs; the tower was like a palace, with orange and light brown walls, and bright blue colours beautifying the floor. Statues and decorative holograms of people, Kalik demons and the planet itself decorated every spare inch.

And the view was I.N.C.R.E.D.I.B.L.E.

Badrick actually got a little dizzy looking down from so far up; he was on the fourth highest floor. It felt like he could touch the clouds from up here.

A few meagre belongings were salvaged from his house, courtesy of some very kind Daemonium agents. They brought them to his room and allowed him to make himself comfortable. This thoughtful gesture helped put Badrick's still frantic mind at ease, and made him feel more at home.

And an unfamiliar thought occurred to him.

Maybe, just maybe, he might finally be among friends.

In his opinion it was a long shot; his past experiences didn't leave him much room for hope.

But he had a little bit.

He lost Zale on the evening of the second day. The black-wearing blonde was called away to the Agent Control Room to go over some evidence pertaining to the murder of an agent in the field. With him gone, Badrick wiled away the day in his room, thinking about the events that led him to here, as well as wandering the HQ, finding conversation where he could.

The third day, when it finally arrived, consisted of assigning him to a division. This really didn't take long; as he was already Zale's partner, and because of his status as the Enthraller of a Singularis demon, the Daemonium immediately dumped him into SpecOps.

"Well, drat," Zale told him as a way of condolence. "Your job is everything now, I'm afraid. Nothing I can do, you're among the elite of the elite now. I hope you can take the heat."

Badrick wasn't sure in the slightest.

In fact he had huge reservations about it. He never liked being thrown in at the deep end. But Badrick had agreed to join this Daemonium business.

He was at their mercy and command now.

Once he was inputted into the Daemonium databases, his training schedule was written up.

"Until you're fully trained, you're just a recruit," Zale informed him. "You'll have the black uniform upon graduation, and you'll be expected to wear it. But for the next four years, I will be your instructor. Not like I'm already busy as it is," he muttered under his breath. "But I suppose I'm happy to do it. You seem like a good investment."

"So what's first?" Badrick asked him as he was led out of the HQ and into the Gate.

"Well, the whole point of this place is to train you into an effective soldier and/or agent. To do that you need to learn to control the demon inside you. You are the driver, the owner, and he can't do squat about it. But he can and *will* influence you if your lack of trained control goes unchecked.

"You're lucky you don't have a super powerful Singularis in there. Those ones take years of training, and many fail, the demons taking advantage of their ability to manifest to the extreme."

"Vulrick manifested," Badrick muttered quietly.

"Yeah, I know, I heard. An anomaly. Sometimes demons do it. I've seen Ordinarius get the chance before. It's a fluke. But you learn to control Vulrick, and he won't ever be able to do it again.

"And control starts with knowing your powers through and through. You *must* have absolute control. So we're going to the powers range, where I took you before and showed you mine."

Since the moment Badrick arrived here, he'd been tense, and

ever since he'd agreed to be a part of this organisation he'd remained anxious, terrified, and tighter than a seaman's knot.

But if there was one thing he was excited to know about, it was the fact that he had a power.

Because call it whatever you wanted, learning you had a superpower, no matter the reason behind it, would get anyone excited.

It would give them a feeling of importance, of being special.

One of a kind.

Badrick was determined to get some kind of positive emotion out of all of this. He deserved that, at the very least.

He knew Vulrick had the ability to throw fire. He'd also been told he wasn't going to be all that strong, and that Vulrick was a low-level demon.

But he didn't care. He still had powers.

It was the only awesome thing he'd been told in years.

And so he followed Zale with a kind of zeal he'd never experienced before, and quickly found himself facing the yellow glowing orbs once again.

However it didn't turn out quite the way he'd expected.

Nothing happened after his first try, though Zale said he hadn't expected anything else.

But there was no result after the second attempt either.

Or the third.

Or the fourth.

Fifth.

Six.

Seventh.

And on, and on, and on . . .

Even Zale appeared confused at his total lack of ability to use Vulrick's powers, and as the hours dragged by and Badrick had failed attempt after failed attempt, the novelty of having anything special had completely worn off.

"Dude!" Zale eventually shouted. "Seriously, just concentrate!"

Badrick threw his arms up in the air with frustration, communicating his feelings with actions. "It's been hours! What do you expect me to do!?"

"*I don't know!*" Zale cried back. "I know we've established that Vulrick is very low-level, and you won't be capable of *too much*. But you can do *something*. Now turn your arse back to that target and throw your best."

"Fine!" Badrick snapped, which only ended up making Zale laugh. "But I doubt it'll do much good."

He felt a hand clasp his shoulder and turned to see a now smiling Zale nodding vigorously. "Look, try to reach down to your demon. He's in there somewhere, inside your soul, waiting to work with you."

"Alright, alright. I'm reaching down . . . reaching down so far I'm in Australia . . . " Badrick clenched his fists, closing his eyes tightly, and concentrated on Zale's directions, calling on what he'd been taught earlier that day. He pictured an energy, a darkness, seeping from a bright white light inside him, spreading through his body to his arms and hands.

He concentrated on this image for a few minutes.

When he was ready, his eyes flashed open and he threw his hands forward, stretching his arms to their full extent, his fingers wide and long.

Nothing happened.

Again.

"*God damn it!* Maaaan!"

He expected Zale to comment. To either sigh and moan, or at the very least point and laugh at him.

When no such thing occurred, he turned around, looking for his partner.

He found him a few feet away.

And he was sniffing the air.

"Erm . . . what are you doing?" Badrick asked confusedly.

"Enhanced sense of smell," Zale replied softly. "I can smell something. Something bad."

An eyebrow rose up Badrick's forehead in an unsubtle display of confusion. "You what? You have electric powers, not heightened senses."

Zale wasn't paying much attention to him; he was totally focused on sniffing the air. But at this comment, he half turned back to him and sighed. "Have you forgotten already? Do you pay any attention? I have electro-senses." He paused when he realised how unhelpful that explanation was. "Electrical-based senses basically . . . *Shut up*, I'm busy."

Badrick never got to respond; a sharp exclamation from outside the range stopped him. "Zale!"

His partner's face dropped, and he immediately legged it out the door. Badrick's eyes widened in surprise and he quickly made to follow.

As the door slid upwards and allowed them through, Badrick recognised the face of Sergeant Reynolds peaking up from the bottom of a staircase.

"There you are!" he cried out. He ascended the staircase and approached them in a hurry.

There was something disturbingly different about the sergeant; he no longer adorned his uniform.

In its place was armour.

Red armour.

It was brighter and cleaner than Vulrick's, *almost* identical but for the much smoother pauldrons and the straps of shotgun shells and grenades draping Reynold's shoulders and waist, as well as the helmet, which looked a lot like a biker's, and was currently under his arm.

Badrick stopped in his tracks.

What was this?

"What's going on?" Zale asked, oblivious to his surprise.

"The Apos are attacking the HQ!" Reynolds checked around himself, almost as though he expected a mugger to surprise him from behind. "They're past the wall!"

"Holy—" Zale didn't say anything else, cutting off his own words as he followed the sergeant out of the hallway. Surprised at his sudden abandonment, Badrick scoffed and made to follow.

Three minutes later, Badrick waited in the elevator impatiently as it ascended the Quarters Tower.

The sergeant had left them; he'd headed for the grounds, but for some reason Zale hadn't gone with him. Badrick watched him charging into the ground floor lobby of the tower, and deduced he was heading for his room.

The doors opened on the fourteenth floor, and he barged out, charging straight for the bedroom.

He skidded to a halt the moment he stepped over the threshold.

Zale was half naked, his legs and waist covered by a leathery material. As he hurriedly zipped it up, Badrick realised it was the exact same under-suit.

His partner wasted no time. He immediately made for a panel on his wall, and slapped it.

The wall hissed, and separated, revealing an opening.

Inside it was another suit of armour.

It wasn't red this time—the helmet and chestplate were grey, as were the two large shoulder pads and parts of the arms and legs.

But the boots, knee guards and sections of the arms were what Badrick recognised as a vivid Persian Blue.

But the differing colours did nothing to ease his surprise and anger at seeing it.

Why did they have armour like his demon? What did that mean? What had they hidden from him?

"What is this?" he asked tightly.

"My armour," Zale replied quickly.

"My demon wears armour like that," Badrick muttered, as he watched Zale strap the metal chestplate to his body.

"Your demon doesn't wear anything. He's currently a metaphysical being trapped within your soul."

His head disappeared underneath the helmet, which too looked a lot like the kind a motorbike rider would wear, only heavily armoured and with a lot more equipment attached.

As it obscured Zale's face, Badrick was surprised to see the gold colour of the visor suddenly spark and change to electric blue.

"We'll talk later. Wait here."

And with that, Zale was gone, running past and grabbing a gun Badrick hadn't noticed before from its placement on the wall.

For a moment, Badrick just stood there.

Then, with a huff, "Screw that!"

He pushed the door open and followed Zale out of the tower.

Zale emerged into a bloodbath. The sound of gunfire was deafening, though it was intertwined with the strange noises of powers being utilised. Energy balls flew everywhere, exploding against dirt, concrete and bodies alike.

Lasers and plasma and clouds of toxic gas.

It was chaos.

Red armoured soldiers bounded across the battlefield, jumping impossibly high and firing into the crowd of invaders.

And he could see *them* doing the same, leaping over the

protective wall, just soaring right over, and reminding him just how behind he was on developing a shield for this issue.

A trio of powerful Enthrallers soared over him, actually flying into the sky in a V formation, and raining green death upon the invading force. The rippling plasma blasts tore wide holes in the enemy's ranks.

To his left he could see Sergeant Reynolds grappling with one of the Apos bastards who'd gotten further into the grounds than his fellows. Zale was about to aim his auto-rifle and give the sergeant a hand, but relented when he saw Reynolds pull his arm back; a white light brightened around his fist as the sergeant hammered it into his foe.

The Apos' helmet shattered into oblivion and his corpse was thrown backwards, his neck probably nothing but dust now. He flew a good few feet before coming to a stop in the tall grass.

Zale smiled; Reynolds' speed-fist power had always impressed him.

Wasting no more time, he raised his weapon once again and charged into the fight, slamming his shoulder against the concrete barriers beside his fellow soldiers. Zale counted to three, then stood and opened fire.

Badrick stopped in his tracks as he crossed the threshold of the Gate and the bloodthirsty massacre assaulted his senses.

Bodies and blood everywhere, marring the otherwise beautiful grounds.

Guns and other weapons lay amongst them and the landscape scarring was unreal.

Everyone was wearing the same armour. An ocean of red soldiers pummelling rounds and powers into a scattered regiment of brown enemies.

He jumped in fright as a grenade went off nearby and three armoured figures, two red, one both red and blue, charged past him, heading deeper into the fight.

"Get to the wall!" the multicoloured soldier shouted. "The Wall Entrance must be defended!"

They vanished into the fray quickly, and Badrick could no longer tell them from the others. He couldn't even see Zale out here. It was just a mess of blood, and bodies, and death.

Badrick regarded the scene with horror.

It was *terrible*. People screaming from slow but fatal wounds, others hiding behind barriers and lobbing explosive after explosive.

He saw a Daemonium soldier tear an invader in half with a whoop of glee.

Another roared abuse as he fired his sniper rifle into a crowd of enemies.

One of the so called Apos punched a red soldier in the back of the head, and shoved a knife through the under-suit over his neck, blood spattering violently.

Before he could straighten, he was pinned to the earth by another vengeful member of the Daemonium. He screamed in agony as his chest was ripped open by bullet after bullet, the soldier reloading just to continue shooting him.

In the midst of all the chaos, Badrick had the horrible feeling that some of these people were actually enjoying the killing.

Was this what he'd signed up for? A life of *this*?

Badrick shook his head; he couldn't dwell on it now. It was awful, but if these attackers got through the defenders then it wouldn't matter what he'd signed up for, because he would surely be killed.

He had to find a way to help. He had to do *something*.

Badrick spread his feet apart, disturbing the dirt and chipped concrete beneath them. He shook his hands roughly, thinking back to the meagre lessons Zale managed to provide before this interruption.

He imagined Vulrick lurking somewhere deep within him, waiting to help, to give Badrick his power.

He imagined the darkness spreading from the light that was his soul.

There was no way to determine what kind of power exactly would be unleashed if this was successful, but Badrick hoped it would be useful.

If only he could figure out how to throw fire . . . that would help *immensely*.

He hesitated for just a moment before throwing his hand forward, roaring with effort for added measure.

It quickly changed to a yelp of alarm as something seemed to grip him from behind and lift him off the ground. He didn't go very far, and he was able to land on his panicking, flailing feet as he fell back to earth, but it shocked him so much that his heart was now pumping ferociously.

He took a deep breath, calming his stunned body.

He'd felt it.

An energy, moving from somewhere inside him to his hand.

It had thrown him forward.

His elation at having finally achieved something was stamped out of existence by the realisation that being able to hop ten feet would provide no help at all.

He would have to find something else if he wanted to aid the Daemonium in this fight.

A Daemonium soldier narrowly missed his target, the bullet smashing into the metal behind the brown invader. He cursed angrily, and attempted to charge the Apos, intent on killing him up close.

He was blasted away by the Apos' shotgun for his efforts.

A rush of anger flooded Zale's senses upon witnessing this event and he immediately about faced, leaping upon the wire spool the Apos was taking cover behind.

He jumped down, crushing the bastard beneath his feet, and reached for his head, snapping his neck. The Apos made a small choking sound as his life left him and his motionless corpse stopped struggling, resting upon the rustling grass. As he stepped over the body, Zale psychically sensed the man's demon depart and vanish, finally free of his or her human cage.

"Zale!"

It was Reynolds, calling him over from behind a barrier. Zale made a beeline for his position. A bullet zipped past his head, making him duck and slide into cover.

He hunkered down with Reynolds, pulled the pin on a grenade the sergeant handed him and lobbed it over their cover. The resounding explosion could barely be heard over the ruckus of battle.

"Zale, we have to take these guys out fast, else they'll overrun us."

Two more Apos fell from Zale's automatic rifle before he cried, "They're Apos. They've never been this organised."

"Zale, they have a damn tank!"

"They have a *what!?*"

Almost as if marking Reynolds' announcement, Zale heard an almighty explosion that drowned out all other noise and he actually felt the colour drain from his face.

"It moved off around the base after it breached the Wall Entrance. Sounds like it's coming back around."

"We need to get rid of it," Zale muttered, still half in shock.

"We currently don't have the ordnance to take it down." Reynolds ducked rapidly as a grenade rocked their cover. "We need some supernatural firepower."

"Where's Karl?" Zale shouted back. "He can throw massive, half-nuclear energy balls. Where is he?"

"He's pinned down, out of reach on the other side of the base. He won't last much longer if we don't take care of the tank. Neither will his squad. Our only option is you." Zale knew exactly what Reynolds would ask of him even before he'd uttered the words; "You need to use your power, Zale. A full blast!"

"Dude!" he hollered in response as bullets hammered their position, keeping them from even looking over the barrier. "Do you know how much that takes out of me? How much that bloody well hurts?"

He couldn't see the sergeant's expression through his visor, but the man put a hand on Zale's shoulder and nodded sympathetically. "I understand, Zale. But we need you."

He told Reynolds exactly where he could shove his understanding, but nonetheless nodded reluctantly, snapping, "Fine! Cover me, ya bastard."

They were in the heat of battle, so Zale didn't have time to focus on his feelings about what was being asked of him.

Nevertheless, he had some trepidation.

Slamming his back into the barrier to stabilise himself, Zale used his powers to send electricity to his ears.

He took three deep breaths, then held it, listening intently.

He could hear them all now; everyone on this damn battlefield, their breaths, their heartbeats, the clicks of their triggers as they scarred this beautiful place with fire and smoke.

But he ignored them all. Instead Zale focused on the sounds of the bullets shattering on his cover and flying over his head. Within moments he had determined the location of the shooters, thirty meters away.

Two of them, and both had just reloaded, slamming in fresh magazines.

They continued their assault, confusing Zale as to the point. What did they hope to hit firing like this?

Either way, if he moved at the wrong moment he would probably be cut down, no matter how incompetent those shooting the rounds were. So he gave Reynolds a 'wait' signal, and held his position, biding his time.

Two seconds went by.

Three.

Four.

He heard the click of triggers being released, and magazines ejecting. Zale immediately indicated to Reynolds and bolted from his cover. At his signal, Reynolds also darted out and lay down covering fire from his single-rifle.

The shouts of alarm and agony from their attackers signalled their deaths.

Zale didn't stop to look, or even aim at anyone else. He kept on going, following the sound of tank treads grinding the stones.

He ran for what felt like days, past all the fighting, until he finally found his target. He skidded to a halt and hunkered down behind a pile of Apos bodies.

The tank was right in front of him now, about twenty metres away. The war machine fired into the Daemonium building, but the shell didn't do much damage.

Zale wasn't sure how long it had been trying to breach the facility, but he knew it would take a lot longer than that to get in. Walls that thick, made from demonic materials, weren't going to give way to something as pitiful as a human tank.

Zale discontinued the electricity flowing to his ears and stopping the super-hearing. He sighed thankfully as the noises around him returned to a normal volume. He hated using that power. It gave him such a headache, the noise was deafening.

The tank fired again, this time into a group of Daemonium soldiers. The explosion obliterated them, what remained of their corpses flying left and right.

It was a powerful war machine in its own right, and Zale needed to deal with it quickly. Studying it, he recognised designs in its chassis based on the Daemonium's own ideas. He tutted angrily; the bastards must have stolen a blueprint or something from one of their production facilities.

It was huge, bigger than any tank used by a human military. The barrel was positioned directly in the middle of the chassis, elevated slightly for better range, able to swivel and fire in any direction.

And though the armour was thick, Zale was able to see that the Apos had implemented their customary failings into its creation.

All the armour was at the front, whereas the sides looked particularly weak.

Having figured out where to hit it, Zale dropped his gun into the dirt, jumped to his feet, and called out to Horas. Electricity generated from somewhere deep within him, right to his arms, and they started to spark and flash.

Building the charge for as long as he possibly could, he threw out his hands and let rip with the biggest blast he'd ever conjured.

The voltage slammed into the tank treads, and the entire vehicle shuddered, electricity moving through the metal at an unforgiving rate.

The effort was *excruciating!*

Zale's heart was racing, his legs felt like they were going to collapse, and his chest seemed eager to explode.

He almost dropped to his knees, his body shaking, but he valiantly fought the weakness trying to overcome him. He kept the flow of electricity going, refusing to back down until the tank was destroyed.

He pushed harder, increasing the voltage despite his body's demands that he stop.

He roared in agony as the metal ripped apart, the treads melted, and the barrel swivelled in every direction as the operator panicked and tried to locate the source of the barrage.

A shell came very close to blowing Zale apart, and though the heat from the explosion was painful, he was able to ignore it. The driver was too disorientated to do too much damage to anything but the dirt; the enclosed space would be reaching insane temperatures now.

There was a loud scream as the top shot open and a brown figure tried to climb out. The Apos' stolen armour looked half melted, and he was writhing so much that he never made it out; the tank violently exploded, taking him and anyone else inside with it.

The current of electricity stopped and Zale let his arms fall. He was unable to stop himself from falling back, collapsing to the grass, where he stayed, too weak to move.

Taking a few deep breaths, gasping for air he could barely reach, he laughed gleefully, muttering, "Gotcha."

Over his radio he heard Reynolds' voice rallying the troops. "The tank is down. All units advance forward!"

Zale didn't move. The rest of the army would have to continue the engagement without him. He was sure they could mop up the remainder of the Apos without his help.

Because he was utterly spent.

Badrick heard a devastating explosion as he hid behind an overturned car, and saw a pillar of fire erupt into the sky. He stumbled back, only now noticing the small figure in the distance, blasting something he couldn't see with a humungous surge of electricity.

The figure collapsed to the floor as the fire dissipated, and in response the other soldiers leapt over their covers and started pummelling the invaders with everything they had.

Badrick breathed a sigh of relief. It appeared the battle was coming to an end, and they were winning.

He stood up so that he could survey the aftermath, feeling safer now that the Apos were being pushed back.

That was when he felt the impact on his back and he was sent sprawling to the concrete. He cut his hands on the hard surface, and rolled over angrily to shout at the idiot who'd knocked him over.

His fury ebbed away when he saw who had run into him.

In his panic, one of the Apos had tried to flee only to find Badrick in his way. They'd collided, and were now staring at each other intently.

Where the hell had he been hiding, Badrick thought, *for him to have been running away this close to the base?*

Before Badrick could even think about figuring the answer out, two more appeared around the corner, spotted them immediately, and helped their comrade to his feet.

He angrily picked up his weapon, and all three aimed their guns right at Badrick.

"Kill this dog," he snarled, "and let's get out of here."

chapter
SIX

⟨⟩ Ψ Ϻ

Badrick had never felt such fear.

He thought it was all over for him.

Already.

And it would have been, if not for the sudden intervention of a blinding flash of electricity hitting the chest of the lead villain.

He fell back, dead instantly, as two more blasts took care of his fellows.

Before they'd even hit the ground, a final surge struck Badrick in the foot. It was weak, and barely left a singe mark on his shoe.

But it *hurt*.

He bounced on one leg, crying out in pain and alarm. "ARGH! Son of a—"

"Sorry!" came a call from the other side of the grounds, barely audible over the now dying din of the gunfire. "You're lucky I'm drained. Could have taken your foot off!"

Badrick communicated a very rude gesture involving his middle finger, which only seemed to amuse the electric Enthraller.

"One day," Badrick muttered darkly, massaging his ankle, "I'll shoot you in the foot with a fireball and see how funny it is.

With the battle over and the Daemonium troops preoccupied with the clearing of bodies, Zale watched peacefully from a stool that had been propped up on the dirt, strangely bored now his life was no longer in peril.

Several times he tried to get up to find something to do, but each and every time he was pushed down by the medic tending to his arm.

"Down!" she shouted for the third time, ripping his helmet from his head. "My goodness, what recklessness is this? Using your power in such a way after taking a bullet to the arm? How stupid are you, Hood?"

"To be fair, I hadn't even noticed I got shot."

It was true; with the adrenaline from running through the battle and the focus on his hearing, he hadn't been aware of the stray bullet lodging itself underneath his left pauldron and piercing his skin until after he saved Badrick, where the pain had finally flared and caused him to misfire, hitting his partner.

His armour had saved the wound from being a lot worse, and he'd gotten away with only a small hole in his arm, the bone unharmed.

He wasn't even sure when it happened, except for that it had to have been around the time of the tank debacle.

But he didn't really care.

It was such a small thing, it was hardly worth a mention.

"Well done," a voice sounded, the owner clasping his exposed shoulder gratefully.

"Argh!"

The hand instantly withdrew. "I'm sorry!" Reynolds exclaimed. "Were you hit?"

"Only a little."

Reynolds smiled, relieved, and gave the pauldron still guarding his right shoulder a firm whack. "Take the weekend off, Hood. You deserve it."

"What about Badrick?"

"He's not going anywhere, and he'll keep until Wednesday," Reynolds said dismissively.

"Wednesday?"

"Aye. This attack was serious, Zale, and it brings to light our desperate need for a—"

"I know, I know!" Zale cried quickly. "Malcolm and I are trying, but his power just doesn't want to adapt to the tech."

"Well, I'm giving you all of Monday and Tuesday with no distractions to try and figure out a way to get his shields over this base without his limitations or the need to have him nearby."

"Shouldn't I use the weekend too?"

"The Apos need to recruit now. That was a huge assault force. They won't be attacking for a long time. There's no immediate hurry, so you can have your days off, but we do need to make it a priority."

"Why do you think they attacked so suddenly? So massively?"

Reynolds only shrugged in response. "Will the allocated time be enough for the job?"

"No promises, but it helps a lot. Thanks."

"You did well. You've earned it." Reynolds pointed into the distance and added, "Looks like you have a visitor. I'll leave you to it."

Badrick saw Reynolds pivot and hurry away just as a huge mess of long, curled hair crashed into Zale, smothering him in the golden locks.

Intrigued, he hurried to get over to them.

"Zale, are you alright?" the hair was shouting frantically.

"I'm fine, Carla," Zale told her, hugging her back until the moment she finally removed herself. "What are you doing out here?"

"John and I were caught in the crossfire. We were just getting back from our mission."

"Holy crap, are you alright? Did you get hit?"

"I'm fine." She waved away his concerns. "Though John got hit in the leg. He's fine, he's fine, the big baby."

Zale laughed, and the pair clasped hands in a show of militaristic affection, their leathery gloves rubbing noisily.

The girl called Carla pulled something on her armour, and the chestplate fell away, allowing her to stretch unconfined. Her torso flexed, and her chest pushed out, revealing—

Badrick's mouth fell open.

The size of them!

This girl was *incredible*!

Now that her chestplate was gone, Badrick had a full view of her upper body, the figure hugging under-suit leaving nothing to the imagination.

And when he looked, even the armour around her legs and waist could not hide the perfection—

Badrick stopped gawping when he noticed both the girl and Zale looking at him.

"Er . . . " he said, his cheeks reddening.

"Who's the gawker?" Carla asked, an expression on her face

that Badrick did not expect; amusement.

As he stood there, stuttering unintelligibly, Zale chuckled and told her, "My new partner."

"Ah, the new kid!" She took two steps closer and punched him on the shoulder in welcome. "How you doing?"

Badrick couldn't answer. Any attempt to would have resulted in him shouting in pain. She had a mean punch, coupled with the fact her fist was reinforced with armour.

Agony!

Zale gave the girl another quick hug, before allowing her to fuss over his wound, much to the irritation of the medic.

Unsure of where to put his eyes now, Badrick darted them left and right uncomfortably, until they finally rested on the medic herself.

He immediately looked away when he realised that she was just as beautiful and physically perfect, not wanting to be caught gaping at someone else.

Were there no ugly people here!?!

"How are you, man?" Zale asked, helping him to focus on someone without breasts. "Didn't get hit, did you?"

"No, thanks to you, though my foot still hurts."

"Sorry," Zale cackled. "Aiming while lying in exhaustion on the floor, with my perspective literally upside down, is not as easy as I thought it would be."

"Oh no?" Badrick retorted sarcastically.

No one said anything for a while after that. Badrick watched Carla pressing a wet cloth to his partner's bleeding arm, with the medic fruitlessly directing her. When he could stand the silence no more, he grappled for the first thing he could think of to say.

"Are you two together?"

Both Zale and Carla laughed.

But, though Badrick wasn't well versed in this stuff, he couldn't help but feel like both of them had suddenly become very nervous.

"No, we're just best friends," Carla said.

"We used to be partners," Zale informed him.

"Zale's amazing. A genius! Don't pout, you modest girl, you know you are. But I wasn't happy being in the SpecOps div. No free time, and I like having a life. How is a girl supposed to find guys when she's working all the time?"

"You can change divisions?" Badrick asked quickly.

"Only if you prove yourself," Zale laughed. "So no. Sorry. For now you're stuck where you are."

"So now I'm an agent." She indicated to her armour. "Hence the blue."

Badrick seized the subject immediately and pointed to their helmets. "Speaking of that, what the heck is this? Why do you guys have the same armour as my demon?"

Zale and Carla shared an amused grin, further irritating him, but he kept his tongue as Zale explained. "We aren't wearing the armour of your demon—Ow! Careful, Carla. We're wearing the standard issue combat suits of the Daemonium. Well, *she* is."

"We're pretty well known among demon-kind," Carla explained. "Whenever they show themselves to us, they have a habit of emulating our armour in their images, with their own flair thrown in of course. That's what your demon is doing. They *all* do that, even those who aren't part of this orgy."

Zale tried to stand up again, moaning that his legs were aching, but he was once again pushed down by both Carla and the medic. He tutted in frustration, but had no choice but to do as they commanded and so continued the explanation. "Remember, buddy, everything Vulrick has done has been in aid of getting you to us. In his case, his appearing in our armour is most likely part of that plan."

It made no sense to Badrick. Why would the demons bother? Why wouldn't they just appear as they did when in their own bodies?

Almost as if she had been reading his mind, Carla added, "We've been involved with demons for centuries and centuries. We've probably been influencing their culture for just as long. The armours are made from demonic metals, after all. They might even make their own down in Hell now."

"Maybe some of the demons actually emulate armour they've made themselves. That could be true," Zale nodded. "These suits, though, are amazing." He twisted off a forearm piece and handed it to Badrick, who turned it over in his hands, studying it. "Agents of the Daemonium wear a default issue set of blue armour, and—"

"The army wears red," a voice interrupted him. Badrick turned back to see Reynolds had returned. The sergeant gave him a quick smile, nodded to Carla in a friendly fashion, and called to the medic, "We need you over here."

"But my patient—" she argued.

"Is fine," Reynolds tutted. "He's faking the pain for female attention. I think he has an abundant amount, don't you?"

The medic grumbled and scowled at Zale. She picked up her med-kit and was gone in an instant, following Reynolds to God only knew where.

"As I was saying," Zale sighed, apparently unabashed by Reynolds' accusation, "agents wear blue, army wears red, but we SpecOps guys are special."

Carla made a face. "The higher ups think they're so important," she drawled, "they require special treatment, a way to identify them as 'the elite of the elite'."

"We get to have our own armour and choose *two* colours." Zale grinned smugly. "I designed mine myself. Custom."

"And I have my old SpecOps armour in my room," Carla told Badrick. "I wouldn't ever give it to someone else, even though they tried to make me, which they regretted. This idiot made it for me." She gave Zale a shove. "I love it."

Badrick's partner was certainly right about his armour; it wasn't just the colour configuration that was different. His pauldrons were bigger than the default version the other members sported, not as square, more like a plus sign that had been enlarged and fattened.

That was the best way Badrick could describe it.

The knee guards were also thicker, covering more space and hugging the under-suit tighter than Carla's did.

And the helmet had an extra piece, just above the visor, something like a mudguard on a bike helmet.

"Why does it turn blue when you put it on?" he asked, looking at it now and pondering on its return to gold.

"Same reason as these," Zale laughed cockily, pointing at his eyes. "My demon. Only Enthraller to ever have physical attributes associated with a hellspawn."

"And that ridiculous hair?"

"Nope, that's all me, baby. I'm just *that* good looking."

Carla gave him a push on the head for his cockiness, and, having finished wrapping his wound in a bandage, allowed him to zip his under-suit back up.

Then she promptly thrust his pauldron back on his arm. He grimaced from the discomfort and gave her a pained wink.

"You look after that arm, you hear?" Carla told him. "I don't want you ripping open those stitches."

"Are we sure you didn't just do that?" he chided her. He jumped slightly as she put a commanding finger right in his face. "Yes, miss," he laughed.

She blew him a kiss, winked at Badrick, then picked up her

chestplate and helmet. "Bye boys."

They both stared after her as she left.

"She is *so* your girlfriend," he cackled at Zale.

"Naw, man." His partner stood up painfully, swaying slightly. Badrick held out his hand and steadied him, receiving a smile as thanks. "She is hot though, right?" Zale's smile turned into something far less innocent.

"Most stunning creature I've ever seen," Badrick nodded. "*Ever.*"

Zale bent and picked up his helmet. He turned it over and moaned. "Damage to the radio. I thought everyone sounded fuzzy."

He still looked very weak, pale, his eyes misted, and though Badrick could only guess it was because of the huge blast he'd summoned, he nevertheless didn't bother him by asking, instead helping him walk across the grounds, into the HQ and all the way back to his room.

"*Grazie,*" the agent sighed, falling to his bed, where he slowly began removing pieces of his armour.

He was almost down to nothing but his under-suit when Badrick finally found the courage to ask, "Zale . . . who were those guys?"

After everything he'd seen he wasn't sure if he wanted to know who these new villains were.

But he had to ask.

He had to know.

"Those guys," Zale breathed, "were the Apostaticus."

"The what?" Badrick almost shouted with infuriation. *Another mental name!? What is with these people? Why can't they just call themselves something simple?*

"The Apostaticus," Zale repeated. "A bunch of a-holes, if I do say so myself."

Badrick threw his arms up in despair, but decided not to question it. He didn't want to get stuck discussing the pros and cons of titling.

Zale continued, "They're a bunch of Enthrallers who oppose us. We don't know why, or what we did to offend them, but they seriously hate our guts. A decade ago they stole the designs to our armour and the secrets to mining demonic metals."

"What do they want? Why did they attack us?"

"We have no idea," Zale said. "Sorry," he added at Badrick's frustrated expression. "They just hate us. We don't know where they came from, how they organised, or what their motivation is. They appeared around a hundred and fifty years ago, if my count is correct. They've been hassling us ever since."

"And they're all Enthrallers? They all have demons?"

"Oh yes, strong ones too. Some of us think that the demons are behind it. That some don't like our organisation teaching humans to control them, and have started a rebellion. That theory does have some stock, but I don't know. Demons can't control their Enthrallers."

"They can influence them, though."

"To get angry enough to kill, yes. But . . . I don't know. Who cares, really?"

Badrick mulled on this for a while as Zale yanked the last of his armour from his body, sighing gratefully.

He wasn't so naïve to think that he was clever enough to figure it out, but it worried him that the Daemonium didn't know what the Apos wanted out of it all.

Did they just want to destroy them?

Or was there more to it?

"So," Zale interrupted his train of thought, "now that you've seen all of *that* how has that affected your decision?"

Badrick smiled softly. "How do you know it has?"

Zale shrugged. "I'm clever."

For a moment, he gave no answer. Though Badrick knew exactly how he felt, he was, for some reason, slightly hesitant to voice it.

"I . . . " he began warily, "didn't enjoy seeing it. And to be honest, what I saw was terrible. Disgusting."

"Blood is never pretty."

That wasn't what Badrick was referring to, but at Zale's words he decided not to go into more detail about his true feelings. Instead he simply said, "Listen, I didn't like what I saw. From the look of it, I have a future of killing, ended by my premature death, to look forward to. I'm pretty sure I decided to leave when I first saw it.

"But now . . . it's weird. I still want to stay, and not just because I have nowhere else to go. I don't know why I want to stay, I just do. Does that make sense?"

Zale nodded knowingly. "People like us tend to have slightly warped morals. What you saw doesn't bother you as much as it should. Side effect of having the pinnacle of all evil in our souls." He stood up and, with a sudden burst of warmth, gripped Badrick's shoulder firmly. "The trick is to keep a line drawn. Use the demon, don't become him."

He gave Badrick one last grin, then yanked at the zip of his under-suit, revealing his chest. "Now, I have the weekend off, thanks to Reynolds, and work on Monday and Tuesday. That means you have *four* days off. I think that's a good idea after what you've just seen. Pick this up on Wednesday?"

Badrick smiled tightly—not minding in the slightest—his mind still on the Apos, and nodded.

"Good!" the Enthraller exclaimed. "Now vamoose! Only unfairly hot women get to see me naked."

Badrick left the room, Zale banging the door shut behind him.

He stood there for quite some time, gently running his nails along the orange walls, deep in thought.

He couldn't stop thinking about what Zale had said. That Enthrallers had warped morals, and that was why the combat hadn't disturbed him.

Badrick didn't entirely agree. He felt strangely calm about the violence for different reasons; in a sense he'd always known this would be a violent place, and fighting demons would obviously involve some disturbing things. Knowing that had prepared him, and he'd already come to terms with it.

It wasn't as though his life hadn't been one big violent horror film to begin with.

But he hadn't meant the violence when he'd spoken; he'd been talking about the fun the soldiers were having. As if the killing wasn't a necessary evil, but a sport to be enjoyed.

Badrick didn't feel like he had warped morals, because he found *that* disgusting. If warped morals turned people into that then he did *not* have warped bloody morals.

With a start Badrick realised he'd left the hallway, his hurried thoughts inspiring his muscles to move, and was now approaching the window overlooking the grounds far below.

Badrick had been so deep in thought he was not even aware of when he'd started moving.

The cleaning was almost finished. Badrick could see them wrapping up down there through the window, the soldiers either pulling back into the base or returning to guard positions along the wall.

And although the vicious fighting had hurt the landscape, the grounds still retained their beautiful resonance. They were resilient, that was safe to say.

He realised his hand was jerking, and he reached to steady it. This fight had definitely shaken him up, but he knew he'd be alright now it was over. If only it hadn't been so big of an attack—the damn Apos had broken right through the wall guards—who would have given their lives fighting them off—by the time he got there.

But it didn't matter now. They were safe once again.

Badrick didn't leave the window until much later that evening. He stayed, watching the sun drop, unable to stop pondering on the day's events.

Zale vacated his room shortly after Badrick, and through the glass he saw his partner leaving the base, presumably to start his days off elsewhere.

He zoomed away on what appeared to be a motorbike. Zale didn't even bother waiting for the Wall Entrance to open; he drove the vehicle up a set of stairs heading to the battlements before launching it over the side, landing neatly back on the dirt and speeding away in an instant.

The guy was crazy.

chapter
SEVEN

Badrick sat silently on the spare chair in the corner of the BCR, watching as Reynolds paced with frustration, back and forth, over and over, and disturbing the Agent Commanders, much to their irritation.

Periodically he would turn and shout, "Where is he?" or "I'll hide him!"

And it wasn't until eleven a.m. that the cause of this behaviour finally stumbled in, swaying so much Badrick was surprised he could walk at all.

"What the . . . Are you hammered?" he asked.

"No . . . dizzy," was Zale's reply.

Reynolds' next shout was such a roar that it made several of the BCR agents jump in their chairs. "Where in the *hell* have you been!?"

"London," Zale grinned back.

"You're late! *Very late!*"

"Sergeant," Zale drawled, "a king is never late because he decides the time of his arrival—"

"This *'king'* is going to get punched in the face if he doesn't stop being an arse and gets back to work."

"*Yessir!*" Zale gave the sergeant a sharp salute. Reynolds rolled his eyes, straightened his bright red uniform, and briskly hurried away, presumably, if Badrick had to guess, to punch a picture of Zale over and over.

With the laughter that had taken hold of him finally under control, Badrick took his hands away from his stomach to wipe away his amused tears. "What do you mean *'king'?*" he asked. "What have you been doing?"

"I, my son, am a king in the art of seduction."

"Hahaahaaa, what!?"

Zale's eyes misted dreamily, and he raised a hand, stroking the air as if he could actually touch the memories. "One had dyed blue hair, the other had beautiful bright dyed red hair, and neither were shy. Neither were very *Christian* at all. Was awesome."

Badrick's laughter resumed, and he almost fell from the chair as his stomach convulsed.

"*What's* so funny?" Zale demanded.

"You got down and dirty with the Daemonium." When his partner frowned in confusion, Badrick elaborated, "One red, one blue. It's the Daemonium. I think you have issues."

The look on Zale's face was priceless. *"Dayum!"*

*

Wednesday took an age to come. Badrick didn't see Zale at all during the rest of Monday or Tuesday; the SpecOps operative was kept busy working with Malcolm, the jailor.

Badrick didn't mind. He knew some severe hardships were coming, and soon, so he was thankful for as much time to himself as he could get.

And though he got a little bored, he was able to kill several hours a day playing basketball in the grounds with Carla.

He was ashamed to say she completely kicked his arse.

But at least he got a good view of hers every time she pulled off a perfect slam dunk, and seeing her in sporty clothes was the best thing to happen to him since *birth*.

Eventually the four days ended, and Zale re-emerged, kicking his way out of one of the labs and draping his arm over Badrick's shoulders.

They were in one of the three recreation rooms. Badrick had been reading some kind of old fiction book about dragons when his partner barged in.

"Hello," Badrick greeted him, eyeing his exhausted form.

Zale gave a heavy sigh and looked him right in the eye, his face only inches away. "Phew . . . You ready?"

"Guess so," Badrick answered truthfully. "Did you do what you were trying to do?"

"Nope, not even close."

Zale looked like he hadn't showered in days, and he was panting like he'd run a thousand miles in eight seconds. "You alright?" Badrick half laughed.

"Yeah." Zale pointed to his brain. "I never thought using this could exhaust someone so much. That, and not having slept since the weekend."

"I think you got enough sleep for the both of us at the weekend."

"I find it adorable you think that," Zale laughed loudly, and looked like he was about to add something when he was interrupted by a deafening shout.

"No! It's mine! Mine, I say!"

A frown ruffled Badrick's brow, and he made for the large window that overlooked the Main Hall. As Zale came up beside him, he found the cause of the commotion.

Someone was running through the Main Hall, hands tightly gripped over something Badrick didn't recognise. Behind, blue uniformed Enthrallers chased him everywhere he went, leaping forward and trying to grab his feet, but every time he would jump or duck out of reach.

"What the hell is going on?" Badrick exclaimed. A second later a woman managed to grab the running man's arm, only to lose her grip and fall heavily back to the floor. "Give us that orb, you freak!"

"Oh, don't mind him," Zale sighed tiredly, ignoring the woman's outburst. "He's crazy. And I mean actually crazy, caused by demonic forces. We're stuck with him, I'm afraid."

"Wa-wa-wa-woooo!?" the man screamed, moments before shooting straight up as though able to fly and disappearing into the shadows of the ceiling.

Zale cut off the laughing Badrick with a finger and a stern expression. "It's funny now, but demonically caused insanity is a horrible thing. Pray it never happens to you."

"Er . . . How would it happen to me?"

"Someone with the power to do it to you, is how. We'd look after you if you were affected, put you out of your misery if you'd be better off. Either way, they go through torment."

Badrick took a horrified step back. *"Jesus."*

"Welcome to the real world, man," Zale said sadly. "It's grim."

Both of them pondered on this sudden turn into morbid their day had just taken, neither speaking to the other. Badrick watched the Enthrallers grumbling at the loss of a jetpack to the crazy man.

He listened to the harsh words they communicated, every syllable perfectly audible even from this distance, frowning in anger at the cruelty they were exhibiting.

The crazy man was nowhere to be seen. He had completely vanished into a corner so high even the floodlights at the very top could not pick him out.

"He'll be OK up there, right?" He heard one of the agents call the man a *very* offensive name and felt his angry frown tighten.

"He's fine," Zale assured him. "He's the least affected one we've ever seen, which is why he was never put down. He's just a bit mental."

The way Zale talked about putting *people* down so easily, as if they were animals, sent flares of rage through Badrick's mind, so strong that he could even feel it in his chest.

But he didn't call his partner on it.

Zale hadn't been cruel with his words, only speaking the truth as it was. There was no point starting a fight because of that.

"Now." Zale clapped him on the shoulder. "We actually have work to do. You haven't managed to use a power yet, apart from that manic jump thing you told me about when I got back on Monday. That's not great. But I think if we put you through some physical training, it might loosen you up a little."

Badrick did his best to put the flying man out of his thoughts, and replied softly, "What kind of physical training."

"Free-running, mainly."

His face must have lit up because Zale grinned and added, "Cool, right? This place has its moments. Now free-running isn't simple, but your demon can help you with it. The buggers aren't just powerful, some of them are incredibly athletic beings, and we can tap into that as well as their powers.

"Vulrick will help you. Eventually. All our demons help us

here, which I've never actually understood. Why would the demons help the people they're trapped in? It sounds like torture to me."

Badrick nodded, but said nothing.

"Anyway, we'll start with a basic . . . "

He never finished that sentence. He slowly trailed off, as if his attention had been diverted.

Turning to see what he was looking at, Badrick spotted a group of Enthrallers hurrying through the Main Hall, murmuring in low voices.

They disappeared through an archway, and the hall quietened once more.

But Zale didn't tear his eyes away. He was staring at the archway with squinted eyes, as though he was deep in thought.

Badrick started to ask him what was wrong.

But, without warning, he bolted away, charging through the door out of the recreation room. Surprised—and a little alarmed—Badrick sped after him, utterly confused.

What was going on?

He traced Zale's footsteps all the way to the top floor, running for what felt like hours. He was entirely out of breath by the time Zale stopped and slammed his fist into a door.

It opened, and he jumped through. Cursing the size of the Daemonium facility and his own unfitness, Badrick stumbled after him.

Looking around, he saw that they'd arrived at an incredibly crowded room. A few dozen people in blue, red and black uniforms were jostling around a rounded, oblong table, all talking over each other, fighting for the right to be heard.

The room was an incredible sight though Badrick wasn't able to appreciate the interior design a whole lot. He could tell it was a lavishly decorated room, but the presence of so many people was obscuring his view.

Badrick recognised a few of them, people he'd seen walking around, as well as Reynolds, who was at the far end of the table, his chin in his hand and the other supporting that arm.

"This meeting has been postponed long enough!" The sergeant's shout was loud enough to pierce the din and stop the arguing. Everyone shut their mouths and turned to him, some looking slightly stunned at the sheer volume of his roar. "Thank you." He sighed heavily, rolling his eyes. *"Christ!"*

"Where is the Hierarch?" someone asked from amongst the crowd.

"He's entrusting the matter to us," Reynolds responded politically.

"I haven't seen him in a week," snapped a woman, who was actually wearing her armour. The custom white seemed strangely contrast to the various bright colours in the room.

SpecOps, Badrick thought.

"He's up in his penthouse suite," an agent scoffed.

"No one's seen him," added a soldier.

"Not since . . . " Whoever was speaking trailed off.

And then everyone looked at Badrick, suddenly noticing him there.

"Anyway," the sergeant sighed, bringing them back to the meeting, "this is a serious concern. Their armaments were far more up to speed with ours this time, and that tank was clearly a rip straight from our design."

"We didn't have any heavy weapons to fight that thing. This needs to be addressed, Reynolds."

"A lot of things need to be addressed!" Reynolds bawled, holding his hands out to everyone as they started arguing again. "One thing at a time! What we can agree, is that we're all seriously worried."

"When *aren't* we?" Zale suddenly piped up. Badrick saw him leaning against the wall, watching them all as if they were beneath him. Many of those present gave Zale, not to mention Badrick himself, hostile glances that suggested they weren't entirely welcome in the room at this time.

But Reynolds nodded welcomingly at the sight of him.

Even though he was only a sergeant, Reynolds appeared to be the spearhead of this meeting. Badrick was impressed. He appeared to be greatly respected.

"A lot of things must be addressed, it is true," he continued. "Firstly, our heavy armaments are on their way. We should get them by the end of the month. Our production facilities cannot get the work and the transit done any faster than that, but a second attack during that time is highly unlikely.

"The Apos were never the biggest organisation in the world, or the smartest. It is likely that their forces are expended for now, and they will be looking to reinforce for quite some time.

"Unfortunately, they have beaten us to the metal deposits the last six times. We've lost a lot of good men in those skirmishes. We have to be faster. When those metal deposits materialise we have to work on setting up a forward base faster than we have been.

"It's getting too hard keeping the world's scientists from discovering the demonic element and preventing it falling into Apos hands. They don't care about it being discovered by normal humans, and if that happens . . . you can imagine what else will be exposed. We have to do better."

Following Reynolds words, a tense silence ensued. Everyone mulled it over, exchanging glances with one another.

"That's not such a big ask," a voice spoke over the quiet. "If we organise practice drills for the army we should be able to increase efficiency."

"Practices with our scanning software wouldn't go amiss, either," said an Asian soldier, his accent diluted with undertones of English. "Failing to identify the deposits sooner is one of our biggest problems."

Everyone present nodded their agreement.

"Lieutenant Johnson and I are sending a contingent of our platoon to the production facility in charge of heavy weapons," Reynolds informed the room. "Just in case. Can anyone else spare any men?"

Two hands rose into the air, and within minutes a plan had been drawn up for the redeployment of fifty or so soldiers for protection duty.

"You're forgetting about us," spoke a dissident voice over the clamour. "Sure, if everything goes according to plan we'll have heavy weapons again. But what if it doesn't? And what about now? Can we be sure the Apos are weak? We're currently recruit heavy. Sometimes it feels like there are more of them than us actual veterans. They can't protect us the next time the Apos attack."

The sound of indistinguishable argument erupted once again, and Badrick quickly lost track of the conversation, try as he might to keep up.

As the higher-ups shouted and insulted each other, Badrick heard a much lower voice to his right, and turned to see a blue uniformed man, who looked like he was in his late twenties, giving a terse greeting to Zale.

"Who was that?" he asked his partner, once the man shuffled away.

"Zach," Zale muttered. "My rival. Hates me."

Badrick was unable to question in what capacity Zach was his rival as Reynolds had just whistled so shrilly it caused several of the room's occupants to slam their hands over their ears, including

Zale.

"Reynolds!" he groaned loudly. "Super hearing . . . Come on now."

"Comrades, please," the sergeant called. "Why are you fighting among yourselves? Remember who the enemy is. The Apos, the Kalik, the Forsaken."

"The royal family," a woman added.

Reynolds sighed. "Yes . . . the royal family."

Royal family? Badrick's inner voice parroted. *The English one? They're our enemies? Are we fighting the Queen of England?*

"But Johnson is right, this latest attack calls for action. We need to act now. The proposition put yesterday of advancing the training program is the best idea put forward. I agree, it'll be risky, but I think we need to do it."

Some of the soldiers present nodded agreeably. "It's been done before in a crisis."

Someone leaned in and whispered in Reynolds' ear.

And both of them looked at Badrick, their faces stern.

Their piercing eyes made him shudder, and he got the horrible feeling they were talking about him specifically.

After an elongated moment of yet more silence, Reynolds looked to his right, and ordered, "Zach, we want you to take your task force and try to figure out where the Apos are getting their armaments from. We've recorded no thefts, not of actual weapons, and they don't have the skill to construct them themselves. Not to that quality."

"Of course, sir." The agent named Zach left the room, nodding concisely at Zale and giving Badrick a once over as he passed.

"Zale, gear up," Reynolds called across the room. "We're giving you an assignment."

Zale's eyebrows rose as Reynolds spoke. "Really?" he said.

"About time. How long's it been? Three months? Glad you're finally giving me my seventh *proper* assignment and not just throwing me dumb-arse investigations."

"Dumb-arse investigations?" Badrick parroted, utterly confused now.

Was Zale a detective?

He hadn't mentioned anything about that.

But, then again, they'd only known each other for a week. There was still a lot they had to learn about one another.

"You'll be hunting down a Forsaken," Reynolds informed him, "and neutralising him before he hurts any innocents."

"Got it."

"Last know location was in this sector." The sergeant revealed his arm computer and tapped on it. A hologram of some kind of mountain flashed into existence over the table, and a small marker indicated to a small section at the base, where the mountain met the dirt. "It's pretty close by, so he shouldn't be hard to find."

"Awesome." Zale's expression suddenly changed, and he added, "Actually, what about Bad—"

"Badrick will be going with you."

With that, Zale exploded. Any joy he exhibited at being given an assignment vanished in a flash, replaced with complete and utter outrage.

"He's *what!?*"

Reynolds gave him a hard look and held it for several moments before saying, "Badrick has joined the Daemonium and therefore must be prepared to accept any assignments given to him. His training is being sped up along with the rest of the recruits. We're sending him out with you to kill the Forsaken."

Zale shoved everyone out of his way to get closer to the table, where he put his palms upon the wood and stared right into Reynolds stubborn face. "He hasn't even managed to use a power yet. We haven't even gotten to weapons training. He has *nothing*. It's been a goddamn week. You can't do this to him!"

"No arguments! We need everyone!"

Getting quite furious that he was being talked about as if he weren't even there, Badrick dared to utter, "Do I get a say in this?"

"No!" was the reply from everyone.

"Zale, take him to the armoury. Let him choose his primary weapon. I trust his armour is completed?"

The nineteen year old didn't answer for a moment. He continued to glare at Reynolds in disbelief.

But eventually he took a defeated, slow step back and nodded in confirmation. "I did the designs the day he got here. The lab finished the build yesterday."

"Good. Get to it."

Zale swore at them all, quite loudly, then about-faced and marched out of the room. "Come on, mate," he muttered.

At those words, Badrick stepped after him out into the hall.

"What's going on?" he asked, struggling to keep up with the storming Zale as they made their way down staircase after staircase.

"Something stupid," was the only reply he received.

Zale led him all the way down, across a bridge in the Main Hall and into the other half of the HQ. From there they ascended once again, before heading into a large open room.

Badrick stopped short at the sight of what was inside.

Dozens of tables—every single one adorning a multitude of weapons.

Guns, blades, grenades.

"Whoa . . ."

"Yep," Zale sighed. He wandered dejectedly between the tables until he reached one at the far end of the room, picking up two weapons, one in each hand, and holding them up for Badrick to see.

One looked exactly like the weapon Zale used during the battle with the Apos. The other was stockier, with a much longer barrel and sporting a small scope.

"Alright," Zale began, "first things first; choose your weapon." He shook the longer barrelled weapon. "This is a single-rifle. It fires a single, precise shot at medium to long distances." He shook the other. "This is the auto-rifle, short to medium. The name speaks for itself."

Zale placed them back onto their table at the same moment Badrick asked, "I have to choose one of these?"

"Every Enthraller chooses a primary weapon out of these two, depending on their preference. You can choose either."

Badrick had no training with either weapon—or any weapon, for that matter—nor had he ever seen a gun before coming to the Daemonium, so how was he supposed to know which better suited him?

"Why do you use the auto-rifle?" he asked, hoping Zale's answer would aid his choice, as silly as that idea was.

"I was a sharp-shot when I was training," Zale sighed, "so I chose the auto-rifle to expand my area of expertise. I don't like having a weak spot in my skill-set."

Badrick marched between the many tables, passing pistols and grenades and long, razor sharp combat knives, Badrick quickly picked up the single-rifle, hefting the heavy weapon with difficulty. "I think this one," he muttered.

"Choose carefully, Badrick."

"I'm certain. We're partners, right? Something tells me having both types of primary weapons in our duo will work to our advantage."

A small smile spread across Zale's face, and he nodded, acknowledging the statement. "I think that's fair logic," he said quietly.

Though his smile became strained at the sight of Badrick struggling to even keep the weapon held upright. "Oh boy," he muttered.

"So what next?" Badrick swiftly queried, moving the process along and pretending he didn't notice Zale's concern.

He didn't need to see that, not with how he was feeling at that moment.

Badrick had the distinct feeling he was being thrown even further into the deep end, and that it could result in his death.

His heart wouldn't stay still.

And his stomach was moving.

A lot.

"Do we go on this mission thing?" he continued.

"Not yet. First you need your armour." With that, Zale indicated behind him.

Upon turning, Badrick came face to face with the coolest thing he'd ever laid eyes upon.

"Hope you don't mind," Zale brushed past him and put his hand lovingly on the shiny new armour that stood before them. "I designed the colours and style for you."

"Dude, it's awesome! It's really for me?"

"It really is."

Badrick approached the armour, which, now he was closer, he could see was propped up on some kind of display pole. He imitated Zale, stroking a hand across the chest-plate, feeling the hard metal.

Whereas the default version of the helmets around here were somewhat angular, like a motorbike helmet, Zale had chosen a more rounded design for his. The visor looked like an oval, which had been bent around the front.

The pauldrons were unique as well; two big H shaped pieces

that protected the shoulders and upper arms.

As for the colouration, the primary was an olive green, covering most of the armour, much like the grey covered Zale's. But his partner had chosen white as the secondary, which adorned the boots, parts of the arms and the knee guards.

In Badrick's opinion, it was the best combination of colours Zale could have chosen.

There was nothing to say about the leather under-suit. That never seemed to change.

"You sure you like?" Zale asked. "Our armour is important. As SpecOps it defines us as people, reflects our personalities."

"Dude, it's sweet. Thanks."

Zale gave him a big, relieved smile, and took a bow.

The next few minutes were spent teaching Badrick what the armour could do. Zale proceeded to show him how to properly suit up, encouraging him to make a few quick attempts at doing it as fast as he could.

But eventually time caught up with them, and an agent interrupted to tell them to hurry up.

Zale handed Badrick his helmet, and he gently placed it over his head, completely encasing himself. If he had to scratch now, there was nothing he could do about it.

"The helmet is where the technology is," Zale taught him. "The rest of it is just leather and metal, but inside the helmet you have a radio, a scanner, a radar, rebreather, and the visor will automatically darken to blot out lights that get too bright, as well as brighten to light up the dark."

He was instructed on how to activate the rebreather. All he had to do was chin a hidden pad on the inside of his helmet, which would require a sharp jab. The helmet would seal itself to the under-suit, providing an air tight seal, and would then begin to provide oxygen.

It was only limited and not recommended for deep sea diving, but Zale assured him that in a situation where gas was employed, or if Badrick fell into water, activating this device was the surest way to survive.

"Of course if you fall into water, detach the armour as quickly as you can, and keep only the helmet. There's no way you're swimming with all that on."

"I could just walk on the floor until I got to the surface," Badrick suggested.

"Try falling into a tank of water, with nothing but glass on all sides. Not fun, buddy. Trust the Hood."

The scanner and radio were easy. It was all voice controlled and Badrick had the hang of it within minutes.

Once Zale finished briefing him on all his equipment, including on how to use his weapon properly, he was sent to the Main Hall, where he awaited Zale's return.

His partner had to shower before leaving, and get ready himself. He hadn't done any kind of self-hygienic activity since returning from his *intimate* weekend, and there was no way, in his own words, he was going on a mission in that state.

Reynolds and the rest of the Daemonium 'be damned'.

He wasn't gone long though; despite his somewhat prurient personality Zale was more vigilant in his role in the Daemonium than most of the higher-ups seemed to be.

Badrick could tell he took his work very seriously, and could always be trusted to get the job done. He was thankful fate had gifted him with Zale as a partner.

Although, in truth, he kind of wanted Carla.

Pretty soon they were heading out, both of them clad in their armour, weapons in hand.

Zale led them through the grounds and into the vehicle depot, pulling out a set of keys and unlocking the doors to a very stylish car.

As they piled in, Zale started the vehicle, then sat back and consulted his arm.

It took Badrick a moment to realise that he had his little computer thing with him. He'd unstrapped it from his bare arm and slotted it into a place in the metal obviously designed to house it.

"When do I get one of those arm computer things?" Badrick asked, eyeing it jealously.

It looked so cool.

"When you grow up," Zale laughed.

"Funny."

"It's called a port-pad, and you'll get one when you finish your training." Zale finished tapping on the screen and put his hands on the steering wheel.

"Hold on to your stomach, Badrick," Zale warned him. "I drive way too fast."

"Yeah," he muttered, quickly taking a hold of the chair with one hand, and the dashboard with the other. "So I've seen."

chapter
EIGHT

The drive to the Forsaken's location was tense, and Badrick could feel his heart racing faster and faster as they drew ever nearer. Zale briefed him on the mission as they went, which, with his habit of overly describing the gory parts, didn't help ease anxiety.

The questions that tormented him in the last hours had been quite forgotten some time earlier, but although everything he wanted to ask was now coming back to mind, he felt far too anxious to bother.

At this point he no longer cared if he ever got the answers.

His anxiety had completely overridden his usually questioning personality.

"A Forsaken is a powerful entity, brother," explained the veteran beside him. "It's an Enthraller whose demon has basically said, 'No, thank you' to the whole being ripped-out-of-Hell-and-squished-into-a-human-soul thing. The moment the Enthraller comes into his or her powers, the demon actively drives him or her mad, creating a Forsaken. Its entire existence is spent being influenced by the demon to get itself killed.

"We have no choice but to comply. They are monsters, Badrick. Complete animals; growling, spitting, savaging, all of it. They will kill you and never ask questions. They will eat your flesh from your bones for dinner.

"All you can do in the face of such savagery is fight for your life, and be very thankful your demon isn't doing the same to you. As far as I'm aware, most demons don't bother because they'll just be stuffed back into another human upon another birth, making the entire effort pointless.

"They stick it out now, for better or worse. Who knows . . . maybe they've grown to like it."

"You guys suck," Badrick muttered simply. His stomach was churning like never before, and he felt like he was going to be sick all over the windshield.

"I don't tell you this to scare you. I'm telling you so you're prepared."

"Yeah . . . thanks."

Zale watched Badrick out of the corner of his eye. He couldn't see his face through his shiny new visor but he could tell from the teenager's body language that he was terrified.

Terrified, yet calm, and though Zale was still fuming at the unjust deployment of an untrained recruit he felt himself cool a little in the face of Badrick's composure.

By rights he should have been freaking out. He was about to enter a violent fight without any preparation whatsoever. It was *insane!*

"I must admit," Zale voiced, speaking his thoughts, "I'm surprised how calm you are. Most people would be bouncing off the walls right about now."

Badrick didn't answer for a moment. He fiddled with the barrel of his single-rifle and stared at the scenery as it flashed past.

But then he sighed and muttered, "I was serious about agreeing to join. I want in. And I *am* freaking out. Just . . . on the inside."

"Fair enough."

But it was more than that, Zale figured. The tones in Badrick's voice told a different story. Apart from the moment his voice wavered when he'd said, 'I want in', it had otherwise remained smooth and coherent.

Badrick appeared to possess a resolve greater than most other men, Enthrallers included.

The only other partner Zale was ever this impressed by, who'd shown this level of courage, was his Carla. There had been *no one* else.

Reynolds didn't count. The man was like his damn dad.

Zale sped the car around a corner, and rocketed onwards down the country roads, but barely concentrating on his driving.

He was stuck in his head, ranting in his mind.

Why were the higher-ups sending Badrick out now? They said they were speeding up the training regime . . . but this wasn't speeding it up, this was bypassing it altogether.

Where was the logic in sending an Enthraller out into the field with no training, no control of their powers and who could barely lift the weapons they were given?

And now that Zale really thought about it, what was with their fascination with Badrick? All he'd heard the last week was Badrick this, Badrick that.

It was so very unlike the Daemonium Council to focus on one

of their recruits so fervently.

It might have something to do with that energy spike he'd detected. The one that had originated around Badrick.

What had that even been?

There was only one answer; it was related to that time four years ag—

Zale jumped sharply as Badrick nudged him on the shoulder. The car jerked violently and the operative had to fight to regain control.

"Whoa!" Badrick shouted in a half panic. "Sorry."

"No, no, it's fine," Zale breathed as the car stopped careening. "I was lost in my own head."

Badrick pointed out the window and said, "I was just going to tell you that over there looks like the place on the hologram thing."

Zale glanced over before bringing the car to a halt and consulting his port-pad, tapping on it with expert rapidity. "You're right," he laughed. "Well spotted. I gotta start concentrating."

As Zale slammed his foot back onto the gas-pedal, Badrick studied the mountain in the distance. It loomed over the tree line to their right, though it quickly disappeared from view as Zale ran their vehicle down a path that cut through the woods.

Eventually, after much bouncing around on uneven terrain, they stopped. Zale killed the engine, picked up his auto-rifle and stepped out. He looked up at the mountain, which was just visible through the leaves of the trees.

"England has so few actually impressive mountains," he sighed, speaking slowly. "It's a shame this one has to be marred by a Forsaken."

He cocked his weapon, and Badrick noticed the vivid blue visor turn his way. "Let's do this."

The sick feeling in Badrick's stomach threatened to explode, but nevertheless he swallowed his fear, raised his own weapon—with difficulty—and followed his partner through the forest.

They'd stopped very close to the mountain, practically in the middle of nowhere. It was gorgeously vibrant in this place, the trees and grasses a beautiful summer green. From the look of it all Badrick guessed the season sneaked up on them during the days he'd been stuck inside the Daemonium.

He'd completely lost track of time while trapped within its walls, but now he was outside again for what felt like the first time in centuries, he was able to reorientate himself.

As they moved forward Zale would crouch to the ground every few moments, checking the soil for God only knew what. Badrick wasn't sure—he was just following Zale's lead—but it looked like he was trying to find tracks left behind by their quarry.

After an hour of this, however, Badrick couldn't help but say, "Face it, you're lost."

"We're not lost!" Zale snapped in return. "I just can't find the damn thing."

"Well, hurry up. I'm sweating from the heat out here."

"The under-suit is temperature regulated, actually. If you're sweating, it's because you're anxious. Just keep ca—AH!"

Badrick jumped in fright and immediately raised his weapon as Zale collapsed heavily to the dirt. In his panic he felt his hand tense; the trigger pulled back and his weapon fired a shot, the gun bucking so hard Badrick cried out as the bone in his arm practically shattered.

The bullet smashed into a tree, ruining its originally untarnished bark, the impact louder than Badrick imagined.

But it wasn't loud enough to drown out the obnoxious voice that next spoke. "Never be too anxious, but always remember to be cautious."

Badrick wasn't listening. He didn't care what the new arrival had to say, only that he'd hit Zale on the back of the head and was now pointing an auto-rifle at him.

"Who are you!?" Badrick shouted.

"My apologies," Zale's attacker spoke again. "Introductions are in order. I'm a corporal in the Daemonium Army. My name is Mawr."

"You've got to be kidding." Badrick's response hardly did it justice; this guy was certainly from the Daemonium—he had the armour.

And it wasn't brown, which ruled out the possibility of him being an Apos.

Hopefully.

The only problem was that the design was not standard issue.

The helmet was different, less rounded, sharp, and had extra enforcement over the 'eyebrows' of the visor.

The shoulder pads were even weirder; they curved around his arm like some kind of armband that had been cut in half, and each had two 'horns' that stuck up on the top.

What was exceptionally odd was that the chestplate was insanely armoured. More so than any other Badrick had seen.

The extra metal had no paint job; whereas the newcomer's colour palette was a combination of blue and red, the add-ons were grey and dull.

With all that extra stuff, Badrick's knowledge told him that the so called 'Mawr' should have been SpecOps, not army, and his claiming to be a soldier rang alarms in Badrick's mind.

"You're lying," he voiced, taking a step closer.

But then Zale's hand grabbed his gun's barrel, preventing Badrick from aiming at Mawr. He stood up and shook his head at Badrick, silently communicating for him to stand down.

"It's alright," he said quietly. "This guy is on the level." He turned sharply to his assailant. "I swear if you damaged my helmet I'm going to sue."

Mawr laughed heartily and let his gun fall to his side. "Kids," he chuckled.

Badrick was squinting behind his visor, trying to discern an accent. For the life of him, he could not figure it out.

Who was this guy?

"I've heard of a Mawr Burakka in the forces," Zale said. "Brilliant, they say, if not arrogant. Has a habit of announcing his presence by clouting people."

Badrick let out a breath he hadn't realised he was holding. "Alright then. I won't shoot you."

Mawr chuckled in response, clearly very confident.

That annoyed Badrick.

A lot.

"What are you doing here?" he snapped. Badrick couldn't help but be agitated. This guy had just smacked his partner over the back of the head. How could he be calm right now?

"I, children, am here to show you how to kill a Forsaken the correct way."

Badrick immediately scoffed. "I think we can handle it," he argued, trying to sound more confident and unafraid than he felt.

"Can you?"

Badrick barely got a chance to jump in surprise at the sight of Mawr pointing his weapon at him before it was rapidly firing. He instinctively ducked, and felt the bullets rocketing over his head.

There was a cry from behind and he swivelled just in time to see a man falling to the ground, dead, his chest peppered with bullet wounds.

"Did you know that a Forsaken can copy itself?" Mawr grunted cheerfully with the air of a man relaxing in an armchair as he unloaded bullet after bullet into large groups of completely identical men that were now leaping from the trees and charging them. Squealing and shrieking like demented zombies eager for the sweet taste of flesh, their inhuman fangs and claws flashed angrily. Their rage-filled eyes—terrifying shades of red and black—leered at them as they tried to tear them apart.

Badrick cried out as the weapon's fire deafened him. Where did these guys come from!?

Mawr continued to speak as he shot each zombie dead. "The demon shreds the human soul, and a soul that becomes that unstable can purge parts to make clones of itself. No matter what the demon is, no matter what its powers are, this ability is always acquired. These clones are commonly employed as guard dogs."

The last copy fell to the grass and, before their very eyes, burst into bright, hot flames. Every other corpse followed suit.

The flames quickly dissipated, leaving nothing behind.

Apart from the blood and scorch marks.

"They're not very smart," Mawr finished, reloading his auto-rifle. "But extremely deadly in hordes."

For a long while there was only silence.

Zale appeared to be studying Mawr.

Badrick trembled back to his feet. "OK," he almost stammered. "So you know a few things. That doesn't mean we can tru—"

Gunshots interrupted the conversation once more as Zale opened fire on a spot inches away from Mawr. The blue and red soldier darted aside and raised his gun, but it was too late; the copy that had crept up on him was already dead, slain by Zale's pinpoint accuracy.

"Thanks," Mawr muttered as the corpse combusted.

"No problem," Zale muttered darkly. He still seemed angry at the newcomer. "So you're here to show *us* what to do, is that right? Well, bang up job so far. We've already wasted time and apparently the Forsaken knows we are here."

"Not necessarily. The copies found us, not the Forsaken. Just because they are part of him does not mean they are connected. He purged them after all."

"I know how it works," Zale growled. "But isn't this against orders? We're supposed to be doing this ourselves."

"If you must know," Mawr sighed, "the Daemonium doesn't know I am here. And they don't have to know. But let's be honest with ourselves. What they've sent you to do is preposterous."

"What's it to you?" Badrick asked.

Mawr simply shrugged. "I don't like it when my Daemonium does stupid things."

"*Your* Daemonium?"

Zale answered this one. "It is rumoured," he sighed irritably, "that Mawr Burakka is a descendant of one of the original eleven Enthrallers that came together to form the Daemonium all those centuries ago. As a result Mawr gets special treatment, a place among the higher-ups, though he refuses to join the Command Council, as well as leniency when it comes to his armour." Zale rested his gun on his shoulder and chuckled dryly. "Based on what I'm seeing it could very well be true."

"Hang on!" Badrick suddenly shouted, making them both jerk in surprise. "I saw you. When the Apos attacked. You ran right past me."

Mawr nodded. "You were standing out there like an idiot. You're lucky you didn't get killed."

Badrick wasn't sure how to reply to this.

Thankfully he was saved having to by Zale. "What makes you think we even need help?"

"Oh, I know *you* don't," Mawr told him. "But you're not ready to lose a partner in battle. Something like that crushes you down to your soul, Hood, and I'd rather fewer agents had to experience it. You *will* lose Badrick if you go in there without knowing everything you possibly can."

Zale didn't reply for a moment, appearing to regard Mawr curiously, as though he was actually considering the soldier's offer.

"Alright," he finally said, surprising Badrick. "What don't we know?"

"For one, where the Forsaken is. He's close, as you can tell from the presence of the security guards. He's hiding out in a cave half a klick away from here to the North. The cave is set deep in the rock, and there are several floors to it. It's quite the incredible natural formation."

"Yes, enough of the nature loving crap," Zale sighed, waving his hand aggressively. "Info."

Mawr appeared to glare at him before continuing. "There are two entrances. One, the Forsaken hasn't noticed yet. It comes out onto the first floor of the cave. This floor curves around through a tunnel that leads to the ground floor, which is flooded with water, about knee deep.

"There is also a large gap in the rock on the first floor, almost like a natural window, that overlooks the ground floor. If you position yourselves near this, you can gain the element of surprise by firing down through this gap. Do you understand me?"

Both Zale and Badrick nodded, though Badrick only did it because his partner had. Personally, he was ready to admit his confusion, and ask for them to repeat it, or at least slow down.

But he didn't want to let Zale down, so instead he bit his tongue and stood with them as Mawr commanded them to check their weapons. Zale reloaded his, but kept the half-empty magazine.

"No need to waste ammunition," he told them.

Mawr then led them through the trees, back the way they had come before careening to the left, up a steep hill that was barely stable under foot.

As they walked, Badrick attempted to open a private radio conference with Zale. Thinking back to his meagre lessons, he eventually found the right command and his helmet quickly obeyed.

He heard the whirrs near his ears as the machinery went into lockdown, preventing sound from escaping and rendering him isolated from the outside world.

"Should we trust him?" he asked.

The reply took a moment. There were clicks of static over the radio as Zale locked his helmet, before his voice finally sounded in Badrick's ears. "The Daemonium is big, Badrick. I don't know everyone. But I've heard of Mawr. Dude's actually quite famous. I trust my instincts, and they're telling me we can trust him."

Zale hadn't led him wrong as of yet. In fact he was the only one who seemed to consider his well-being at all.

So he decided to trust Zale on this too. "Fair enough," he finished, and let the matter drop, discontinuing the conference and lifting the lockdown.

It didn't take them long to reach the mouth of the cave. When it came into view, Mawr darted ahead, sprinting up the hill to the opening and carefully peering inside, his weapon raised and ready.

For a while he didn't speak, only gazed in, assessing. "Alright, ladies, this is it. The Forsaken is right in there. If my incredible abilities are correct, then I'm right in saying that he's resting at the moment, so you should have the element of surprise.

"It won't last long though, so make sure you act fast. The fight will be tough."

"Wait!" Badrick immediately shouted, receiving frantic hand gestures and shushes from both Zale and Mawr for his trouble. "You're making *us* do it?" he hissed, speaking in whispers.

"Of course," Mawr tutted as if Badrick was an idiot. "This isn't my assignment."

"You're supposed to be showing us how to do it the *'correct way'.*"

Mawr started to laugh, but caught himself and quickly stopped. "I told you I'm here to help. I gave you the intel you needed. I warned you what could happen. Doesn't mean I'm going to do it for you. I am not your babysitter. You have to do this yourself. Now get your butts in there."

It was rather harsh, Badrick felt, to warn of impending doom and then force them to go in regardless.

But what choice did they have now?

Badrick heard a sigh come from beneath Zale's helmet, and the electric blue visor turned to look at him. "Well . . . after you."

"Pfft!" Badrick huffed, and instead let Zale lead the way into the dark, cramped space of the Forsaken's lair.

chapter
NINE

They crept through the darkness, Badrick's visor brightening on its own whim, enabling him to see as clearly as if the sun was shining down on them.

Zale led the way, stopping when he reached the gap Mawr described. It was huge and did indeed look over the lower floor.

He sensed Zale smiling as the warrior jerked a gloved finger through the hole and whispered, "Gotcha."

Badrick peeked down, tense and breathing hard and being extra careful not to dislodge any stones.

What he saw was not what he expected.

The Forsaken was sitting in the water, its whole lower half completely submerged. The rim of its shirt was soaked, and the water licked at its midriff.

His head was bowed, giving the impression that he was asleep.

But apart from the odd choice of bedroom, this Forsaken looked completely normal.

Badrick had expected a monster in appearance as well as mentality, like the clones they encountered in the woods. Claws and fangs and monstrous eyes . . .

But it was just a person.

And a calm one, at that.

He backed away from the natural window and leaned against the rock, his stomach once again churning.

"Zale," Badrick whispered redundantly, as he had once again opened a private conference.

"What?"

"It's just a dude."

"It's the Forsaken, man," Zale replied. "We found him."

"No, it's . . . it's a *regular guy*."

His tone finally seemed to penetrate Zale's consciousness, who simply replied with, "Erm . . . "

"Are you serious?" Badrick snapped. "Is that all you have to say? Don't think I've forgotten why we're here! The mission is to kill him. We can't do that."

He heard Zale sigh tiredly, and felt a stab of rage. "Badrick, that Forsaken is dangerous."

"No, the demon inside him is dangerous. It's the demon who won't work with him, not the other way around."

"And that's our fault, how?"

"The Daemonium says they protect the world. How can they say they do that if they just kill every mentally unstable victim?"

Zale huffed irritably, and took a slight step closer. "Badrick, this isn't someone with demonic insanity. That *thing* down there is a destructive monster. It will kill and kill and kill until someone stops it."

Badrick clenched his fists angrily and spat back, "Reynolds said you lot can force our demons out of our bodies. Why can't we just capture him and do that?"

"And sacrifice three of our guys?" Zale almost shouted. "Listen to me, Badrick, and understand me. There isn't time for your moral compass. It's too late, the damage is done. His soul has been savaged beyond repair. Without the demon he'd be a vulnerable monster, but a monster nonetheless.

"We can't waste time with ethics or resources on extracting the demon. We kill the Forsaken, and send his demon back to Hell."

"This is wrong," Badrick sighed, shaking his head dejectedly.

"It's not right, no," Zale hissed back. "But neither is destroying a man's soul just because you can. Neither is letting that man continue to live every day in an agony that can never be healed." Zale lifted his weapon. "We have to help him, and we do that by killing him."

"This is stupid," Badrick called. "Why is this ha—"

He got no further. At his last outburst he'd readjusted to get closer to Zale.

And kicked a stone through the gap.

There was a tentative moment of silence as they both watched the stone fall. It seemed to tumble in slow motion, rolling as it fell.

Then it hit the water.

And the situation changed entirely.

With a splash, the Forsaken leapt to its feet. It turned sharply, snarling and hissing inhumanly, left and right, attempting to find the source of the disturbance, before finally gazing up at the first floor.

It saw Badrick and Zale.

It went *mental*.

Spreading its arms and screeching, Badrick was now able to see the Forsaken in all its glory.

It was red and bloody from what appeared to be self-inflicted scratches, and its ordinary human shirt was barely recognisable. There was a disgusting open wound in its side which was so big the bones inside were visible, and Badrick could now see, where he hadn't before, the red stains in the water.

The wound didn't seem to hinder the Forsaken in the slightest, and Badrick's eyes widened as it reached within the folds of its own flesh and rummaged inside.

He almost vomited as it pulled something out that dripped with blood and gore, but jerked back when he realised what it was.

Just in time too, as the Forsaken started firing the pistol it had stashed inside its own ribs with a speed that seemed impossible.

Now it was awake, the human façade was vanished completely. It snarled, hissed and gibbered crazily. The teeth were elongated just the same as its clones, and though it lacked the claws and the eyes of its puppets it was certainly far more terrifying.

Its screeches reverberated throughout the entire cave, they were so loud, and it glared up at their position as it fired relentlessly, the anticipation of killing consuming its consciousness.

Badrick couldn't stop screaming, and gulped in terror as a bullet ricocheted off his arm, sinking into the rock above them.

"Lucky for you that's a regular human gun!" Zale shouted. "If it was one of ours it would have penetrated your armour with ease."

"This sucks!" Badrick shrieked as the bullets continued to fly.

It was never ending; every time the shots stopped the Forsaken would rip out the magazine and jam a new one right in, pulling them from God only knew where.

How many did he have?

"Are you kidding?" Zale cackled in reply. "This is the most fun I've had in ages!"

Badrick instinctively shouted a warning as his partner jumped up and hopped into the middle of the wide gap. The noise from his weapon as he opened fire was deafening, but Badrick ignored it in order to witness what Zale's attack was doing.

The bullets were hammering into the Forsaken at unforgiving velocities, but Badrick felt his face go pale as he noticed that they were simply ricocheting off its skin, as if it possessed naturally armoured flesh, leaving the monster completely unharmed.

Unharmed, but not calm. The Forsaken roared in fury, a high pitched, inhuman din. Without warning it leapt from the water, impossibly high, and soared up to their vantage point.

"Oh dear." With the reflexes of a pro, Zale flipped his gun around and batted away the rocketing Forsaken. It fell back to its hole with a splash, completely dazed.

Zale stepped back into cover just as the hissing and spluttering resumed.

"For the love of . . . " he muttered darkly. "Badrick, take a shot now."

"What!?"

"*Now!*"

At the sound of Zale's urgency, and with his own cry of fear, Badrick felt his legs obey his partner and immediately struggled to bring his weapon to bear, all too aware that he was now out in the open.

The Forsaken saw him instantly and aimed its pistol directly at his chest. Two bullets smacked off Badrick's chestplate, tarnishing the once pristine paint. He screamed in panic and lost his balance, falling to the ground.

As he fell his fingers tightened and his weapon fired a shot. At the exact moment Badrick hit the floor, the bullet had the good fortune to hit the Forsaken directly in the forehead.

The insane creature fell to the water with a second loud splash.

For a moment there was only silence, disrupted by nothing but Badrick's gulping breath.

"Did we . . . " he started. "Did we . . . win?"

Zale didn't get a chance to answer; just as he turned to reply, the sound of a gun reverberated throughout the cave and a bullet lodged itself into the roof.

"God damn it!" Zale shouted as Badrick unceremoniously dashed for cover.

The bullets began flying again, never ending, terrifying.

Why the Forsaken didn't just jump up again and kill them with its teeth, Badrick didn't know. It would be a lot easier.

Either the thing truly was completely mad, or it remembered when Zale had smacked it.

"Use your power!" Badrick cried. "Zap it!"

"And electrify the water? Yeah, clever that. Then we'd be stuck up here.

Badrick's face whitened; it sounded as though Zale was considering going down there to face the Forsaken up close.

"OK," he heard Zale mutter, his voice amplified by Badrick's helmet speakers, "so . . . hardened skin . . . *very* hardened skin . . . heightened jumping . . . object replication."

At that moment Badrick understood where the magazines were coming from—the Forsaken could create them out of nowhere, and was using this power to full effect.

How could they fight something that could do that?

At that moment Badrick was glad it was mad. If it had any brains whatsoever, surely with a power like '*object replication*', it would just create something that would destroy them instantly.

Like a *nuke*.

"God, I hope it doesn't get that idea," he muttered. *Somehow* he felt even more unsafe than before.

Zale wasn't listening; he continued to mutter to himself.

"Singularis, definitely. I'm guessing fifth fissure. We've got a tough one here."

Badrick didn't understand all of that, but right at that moment he was far too preoccupied to care. "Why isn't he dead?" was all he could get his mouth to say.

"The hardened skin is more powerful than I've ever seen," Zale informed him. He paused to duck as bits of stone and dirt fell onto them as yet another hail of bullets soared past. "Our bullets are literally bouncing off him, but I reckon if we get close enough we can get a round in there. I wonder what my dagger will do. God, I wish I had my sword right now. Stupid laws."

He was rambling now, and Badrick felt a surge of indignation that he could be so calm as to lose focus at a time like *this!*

"Oi!" he shouted.

"We'll split up," Zale continued as if nothing had happened. "Badrick, you circle around. The second entrance Mawr mentioned is down there. If you can get around to it we can flank him."

"How?"

"I'll go down the ramp behind you and engage him. You find the other entrance and shoot him in the back at point blank range."

And with that he sped away, ducking the bullets and disappearing down the ramp. Badrick cursed his name loudly, knowing he would hear it.

Nevertheless he shakily got to his feet and hurried out the way they had come.

Zale reached the bottom, splashing into the water and opening fire, wasting no time. The Forsaken looked surprised at being caught at its flank, but it recovered quickly, and that meant bad news for Zale.

Zale was strong, quick, practically a superhuman these days, but even he wasn't fast enough as the Forsaken pushed through the barrage of bullets and smacked the gun out of his hand.

It tried to raise its pistol to his head, but Zale was able to utilise his enemy's loss of balance after its strike and managed to whip out his dagger and confiscate the firearm.

"Suck it!" he shouted, twisting the gun around and emptying the clip into the Forsaken's chest.

But it still wasn't enough and he quickly had to throw it away in favour of his dagger. He ducked his enemy's swiping blow, darting behind him, and thrust his weapon towards the undamaged rib, aiming to cut open the flesh as much as he could.

But the Forsaken proved faster still, and it caught his arm in its grip moments before the blade pierced the skin.

With a violent shake the dagger fell from Zale's fingers.

And the Forsaken's fist found his visor.

The blow was so powerful that the acrylic glass cracked and Zale's head bounced painfully around inside the helmet. His mind went fuzzy and he was only dimly aware of falling into the water.

His head ached like a bitch, and he could barely focus. But Zale was a trained professional. Not only that, he had been one of the best in his class.

And so he was able to shake off his dizziness within seconds.

Unfortunately he was only able to focus just in time for the Forsaken to jump on him, pinning him to the ground, its pistol back in its jerking hands.

A fresh clip was summoned from thin air and loaded into the gun.

The Forsaken pressed its weapon into Zale's neck.

There was nothing he could do; the weight of this monster was too much for him, he couldn't wriggle free.

He couldn't quite believe he'd allowed this to happen, but had no problem figuring out why it did.

He'd allowed himself to get too cocky.

Zale reached up and tried to push the beast off him, but the Forsaken only roared in his face as a reply, and pushed the barrel harder into his throat.

They were interrupted by a loud shout of panic.

"No!" Badrick's vocal chords ripped as the shout pierced the nauseating silence. The moment he'd heard it go quiet he feared the worst, and had rushed in through the entrance despite his terror of their enemy.

Cascading into the water, his eyes met the scene before him, and the Forsaken quickly turned its attention his way. The pistol was now aimed in his direction.

His faith in his ability to use his own weapon tarnished from the memory of how he'd handled it only minutes ago, Badrick did the only other thing he could think of.

He tried to use a power.

But he didn't throw his hand forward, and he didn't attempt to summon fire.

Instead he felt a pressure in his mind, as though someone was prodding at the correct synapses in order to influence him to do as they wanted.

Without knowing at all what he was doing, Badrick made a fist and brought it crashing to the ground. He crouched and plunged his hand into the water. As the material of his under-suit met the rocky bottom and ripped, revealing his knuckles and cutting them, a surge of agonising energy flashed through his body, electrifying his bones, his veins, the muscles under the skin.

His hair stood on end and ruffled beneath his helmet,

whipping so violently the strands stung his forehead.

And he could see a blue light—*demonic energy*—surrounding him, rippling, fizzling like ten thousand volts, pulsing, blinding. Badrick roared in pain as the sensation of power—a cruel, unholy power—built up in his soul.

He could feel it. Actually *feel* his soul, as if it was there and he had always been aware of it, like an organ or a bone.

His head was pounding, his heart racing.

And then, without warning, just when he thought he couldn't handle it anymore, he let it all go. Everything went white and silent, all sound ceased, and he was completely blinded.

In his head, against the white that filled his mind as well as his vision, Badrick saw something appear; a symbol flashed, clear and bold, black and orange in colour, forcing its way into his consciousness as if someone had aggressively placed it there.

Eventually his vision cleared. As the white dissipated and the world swam back into focus, Badrick realised he was back on his feet, with no knowledge of how he'd gotten there.

And the Forsaken was dead in the water.

He stared at the corpse for a moment, watching it bob gently in the still storming water. As the waves began to calm, no longer being thrashed by power, Badrick tried to lift his head, quickly learning that it was extremely painful. His eyes found the sitting

Zale, who was staring straight at him, helmet off, his eyes wide and unmoving.

"Ow," Badrick whispered.

Then his legs turned to jelly and he crashed to the floor, his armour clanging loudly as it impacted against the rock.

"Badrick!" He heard Zale splash to his feet and saw his electric blue eyes appear in his field of view. "Badrick?" Zale shook him. "Jesus. Mawr! Mawr, get in here! Something's wrong with Badrick!"

There was a second splash, and Badrick strained his neck to look at the newcomer. The blue helmet of Mawr gazed down at his limp body.

And that was the last thing Badrick saw before he gave in to his exhaustion, and darkness consumed him.

chapter
TEN

The next thing Badrick knew, an unfamiliar white ceiling was swimming into focus, and his head was thumping with an unforgiving beat.

He put a hand to his forehead, only vaguely realising his armour was gone, and moaned in agony. "Agh! My head!"

Half a second later an easily recognisable voice called, "Badrick!" and he achingly glanced over to see, not only Zale standing nearby, but Mawr as well.

His location finally dawned on him; he was back at the Daemonium, in what was probably the medical wing.

Badrick gave a small, inaudible sigh of relief. He was safe again. Well . . . safer.

His comrades were at the end of the bed he had awoken on,

still adorning their armour and helmets. Zale gave him a thumbs up. "Thank God you're alive."

"Of course he's alive," Mawr chipped in, attempting to sound amused and nonchalant, though the relief was as evident in his voice as much as Zale's.

Badrick tried to sit up, but a pair of hands gripped a hold of him. The face of the medic from the battlefield came into view.

"Don't move, you idiot," she snapped, grabbing his forehead and forcing him back down.

"Agh!"

"Well, that's what you get!"

"Perhaps a modicum of carefulness, Melody?"

Silence ensued whilst everybody watched her remove a drip from Badrick's arm and slap on a flowery plaster. Badrick leered at it, not sure whether to laugh or scowl. *Well, at least she has a sense of humour.*

When the medic left, giving orders for Badrick to stay still for the next hour on her way out, he quickly ripped it off and threw it to the floor, sitting and propping himself up on the pillows.

He massaged his shoulder, groaning and wincing sorely. His gaze caught that of the emotionless visors of his companions, and he briefly wondered what they were thinking inside those helmets. The crack running along Zale's forced him to wonder just what exactly happened in the cave before he got there.

"What happened?" he asked them. "Last thing I remember . . . " He trailed off, unable to finish that sentence.

Zale and Mawr appeared to share a look, though he couldn't be certain due to their faces being obstructed from view.

Mawr shrugged and indicated to Zale. "After you."

Zale sighed, reached for his helmet and removed it, revealing his handsome face and unfairly awesome hair. "You opened the fourth fissure," he said softly.

Badrick simply stared at him; though he remembered his partner mentioning a fissure during their fight with the Forsaken, he had absolutely no clue as to how it related to him in any way. "I'm sorry, I did what?"

"The fourth fissure of demonic enthrallment," Mawr added unhelpfully.

"The fissures are rips in souls, Badrick," Zale explained, his hands waving dramatically, emphasising each word. "Specifically, *our* souls. Each Enthraller is born with just one. It is the link between our bodies and the demon inside our souls. It's what connects the two. The fissure lets the power of the demon flow into our bodies, like air through a crack in the rocks."

Mawr continued, "As we use our powers more and start to gain control it puts more strain on our souls. Mortal bodies are not meant for immortal powers, and the gravity that puts on us is immense. As a result our souls tear to relieve the strain, though ironically granting us more of the thing that is hurting us."

Badrick knew his eyes were wide, but he didn't care. What he was hearing was *insane*.

"How many times can we tear our souls?" he asked, aghast. "There must be a limit."

"No one truly knows," Mawr told him.

"But it is theorised that there's thirteen," said Zale. "Based on old texts that no one knows came from where."

"No one has survived past eight."

Badrick ran his hand through his hair and thought about that for a minute. It was becoming a common thing, for someone to just throw a new bit of life changing information at him as if without care. How much more was there to know? How much of it was as awful as this?

Probably a lot of it.

Probably all of it.

"So . . . " he began, trying to make sense of it in his head, "I advanced to the second fissure?"

"No," Zale sighed irritably. "Didn't I *just* say you ripped open the fourth one? In that cave you did something which shouldn't have been possible. We've *never* seen it before. You tore your soul three times in one moment."

"That's why you blacked out," Mawr told him. "Your body simply shut down from the sheer strain of it. You're lucky to be alive, but you may have more power than everyone thought."

"Much more," Zale scowled, "and this is why recruits should never be sent out without proper training!"

"Yeah," Badrick sighed, "you said that . . . several times." He rubbed his shoulder again, trying to massage the stiffness from it. "How did I get back?"

"Mawr carried you," Zale smiled. "All the way back."

Badrick shifted his gaze to the red and blue soldier, unable to hide his embarrassment. "Thanks."

"No problem. Just . . . try to be more careful from now on. No more multiple tears. You've only four left before it burns you up."

"Encouraging, thank you." Badrick rolled his eyes.

But without really knowing why, he felt himself suddenly fond of the soldier who had apparently carried him to safety. Maybe there was more than the bold exterior the man boasted.

Zale and Mawr were deep in conversation now, debating on the power levels of the Forsaken, though Badrick wasn't listening. His mind was too busy thinking about the fissures, and the effect they'd have on him.

Why had he opened so many of them? It sounded like it would take years of training just to tear open the second fissure, but he'd done three without having even used a proper power yet.

His friends weren't paying any focus to him anymore, so he called to get their attention. "Guys! Sorry, don't mean to interrupt, but I was just wondering what fissures you guys are up to."

"Second," Zale instantly replied.

"The fourth fissure, myself."

And then a third voice sneered, "Ha! That's it? I'm already at the seventh."

The moment this voice spoke, Zale dropped his head and rubbed his eyes, swearing loudly in what sounded like Italian. He turned aggressively and shouted, "Get the *feck* away from here, you disgusting piece of trash."

"Now now," the new voice drawled, its owner stepping closer to Badrick's bed. "Don't be so rude."

Zale didn't listen to him. He shouted something aggressive in French before turning to Badrick and sighing. "Badrick, meet Stefan. Worst SpecOps operative ever. Biggest failure in the Daemonium. Why are you even here, you waste of space?"

"Just here to check out what everyone's talking about." He gave Badrick a cruel sneer. "Can't say I'm impressed. Four fissures? So what?"

Stefan's voice seemed to be incapable of doing anything but drawling, and the snide tone suited the way the guy held himself.

Badrick instantly hated him, despising everything about this guy. Not only that but he felt immediately perplexed at Stefan's boasting of his fissures.

He wasn't displaying any understanding that, in their case, more power meant being closer to death.

Was he an idiot?

Badrick felt the same as Stefan; he was very much *not* impressed; the guy had messy, dirty blonde hair that looked like someone with grease for stomach acid had vomited all over his head. The ugly expression on his face did nothing to soften the sharp features either.

Zale spat the harshest insult Badrick had ever heard right in

Stefan's direction.

"Hey!" their aggravator shouted in response. "Language!"

"Whatever," Zale muttered tiredly. He turned back to Badrick. "He's telling the truth though," he murmured. "Three years younger than me, started three years after me, and has reached the seventh fissure already. He's even been advanced in the training program because of it."

"That's because I'm amazing."

"It's *all* he has, though," Zale continued, a small amused smile appearing on his face. "He's last in every class there is. He's a failure."

"Unlike you," Stefan crowed, "who's so brilliant he doesn't even know where he comes from."

"Get out of here before I beat you with your own disgusting yellow helmet!"

Stefan hissed maliciously. "Tough words, fissure two." He took threatening steps towards them as he spoke. "Can you back them up?"

He was within striking distance when Mawr finally stepped in. The hulking soldier grabbed Stefan by the shirt and threw him at the wall. "Back. Off. Right. Now!"

The look of cruel confidence vanished from Stefan's face as he stared up at the visor of the adult.

Judging from the sound of Mawr's voice, the soldier had, maybe, twenty years on the kid, and was obviously his physical superior. He could, without a shadow of a doubt, wipe the floor with him any day.

And they both knew it.

Mawr released him, and Stefan stepped away from the wall, straightening his shirt. "Fine," he snapped arrogantly, trying to salvage what was left of his dignity. "I'll see you freaks later."

He gave Badrick one last snide once over, muttered something that sounded suspiciously like, "Half-breed freak," then turned and left the medical centre.

As soon as he left Badrick shouted, "Oh my God, he sucks!"

"No kidding," Zale sighed. "He's even worse than Zach."

"If you're talking about Zach Brenner, head of the secondary investigative team, I happen to like him," Mawr said boldly.

"You would."

Mawr chuckled, then suddenly turned away from them, putting his hand to the left side of his helmet. Badrick saw a small section sink into the metal under his fingers.

Mawr paused, then spoke to the air. "Understood. I'll be there shortly." He faced them again. "I have to go, but I'll be back soon. I'd like to teach Badrick a few moves. I think it'll do you good. Zale, you can help me out with him."

Zale gave a sharp salute. "*Yessir.*"

Without another word he quickly darted away, disappearing through the automatic doors and into the massive HQ beyond.

Badrick swung his legs off the bed, only to have them thrown back by Zale. "Doctor's orders," he chided him. "And you don't want to anger her. What you do reflects badly on me, and I can't hit that if you screw it up."

"Always the sentimental type," Badrick sighed, but obeyed nonetheless.

Nothing was said for a while after that. No one came into the medical centre, nor did anyone else leave.

Not that Badrick could see anyone else. It looked like he was the only patient as of that moment, unless there were others hidden around corners. He took the quiet time to examine his surroundings, something he had failed to do thus far.

He had to give an appreciative nod. The room was *amazing*. Everywhere he looked, futuristic-looking tech lined the walls.

And the whole place was white. Even the floor. It was quite a contrast to the rest of the HQ.

Thinking of the HQ reminded him of the Daemonium, thus reminding him of demons, thus also reminding him of the Forsaken, and his mood, which had been steadily rising as he felt better, rapidly dropped once more.

If not for Mawr . . . God only knew what could have happened.

"I hope he comes back," Badrick muttered. "Mawr, I mean." Badrick wasn't a fool; it was obvious the soldier had been called back to some kind of demon related job, and that meant his return wasn't entirely written in stone.

But that was the way it was for everyone here; survival was not guaranteed. Badrick had witnessed this already, having come close to a terrible fate himself with the Forsaken.

"Me too," Zale smiled. He was throwing his helmet around, flipping it in the air and catching it again. "He's grown on me."

"Yeah," Badrick sighed. "Me as well."

"Could be cool to get to know him. Would be nice to have some intelligent conversation for once."

"I'm offended by that, but I agree with the first part."

Zale laughed and gave his legs a boisterous thwack. With the added weight and solidity of his armour, this actually hurt Badrick quite a bit. He rubbed his thigh, grumbling darkly.

Zale didn't respond to his griping, which only added to Badrick's growing sense of restlessness.

"Well!" he shouted. "I refuse to sit here and do nothing. I'm going to the powers range."

"You're doing what!? Dude, you just recovered from injuries due to your own power. Calm the hell down."

"*Dude*," Badrick mimicked him, "I just tore my soul three times. I wanna see what that's done to me. I'm not sitting here." He grimaced. "Though I can't remember how to get there. Help me?"

"No."

"Pleeeeeease!"

"*No!*"

Badrick presented him with his middle finger in response, but nevertheless he conceded.

Sort of.

"OK, fine, let's go to the firing range. That's just learning to shoot, nothing fancy. I just want to do *something*. I'm too filled with energy. Give your libido a rest and help a brother out here."

Zale laughed at that, though he didn't look entirely happy. He gave a heavy sigh, and finally stopped resisting, allowing Badrick to struggle to his feet.

"*If* you can make it to the firing range I'll teach you how to properly shoot that blasted single-rifle of yours."

Determined to beat Zale's challenge, Badrick took slow, steady, purposeful steps out of the medical centre and across the walkway directly opposite the door.

The massive Main Hall greeted him, the ground floor many metres below.

Taking a moment to rid himself of a sudden feeling of vertigo, Badrick gripped the handrail and followed Zale to the ranges.

"You," Mawr said sternly, pointing a finger at Reynolds, "have got to stop recruiting kids."

"Oh, relax," Reynolds snapped, though Mawr knew he wasn't angry. "There's four of them. It's not like they're taking over the place."

"One of them just broke the rules for everything we know, and another is more likely to blow himself up than feed himself correctly with his morning cereal."

"And the other two are the best agents we've ever seen," Reynolds argued stubbornly.

"I'm not denying Hood and Miss Hunter's effectiveness," Mawr sighed. "Those two are beyond brilliant. They're set to overshadow every agent we've ever had, especially when they work together." His expression darkened, redundant as this action was; he still hadn't removed his helmet. "But Vulrick presents a clear and present danger."

"Why do you think we rushed Badrick into the field?" Reynolds said quietly. "We needed to see what he was capable of—"

"No," Mawr interrupted immediately. "There's more to it than that. There's something you're not telling me. What is it about these kids? They could be trouble."

"Despite some disagreement, it is the majority of the Council's verdict that Badrick is welcome among our ranks and that Zale and Carla's effectiveness is one of our greatest assets Let's not forget some of the inventions Hood has provided us. The jetpacks, the upgrades to our scanners . . .

He's an indispensible asset."

Mawr scowled and crossed his arms. "Your feelings for Zale cloud your judgement, Daniel." He threw his hands in the air with frustration, blowing air from his mouth in a rush of emotion. "Back on the subject of Badrick, are you going to fill me in?"

"Well . . ." Reynolds actually smiled. "Let me put it this way . . . we have a new assignment for you."

Seeing as the sergeant had no clue what his facial expression was, Mawr communicated his confusion through his body language. "You do realise I'm army, not an agent, right? Or have you forgotten that?"

"The only reason I'm giving you this mission is because we're friends," Reynolds puffed indignantly. "And yes, I'm aware. Me too, if you remember. Frankly, I'm getting kind of sick of having to run operations outside of my division."

"Then stop working with Zale," Mawr chuckled, knowing he was hitting a sore subject.

"Careful," Reynolds hissed. "That boy means a lot to me. You obviously know that. I will deal with him for as long as I am here. No one else will."

"As you wish, Daniel. But you know the other SpecOps dislike you ordering one of theirs around." It wasn't a question.

"I could not care less," Reynolds huffed stubbornly. "I will protect that boy for as long as I can. If that means I have to do two jobs, I will. I was simply stating that the Council keeps making me do this crap for other agents."

"And soldiers who shouldn't be doing BCR assignments."

"Like I said, I'm giving you this mission because we are friends. You may be a soldier, but you're a great one. You're smarter than most agents. This job is suited for you."

Mawr sighed once more, an action he seemed to be performing a lot lately. For a moment he felt like continuing the argument.

He *wasn't* an agent. He *was* a soldier. A damn good one, just like Reynolds said.

But that was probably his undoing.

Mawr decided to relent, but only because Reynolds was right; they *were* friends. The things they'd been through together . . . he would do anything for the sergeant. "The mission?" he eventually sighed reluctantly.

Reynolds gave him a very thankful smile, and reached to the table behind him to snatch up a folder.

The vivid blue cardboard was nauseatingly colourful under the shine of the even bluer lights of the BCR. The uniforms of the agent commanders had the same effect, and Mawr was suddenly looking forward to getting out of here.

The presence of Reynolds' red uniform, a disgusting shade of brown in this light, only served to reinforce just how out of place they both were in this room.

He took the folder from the sergeant and flicked through it, speed-reading the notes and instructions.

"The energy spike detected on Badrick," Reynolds spoke. "The one that enabled Vulrick to take over. We need more information on that."

"Ah," Mawr crowed. "More on the subject of which I am not authorised to know about. You call this an answer to my question about Vulrick?"

Reynolds shrugged at him. Mawr ground his teeth.

"If you ask me," he muttered, "there was no energy spike and Vulrick is more powerful than we've ever seen."

"Please," Reynolds scoffed. "It's Vulrick. You've heard the stories."

"Envoy for the demonic royal family, servant and punching bag to the demon, Daemnos, yadi-yadi-yada."

"Something happened out there," the sergeant continued, ignoring his mockery. "We just need a better look at what, and if it is still affecting Badrick. Are you clear on your orders?"

Further explanation from Reynolds was not required; they were there on the page. Mawr took a calming breath and said, "Yes, old friend. They are clear. I shall leave immediately."

"Good work. Carry on."

The soldier was leaving the BCR now. He could see him. He'd been waiting. Waiting for him to depart so he could follow.

Because that was what he had to do. Those were his instructions.

Burakka left by the main door, striding through it purposefully.

Stefan watched as the automatic shutters closed behind him.

The half-breed hadn't spotted him as he'd exited the BCR; Stefan had chosen his position carefully.

He was clearly headed out on a mission of some kind. On his own as well, by the looks of it.

It seemed that now was the time to act.

But . . . what did *that* mean, Stefan was no longer required? He frowned angrily and turned to glare at the man sitting beside him, calm as the surface of an undisturbed lake, and acting as though Stefan's anger didn't bother him in the slightest, maybe even amused him.

The emotionless visor of the skeletal helmet stared back, and a black, armoured hand put a finger to Stefan's lips.

Stefan had no choice. He had to obey.

He would sit this one out.

*

The day would end soon, the sun would sink and darkness would take over.

And Mawr had no intention of being out here during the night.

He *hated* the countryside. Being amongst the plants and trees with the kids was bad enough, but now he was out here on his own.

If not for his ancestors and the only alternative choice given to all humans with a demon stuffed inside them he would have quit the Daemonium many years ago.

It was crap work.

Though there was one silver lining; he didn't have to leave his armour behind when out in the country.

That was the single flaw when working within populated areas.

You had to abandon everything, only keeping a sidearm for

protection. Anything else and you'd not only arouse suspicion but potentially cause a panic at the armed metal soldier, and you'd run the risk of getting bloody arrested.

Not to mention exposing everything they'd worked so hard to keep a secret for so many centuries.

But Mawr always felt vulnerable without his armour, and very rarely took it off, despite the Daemonium's uniform regulations, so he was extremely thankful for the weight of it on his back, as well as the presence of the large weapon gripped tightly in his hands.

Being in a small town like this wasn't a problem. There was barely anyone to notice him, and he expertly avoided anyone who might.

Even so, he wanted to wrap things up quickly.

This place was awful.

He'd already found residual evidence of the power spike in Badrick's home town, and followed it all the way from his school to the therapist's office, the burnt remains of his old house, and finally the confounded church.

He didn't stop to check in with Hans. Mawr already read the report the undercover agent sent in, so he didn't need a recap.

Besides, he had no time for those Enthrallers who spent their lives hiding out in old churches, waiting for the therapists and the doctors and the policemen of the world to unwittingly send potential Enthrallers their way.

As instructed, every single hospital, police station, therapist, etcetera, in the world had explicit, top secret orders to transfer anyone showing specific behavioural attributes to the undercover agents in the churches.

No one but the Daemonium truly knew where these orders came from, but no one questioned it. A hundred lifetimes of pressure, indoctrination and supernatural influencing had seen to that. Even the most powerful presidents in the world considered it *way* past their pay grade.

Anyone who tried to question this got a severe lesson in obedience.

Mawr had despised this method his entire life, having studied its history, from the moment of its conception to the present day as well as its success rate, personally feeling that it gave the Daemonium too much power.

Unofficially, unbeknownst to anyone else, they were the largest power on the globe. No government held any authority over them.

Mawr understood the necessity of it all. But he would never give his consent; their job was to find new Enthrallers and police them, not wait for *them* to come to the Daemonium.

And it wasn't to override the human world's leaders and govern it for them.

As far as Mawr was concerned that was far too close to a hostile takeover leading to a police-state.

He spent a while staring at the ornately decorated windows of the church as he mused over the Daemonium's workings, but still refused to step inside. He skipped the building and continued tracking the energy trail.

Half a second later it dawned on him, the strangeness of this.

Why was the energy going past the church at all? Badrick hadn't walked past, he'd gone inside it.

Mawr followed it for a few more moments, frowning tightly, before stopping, wondering why the energy was now leading him down a nature trail, away from the town.

He hadn't imagined he'd find *this*.

Had Vulrick caused this, coming out all this way when he manifested? It could be the result of an explosion of energy when the event occurred, with residual spikes trailing out randomly.

Or was Reynolds telling the truth, whether intentionally or not, and the spike had been external?

It felt . . . different . . . like it had a different 'taste'.

Though, at the same time it was the same.

Whatever the real cause, Mawr discovered he wasn't the only one interested.

He found him half an hour later, digging through the dirt, his weapon propped up against a rock; an Apos. His armour was even browner from all the dirt he was kicking up.

He was in the exact spot Mawr sensed the power converging, and he had no doubts the Apos was also here because of the energy spike.

There was no way Mawr was going to let him get his grubby little hands on whatever it was, and so he had no choice but to pull his sniper rifle from his back and shoot the Apos dead.

He put in a call for the body to be collected before it was discovered by a hiker or something. Being able to make good use of the demonic materials salvaged from the Apos' equipment was an added bonus.

Mawr gave the scumbag an irritated kick, then ducked down to see what he'd been digging for.

It took only a few moments for his skills to determine that the Apos had been on the right track, but not the right trail.

His natural ability to sense demonic traces was telling him there was something buried close by, which was the reason behind the Apos' digging. It wasn't a physical object . . . more like an air pocket under the earth that had trapped traces of energy.

Though it continued to trail, phasing through the dirt back to the surface, and stretching even further on.

What a strange thing for it to do. Someone was doing some weird stuff with their energy.

But though Mawr had no idea how this phenomenon happened, he couldn't have cared less. All he wanted was to finish this mission as fast and thoroughly as possible. At this point he didn't even care if his search yielded any result; he just wanted to get in before dark.

He took slow steps, feeling the energy, following it carefully until he found himself at the edge of a *very* high cliff.

The sudden appearance of it surprised him. Mawr had never been afraid of heights, but even this was higher than he was used to, and it unnerved him to realise that what he was seeking was buried within the ground at the base of the drop.

"Well, how am I going to get down there?" he muttered angrily. It was times like this that he couldn't help but curse his demon for being the only one in all of known creation who didn't have the power to land feet first and unharmed from massive falls.

Mawr cast his eyes around, searching for a path, though none revealed themselves to him.

He grumbled darkly, quickly understanding he had to do this the demon way.

Though he wasn't sure how he was going to pull this off; his power had such little range to it.

It was a rare thing for a demon of such a low calibre as Mawr's to possess any kind of teleportation, even the limited twenty metre range capability he had. But he was thankful for it, especially at times like this.

Though, it would be difficult.

Mawr would have to jump. He would have to teleport while falling.

No ... That wouldn't work. His momentum would carry through the teleporting and he'd crash into the ground regardless.

What if he teleported rapidly, every second, until hitting the ground? It would stop his body from gaining momentum and saving him from a very bloody impact, though it would be extremely strenuous.

It was a ridiculous idea.

Dangerous, at best.

But sod it; Mawr would give it a try. Anything to get back to the car quicker.

His recklessness was a flaw and a direct contradiction of the lesson he was always grilling into people.

He knew that.

But who really cared at this moment? The sun was starting to go down now, and his mood was dropping rapidly.

He took ten large steps back, allowing himself plenty of room for a run up. He would have to time this perfectly, and the extra time flying forwards instead of falling would be helpful.

He laughed a little at what he was about to attempt . . . then sprinted.

His feet left the ground two seconds later, his powerful legs launching him through the air. Nothingness appeared beneath him, and he had a horrible rush of vertigo. Mawr forced himself to concentrate and counted the time it took for his downward momentum to dominate his forward momentum.

One . . .

Two . . .

Thr—

A searing pain shot through Mawr's spine. He screamed in agony when something belted him downwards. His arms began to flail as he rocketed towards the ground.

He hit it a moment later with the force of a missile. His armour half smashed with the impact and he felt the agony of many of his bones breaking.

Finally the dust settled, and he lay there, gasping for breath, his broken arms and legs twitching, barely gripping to life.

He couldn't move. His face was buried in the grass, his visor smashed to nothing, and he couldn't speak or even clear the dirt from his throat.

It was that moment that Mawr realised he had walked straight into a trap.

The difference in energy back at the church. Neither Badrick nor Vulrick ever came this way. If there was an external cause, it hadn't come this way in the slightest.

Someone had planted energy for him to follow, mixing it among the residual signature and disguising it to read the same.

So expertly even Mawr hadn't been able to recognise it as fake.

There was a deafening noise descending on him. It was getting louder by the second. He recognised it instantly as the sound of demonic flight, and wasn't surprised when he felt the gentle thud of feet hitting the dirt beside him.

There was silence for a moment. Nothing moved or made a sound.

Using all his strength, Mawr was just able to move his neck, and he agonisingly turned it to look at the new arrival. He caught a glimpse of a skull-like helmet before an all too familiar pistol filled his vision. He could see down the barrel, imagined the bullet lodging into place as his attacker cocked the weapon.

There was a blinding flash and he felt his upper spine shatter into oblivion.

He had just enough time to feel the man's hands fiddling with his pouches, and hear him curse with frustration, before the lights went out and Mawr was consumed by darkness.

chapter
ELEVEN

Ever since Badrick arrived at the Daemonium his new partner had always seemed so full of energy. So it was weird to see Zale passing out every few minutes, his head smacking into the table and waking him with a jolt. Each time he would shake his head, a confused expression on his face.

Then he would go back to writing his report on their conflict with the Forsaken.

Rinse, repeat. Rinse, repeat. He must have managed only three lines in the last half an hour.

Badrick watched him with amusement, though only vaguely; his mind was elsewhere. He'd only realised it this morning, and he was incredibly irritated with himself that it had taken him so long to get there, but he finally figured out that part of his memory had a very clear recollection of Zale, from before their meeting.

More specifically, his voice.

Badrick was certain. He'd listened to that voice once before. Somewhere, sometime . . .

But when?

And *where*?

It was driving him mad not being able to figure it out.

In a bid to try and gauge the tones and accent to refresh his memory, Badrick called out, "What's wrong with you? Why do you keep passing out?" and immediately concentrated, trying to place the responding voice.

His partner jerked awake and blinked twice. "Wha . . . what?"

"You look shattered. We went to bed at the same time last night, so what were you doing? Carla?"

"Naw, its fine," Zale yawned confusingly, too tired to catch Badrick's remark. "I was called back into the BCR an hour after we went to bed last night." When Badrick gave him a quizzical look he sighed and continued, "This case I started . . . and . . . well, finished actually, last night, tired me right out. This dude we found was resurrected by a demon a few days ago."

"Whoa . . . really?" With that Badrick's original intention was forgotten.

"Yeah. I had a look at the evidence and located him. But in the end the agents had to put him down."

Memories of the Forsaken swarmed to the forefront of Badrick's mind, and he remembered his distaste at what they'd been called to do. A terrible sick feeling filled his stomach at the thought of the praise that followed their return, which made everything ten times worse.

The attitude of the soldiers and agents was awful. Two days had passed since that horrifying battle, and during that time Badrick had been congratulated on killing that 'scum', 'freak', 'piece of crap', and 'reject'.

There were so many names. So many low opinions of the unfortunate Forsaken.

And it wasn't just them; Badrick continued to hear disgusting conversations about those afflicted with demonic insanity.

The prejudice coming out of their mouths . . .

It horrified Badrick.

And it didn't end there; he resumed his training the day after, and everything worsened even further. The opening of three more fissures had damaged him, but he also benefitted from the event.

His manoeuvrability was improved considerably. He could now keep up with Zale on the obstacle course, and for no reason at all he was incredibly adept at sharpshooting, as if he'd been practising for decades.

As a result, he'd been 'generously informed' by many of the witnesses to this improvement that he'd be killing the *'Apos dogs'* in droves in no time.

It excited them, and that rang deafening warning bells in Badrick's head. No one should ever feel excited to kill.

"Why did you have to do that?" he finally croaked back at Zale, dreading the answer.

His partner jerked awake again and mumbled, "Well, it's weird, and a phenomenon, actually. If a civilian, or anyone really, who is exposed to a big amount of carbon monoxide, then dies at the hands of a demon and is then resurrected, they develop an ability."

"Which is?"

"They can create these tiny little splinter things out of their fingers," Zale yawned. "It's the strangest thing. It's not even like the gas reacts to demonic energy. Carbon monoxide eventually leaves your system . . . I don't know. Even I can't figure it out. But it's not the only one, quite a few different gases and elements have mental, sometimes terrifying effects when mixed with demonic energy. You can thank demonic scientists for that."

Badrick watched Zale bang his head on the table again. He chewed his lip in thought, before muttering, "What do these splinters do? What's the point of them?"

"If the splinters prick someone that person becomes utterly crazy. Remember our resident mental flying man?"

"How could I forget?" Badrick growled through gritted teeth, thinking about the agents' cruelty towards him.

"The problem is that these splinters dissolve approximately twenty four seconds after infection so it can be pretty damn hard to identify sometimes."

Badrick could only stare at Zale now as he struggled to stay awake. They stayed that way for quite some time, and it was only when Zale looked moments away from passing out again that he managed to make his mouth make sound. "That's . . . scary."

"The infected are harmless," Zale reassured him, "but they do become seriously weird. It'd be fine if it didn't ruin their lives. This guy I was talking about was infecting people with purpose. Just people on the street, one after the other. He resisted our arrest and tried to infect agents."

"So they killed him? Man, that's rough."

"It's a rough world."

No kidding. Badrick felt like his world was turning over and over and over. He could barely focus on right and wrong anymore. Everything just seemed . . . *evil*. "What about the crazy people?" he asked slowly.

"Killed," Zale responded without hesitation. "Put out of their misery."

Badrick felt his temper rise, and was about to shout at Zale when he suddenly remembered a certain demon telling him to control his anger.

This was partly why he was in this morally black organisation in the first place. His anger was dangerous and he already knew that if he displayed an inability to remain in control the prison was all he could expect as reward.

He opened his mouth to voice his opinions in a calm manner, but before he had a chance the door whirred open and in stepped a very happy looking Sergeant Reynolds.

"Hello lads," he smiled. "Haven't seen you for days." His expression faltered when he noticed the unresponsive Zale; he'd crashed again, and this time the bang to the head hadn't woken him.

Reynolds rolled his eyes, tutted and instead turned his attention to Badrick.

"Congratulations on the outcome of your first mission, Varner." He gave Badrick a sharp salute. "You did incredibly well."

"Thanks," Badrick replied hoarsely, giving only a half hearted salute in return. The compliment felt like a chainsaw against his stomach. He didn't want any praise for what he did and accepting it felt wrong.

His fidgeting did not go unnoticed by Reynolds, who quickly asked, "Something on your mind, Badrick?"

He shook his head quickly. "No, sir."

The sergeant gave him a humoured smile. He pulled up a chair and sat upon it, presenting Badrick with a knowing look. "A question unasked is knowledge wasted. Speak your mind."

It was strange, the sergeant talking to him like this. They'd never spoken about anything besides Daemonium business, and the last time they'd actually conversed he'd threatened Badrick with imprisonment.

This compassionate side of Reynolds, Badrick had never witnessed before. It was odd; although the sergeant seemed kind, he also took his position in this organisation very seriously. He was often stern, at least whenever Badrick met him.

Seeing this softer part of him, Badrick didn't know whether to be relieved or unnerved.

"I just . . . " When he failed to continue Reynolds gave him a rapid hand gesture, urging him to carry on. "I don't feel like I did a good thing."

"How do you mean?"

"The Forsaken was just a victim," Badrick sighed. "And I killed him."

"You did what you had to do to save people."

"Who gave us the right to make that kind of decision? He was a *victim*."

"We have no choice," Reynolds said. He was studying Badrick with an unreadable expression now. He kind of got the feeling the sergeant was gauging his reactions. "These people can cause indescribable destruction and there is no one else to stop them. I know it's harsh, but when you deal with pure unadulterated evil you can't always consider those who get caught in the crossfire.

"Whatever you may think, you did a good thing. You released that man from his pain and his demon was cast back into Hell."

"Why would it do that though?" Badrick half shouted, frustrated. "Why do some demons do that to people?"

Reynolds shrugged sadly. "Who knows? We don't understand everything. That's why we do what we do. To try and figure it out."

Badrick immediately disagreed. From what he'd witnessed so far it wasn't their job to figure out anything, but to kill anyone unlucky enough to fall into this hellhole, no questions asked.

Reynolds grasped his shoulder and smiled proudly. "You'll be a fantastic agent one day, I can tell. Just do me a personal favour?"

"What?" Badrick asked simply, grumpy from what he considered unhelpful answers.

"Never lose sight of your morals."

He frowned, confused by this cryptic request. Had he said something Reynolds agreed with? Or did the sergeant already know Badrick's other thoughts, the one's he hadn't yet voiced.

Trying to decipher it only made his head hurt.

He was still pondering the meaning when Reynolds threw his hand to his ear and his smile vanished. There was a pause, before, "Alright, I'm on my way."

And then he was gone without so much as a goodbye.

A little stunned at his sudden departure, Badrick stared at the door, mulling over their conversation.

He decided he didn't feel better at all.

Though he *did* understand the need for the Daemonium— demons were the epitome of evil and they needed to be controlled—it did nothing to justify their actions, the cruel words that accompanied them; the prejudice against the Forsaken, the congratulations for killing 'an animal' . . . it only proved that they were fuelled by hate and not a sense of duty.

Zale made a strange noise as he jerked awake once again, making Badrick jump. He glared at his partner, irritated at being jolted from his thoughts. "How are you *that* tired? It didn't take you that long last night, did it?"

Zale gave him a bleary grin. "Well . . . after I was done I had . . . a medical . . . check-up . . . oral examination . . . fitness . . . study . . . you know."

Badrick *did* know.

Zale didn't have to say anymore; Badrick could already tell he'd hooked up with someone.

"Lovely," Badrick jeered. "Well, I hope you wore glov—"

A shrill whining interrupted him, and Badrick painfully covered his ears, glaring at the intercom speaker as if it had paid him personal insult.

"*Attention, Enthrallers of the Daemonium!*" At first he didn't recognise the voice. It was only after Zale commented on how fast Reynolds had gotten back to the command rooms that Badrick realised it was he who was speaking. "*We are saddened to report the death of Corporal Mawr Burakka, official status KIA. The Command Council wishes to convey our condolences to his friends and military family.*"

Zale's chair clattered to the floor as he awoke with a jolt and jumped to his feet, dashing to Badrick's side to stare up at the intercom.

Standing back up—the crash made Badrick jump in surprise—he gave his friend a heavy look. "Mawr is dead?"

Zale turned his blue gaze upon him. "It appears so."

"Did we miss something?" Badrick mumbled. "Was there a battle?"

"There was no fight," Zale mumbled, "and Mawr wasn't assigned to any of the outposts. Which leaves only one thing."

"Which is?"

"He was sent on a mission." Zale sat back upon a chair and started to rub his lower lip with his thumb, his eyes glossed over in deep thought.

"Why would they send a soldier on a mission? The agents do the missions."

"Now isn't that just the question of the day?" Zale's eyes locked onto his. "I know what you're thinking, and it's crazy."

"We're still doing it though . . . right?"

"Of course."

*

The information didn't make sense.

Unless Mawr's killer stashed the body somewhere, he *should* have been right where Zale was standing.

The Daemonium had no record of the warrior's remains, no clue as to where he had gone, and none of them knew where to start. All they had was that Mawr's helmet reported his status as KIA at the base of this humungous cliff.

And the helmets never lied.

The location's proximity to Badrick's home town did not escape Zale's notice, but he kept it to himself. There was no point upsetting his partner by telling him Mawr was killed on a mission regarding him.

A mission the soldier shouldn't have been on in the first place.

Though Zale figured, if Reynolds was forced into giving the mission to an agent as he had been a lot recently, he would have probably given it to Mawr instead, for no reason other than they were friends.

Though Zale hadn't met Mawr before the Forsaken, he knew Reynolds and he were rumoured to be best friends, and Mawr was definitely curious about this whole affair; that was obvious by his decision to follow Badrick, despite his attempt to cover his interest up with what was probably still genuine concern.

It hadn't taken long for Zale to get them to the location. He'd driven very fast, arriving at their destination in only two hours.

Getting to the place was easy. But their task got a lot harder from that point on.

There was *nothing*.

They'd driven all the way out here only to find zero evidence to help solve Mawr's death.

Zale was aware the other agents had already been all over this area.

But there should have been something!

The agents *always* missed at least something, and unless wild animals killed Mawr and conspired to hide the evidence, there should have been something to find.

Whoever *did* kill Mawr was incredibly clever.

It was infuriating.

And he clearly wasn't the only frustrated one, as after an hour of looking around Badrick suddenly called, "As good an idea it was to come out here and find out what happened . . . it was a waste of time."

"I know," Zale sighed in frustration. "There's nothing here. No residual energy readings, no ammo casings, no blood . . . where is everything!?"

He kicked the grass in fury.

It took a surprised shout from Badrick for him to realise he'd actually made contact with something solid.

The olive armour rattled as Badrick scrambled and almost tripped in a bid to catch up to the flying object. He picked it out of a small puddle and brought it to Zale so he could look.

"It's a bullet casing," Zale said, surprised, rolling it between his fingers. "Wait," he added, squinting his eyes. He ripped his helmet from his head and brought the casing closer to his face. "This is a round from one of *our* pistols!"

Badrick was silent for a second, but then he nodded and said, "Right, we design our own weapons. Maybe Mawr fired his gun."

"No." Zale shook his head slowly. "Mawr didn't have a registered Daemonium pistol on him. He had his auto-rifle and a sniper rifle, but no pistol. However, the existence of this casing proves he was attacked, and didn't just, like . . . I don't know . . . fall off the cliff."

"Could he have?" Badrick asked him as Zale gazed up the giant rock wall, his blue visor darkening the bright sun to keep his vision unimpaired.

Deciding this was hurting his neck, Zale lowered his head again and rubbed the pain away. "I doubt it. Most of us can land a fall that high, and even if Mawr didn't have that power he wouldn't be inept enough to fall. Nope, I believe he was shot."

"So whoever attacked him had—"

"Access to our weapons, yes," Zale confirmed.

"But we have no leads?"

"Nope."

Badrick sighed and muttered, "Great." He let his single-rifle drop gently to the grass and took a seat on a nearby rock pile. He punched it lightly.

Zale could only guess what he was thinking.

"You don't think it was Stefan?" Badrick suddenly voiced. "I mean, Mawr did humiliate him."

Zale scoffed. "No way. That guy's too much of a wuss. No way could he take Mawr."

"*But he's at the seventh fissure!*" Badrick cried mockingly.

"So? Stefan's pathetic, Mawr's a professional. If you can't handle the fissures then you won't win, and I have no doubt Stefan hasn't got anywhere near complete control."

Badrick didn't reply, only nodded thoughtfully.

Zale sighed once more, put the bullet casing into a pouch and slapped Badrick on the right pauldron. "Come on, let's get back before they notice us gone. We've done all we can here."

*

The pair of them were in low spirits upon their arrival back to base. Neither had spoken during the drive home, Zale only making sound when he would sigh at people gawking at his strange car with its blacked out windows.

They left their armour in their rooms the moment they got back, and went down to the HQ. After all, Badrick still had training to do. Although he had made leaps and bounds since his encounter with the Forsaken, he still had a long way to go.

His newfound abilities were because of Vulrick, but Zale told him he had to build genuine muscle and learn the skills he could pull off without the use of powers. Not every demon granted physical abilities at the same scale as Vulrick, Zale's demon Horas included, and they all needed to be well trained.

He couldn't rely on what Vulrick gave him for everything.

Badrick didn't want to train right at that moment. He was knackered, and in a solemn mood as it was, bolstered by his fatigue.

And he certainly wasn't in the mood to listen to the congratulating comments from the enthusiastic Enthrallers.

"Hey, it's the man of the hour!"

"Badrick, good work with that Forsaken freak!"

"You'll be a bona fide killer in no time, man! Good job!"

Enough!

It was getting very annoying. Badrick just wanted to forget what happened and never talk about it again.

And amongst all the crap he had to listen to on his way through the HQ, he *definitely* wasn't in the mood for a nasty SpecOps recruit, who called out to them from the other side of the Main Hall.

"There they are. The sappy mongrels."

Badrick easily caught sight of Stefan in his peripheral. It wasn't hard; the guy was wearing his armour.

It was a disgusting yellow colour. Not like the warmth of the sun, or freshness of a banana, but a sickly kind of colour you'd see on a badly painted car, with only a hint of orange.

He stood out like a sore thumb.

It was anger at everyone nearby, as well as genuine confusion at these words, that prompted Badrick to swivel around and roar back, "What the hell kind of insult is that!?"

"A Stefan one," Zale laughed.

"Well, that was a terrible comeback," Stefan cackled, completely unabashed. He reached up and removed his helmet, revealing his snide sneer. "Missing Mawr, are we? You guys are weak, pathetic and emotionally fail. Mawr was a powerless fool!"

Despite not knowing the fallen soldier all that well, anger rose within Badrick that Stefan would dare insult a man who'd been murdered.

And now Badrick was inches from jumping up and throwing Stefan to the floor, intent on laying into that face to permanently remove the disgusting grin he hated so much. But Zale put a hand on his shoulder before he'd managed to take even one step, as if he'd foreseen the outburst. "No, man, he's not worth it. We have better things to do."

It would have made Badrick feel better if he could have at least gotten in the last word, but even this was robbed from him when Stefan gave them a mock salute and waltzed away, disappearing into the mazes of the HQ.

Badrick pointed aggressively at the door Stefan vanished through and hissed with as much venom as he could muster, "I really don't like him."

chapter
TWELVE

Their further efforts to uncover the details of Mawr's death proved futile.

Utterly fruitless.

It seemed like the Daemonium wanted to keep the case to their most senior SpecOps operatives. They put a lock down on all they had uncovered, as well as the notes made by the agents, detailing their thoughts and deductions.

Zale told Badrick that they had it under such a heavy lockdown that getting into the files would be near impossible.

Though Zale swore blind he could do it, he decided against the idea. They didn't have anything he couldn't hack, but he had no desire to get into trouble.

The levels of security on the case files were incredible, and though Badrick's partner seemed genuinely capable of retrieving the info, he wouldn't have been able to stop the system from identifying him, thus giving his hack away.

Besides, he had to focus on Badrick. His recruitment could not be ignored any longer. So, despite their reluctance, they had no other choice but to forget about Mawr and return to their own work.

Over the next three weeks Badrick underwent a gruelling regime of physical and mental training, which consisted of painful sparring with Zale, traversing over increasingly difficult obstacle courses, attention demanding lectures on demonology, the history of the Daemonium and the physiology of Enthrallers, tiring sessions in the firing range with every weapon at the Daemonium's disposal and, finally, long hours of meditation, learning how to control his anger and his demon.

At some point down the line Zale seemed to have deduced exactly how Badrick perceived the opinions and attitudes of their fellow Enthrallers, not to mention his own feelings about it. For hours he would hammer Badrick with cruel yet subtle remarks about the Forsaken and the demonically insane.

He obviously didn't mean any of it. Badrick knew that. Zale was just testing his anger control.

Maybe

But Badrick wasn't doing well—Zale knew exactly how to push his buttons.

Zale would also pretend that the day's training was over, and bring Badrick to the recreational rooms. More specifically, he would find areas filled with Enthrallers talking about those specific subjects.

And Badrick's blood would boil.

Was it because he felt like he understood the less fortunate? He'd spent most of his life a victim after all. A victim to his uncle.

He would get angry, lash out at other kids in school.

Perhaps that *was* the reason . . . but also maybe not.

Despite his anger, he couldn't prevent a niggling feeling that he was wrong. The more and more he heard on the subject, the less confident in his views he really felt. There wasn't anyone who shared his opinions.

Was he just trying to make the Forsaken and the demonically insane out to be victims, that they weren't to blame for their actions, due to his own past? Was he trying to say that *he* hadn't been responsible for his aggression, and it was all because of his uncle's treatment of him?

Was he using them as an excuse to feel better about himself?

Badrick wanted to be one of those people with solid convictions, who knew how he felt about his reasons behind his opinions.

But, surrounded by so much of the opposite, he was no longer sure.

How had Zale figured out what he'd been thinking? He'd never really voiced all his thoughts to anyone.

Even when Reynolds questioned him, Badrick had only spoken a small fraction of his emotions.

Whatever his methods, he just wished Zale would stop bringing him into these areas.

But it was part of his training. He could tell; there was no other logical reason for it.

There was nothing he could do.

Unfortunately it didn't end there. When Badrick proved unable to refrain from scowling at the Enthrallers—even though that was *all* he did—Zale decided he wasn't doing well enough.

He henceforth developed a habit of bringing him closer to Stefan.

Who, for his part, never missed any opportunity to try and

make them both feel as bad as he could.

It was difficult to hold back.

To say the least.

However, even when Badrick did figure out the tactics behind the training, he chose not to say anything. He was pretty sure if Zale learned that he had copped on to his strategy then he'd find some new, more aggravating way to test his resolve.

Although . . . Zale was *far* from stupid. Bringing Stefan into the mix was such an obvious move that it actually wouldn't make sense for him to believe Badrick to still be in the dark.

Maybe that too was the plan; Badrick would figure out what he was doing and get angry at him as well, giving him even more to struggle to repress.

It hurt Badrick's head to think about it.

Again, he felt unsure of himself. He didn't know what was right anymore.

But it didn't matter. *Just in case* Zale hadn't figured out that Badrick now understood what he was up to, Badrick kept it to himself. He knew he was supposed to be testing his limits, but with everything going on . . . he just wasn't in the mood.

So he allowed Zale to continue bringing him to these people and stewed hatefully in silence.

Despite this difficulty, Badrick was proud of one thing. He was doing very well in the physical training, and as far as he was concerned *just not* punching Stefan in the face meant he had his anger under control.

Vulrick wasn't going to use it against him any time soon.

At least that's what he told himself every time he went to bed at night.

Apart from his concerns on what he'd gotten himself into and the kinds of people involved, the only other stress on Badrick's mind was that, even though he had four fissures, he still—*still*—

hadn't displayed any powers.

It was infuriating, to say the least.

Zale began spending more and more time with him at the powers range. Day after day was wasted throwing all manner of hand gestures at the floating orbs before him, with zero results achieved.

It was ridiculous that an Enthraller would have so much access to their demon's power without actually being able to use their damn *powers*.

Sure, he had acrobatics and new combat skills, flooded into his mind like a tidal wave of knowledge. It was like he'd known how to do it all for years, and he felt that with only a few more months of training he'd be at the peak of human physical condition.

Though, that was probably an exaggeration.

It was more of a supernatural condition. He was still working on being physically able without the use of demonic energy. His skills had supernatural origins, not human.

But he didn't *feel* supernatural; as far as Badrick was concerned he was as powerless as ever.

Zale must have felt the same way because he appeared just as confused. He went through several different theories a day, rattling them off at incredible speeds but each time dismissing them as 'balderdashery'.

These so called theories included Vulrick keeping his powers from Badrick, Vulrick was ill or crippled, and Badrick wasn't able to channel demonic powers.

Every time he spoke he would shake his head and throw the idea away.

And so the reason went undiscovered, and the gruelling failed attempts continued without end.

"Keep trying," Zale would tell him every five minutes. "It's either this or another two hours meditating, trying to gain access to your powers through spiritual communication."

"I'd prefer this," Badrick sighed, though he wasn't so sure. At least he could pretend to sleep when meditating.

He absent-mindedly thrust his hand in the direction of the glowing orbs in the manner of *Spider-Man*, expecting nothing and achieving exactly that.

"Sorry, man," Zale muttered. "I don't know what to do, except what we've been doing. I've never met an Enthraller who had this much trouble using powers. If we didn't already have evidence to the contrary, I'd deduce Vulrick's powers were simply physical in nature, which is something you've managed to gain with ease."

"But he can throw fire." Badrick nodded. "He burned down my house."

"Exactly!" Zale sighed dramatically. "And not a cinder since you arrived. If I could see Vulrick and give him a telling off, I would. But alas . . . "

Badrick let his arm fall to rest by his side and took a breather from the endless attempts. He wiped his mouth with his sleeve and turned to his partner, who gave him a knackered smile.

Zale looked rubbish. He'd abandoned his uniform the week before, and was wearing baggy tracksuits, something which Badrick could tell he never wore; they just didn't suit him in the slightest.

"You look as tired as I feel," Badrick chuckled, casting an eye over him.

"Training you is exhausting," Zale laughed back. "Even Carla wasn't this hard to work with when we were partners. And we had to train together. That's always difficult."

"Well yeah, Carla could use her powers straight away, so I've heard."

"And her demon, Acro, isn't a Singularis. It was easier for them to bond."

"Well, tell Vulrick to stop being one then," Badrick mumbled. Zale laughed in response, but otherwise said nothing.

This was because the intercom had aggressively whined, deafening the both of them, and a voice Badrick didn't recognise echoed throughout the powers range.

"Attention, Enthrallers of the Daemonium. It is that time again. The Graduation Trials will commence in two weeks."

"*Sweeeeet!*" Zale whistled, grinning widely. "I always love watching these."

Badrick raised an inquiring eyebrow and asked, "What is he talking about?"

"The Graduation Trials," Zale began, "is exactly what it sounds like. It's when recruits undergo a series of tests to determine whether or not they can become proper agents or soldiers. They hold one every time there's enough recruits who have finished their four years, or are close enough."

"What happens if you fail?" Badrick asked warily, expecting the answer to be imprisonment.

"Usually? You are made to start the program again. From the beginning."

Badrick wanted to discuss it further, but the intercom was still going and the voice hadn't waited for them to quit jabbering.

"Due to time constraints the Command Council has already gathered the names of those waiting, willing and ready to graduate into the Daemonium. The recruits are the best of the best. They have demonstrated remarkable skill and advancement, and we hope to see them all in our Command Centres very soon.

"The chosen are as follows: Adrian Darcy, Belle Bennett, Akihiro Akiyama, Booker Young, Ae Cha Kwan, Avent Chevalier, Stefan Blackwood and Badrick Varner."

Zale's reaction was priceless, though Badrick was unable to appreciate it. His stomach had dropped a thousand miles, creating a hollow pit that made him feel like he was about to throw up all over the place.

An icy chill pierced his heart at the sound of his name, and he felt his eyes widen in barely controlled panic.

Zale's squawk of indignation reverberated around the room. He jerked angrily and screamed profanities at the intercom.

"You have got to be joking!" he roared angrily. He pointed at Badrick with a furious finger. "Don't go anywhere. I'll be back." With that he charged out the door, leaving Badrick on his lonesome to ponder the reasoning behind this unexpected and nauseating turn of events.

*

Zale paused outside the door to the powers range, hesitating for a moment, his brain whirring agitatedly.

The conversation he'd just had with Reynolds wouldn't stop haunting him and he could still hear the sergeant's dismissals echoing in his ears.

"Zale, it's out of my hands. The Council wants to push Varner's training to the final stage. I can't do anything about it."

Zale hadn't let it end there. "No, you had a say. I know you did. You're use of his last name as a way of distancing yourself means you disagree. But you've been at the head of this strangeness since he got here."

Reynolds had given him the mother of all scowls. "Zale, don't psychoanalyse me, and don't talk back to me. The Council has made its decision."

Zale shook his head for a whole two minutes after hearing that. "There is something you aren't telling me about Badrick, and though I may not know what it is, I *do know* it has something to do with that time, four years ago—"

"SHHHH!"

Zale had been sure Reynolds was in the process of clasping his hand over his mouth, but he appeared to get a hold of himself, and refrained from doing what he wanted. Instead he contented himself with scowling even harder. "Look," he spoke quietly, "I can't tell you much, but yes . . . fine, it does. We're worried about the energy spike we detected on him."

"Still?"

"Yes, still! Look what's happened with him. He's advanced faster than any other recruit . . . ever! Even you."

"Hey now," Zale argued, vanity taking over for a second. He quickly refocused. "He hasn't even used a power yet."

"The only other recruit to get past the third fissure during their training is Stefan, and we both know he has very little control. He's weak, but Badrick . . . is something else."

"It's because of Vulrick?"

"Maybe."

"I know who Vulrick is. I looked him up. He's a nobody. A punching bag. So what's going on?"

Reynolds put his head in his hands and sighed. "Zale, I told you. I can't tell you anything else, and the Council has made its decision. The best you can do is get him ready."

"Yeah, that's going to have a great result," Zale immediately growled. "He's *so* not ready."

"Well," Reynolds had sighed, "if he fails it won't be a huge loss, will it? He's only been here a month, whereas the other recruits have made this their home for years. It will hardly count as a setback."

"Either way it's still unfair. I want to see the Hierarch."

"Yeah . . . so do I."

And that had been it. Zale was ushered out of Reynolds' office and left to trudge back to Badrick with the news.

Neither of them had any other choice now. Badrick had a hard two weeks ahead.

Zale stood by the door silently, hand on the wall, dreading having to break to his partner exactly what the Trials entailed.

He wasn't going to like it.

Zale found him trying to use powers again, thrusting his hands towards the targets over and over, possibly in a bid to kill time and stop himself from dwelling on what he'd heard over the intercom.

"Hi," Zale croaked.

"Hey." He continued thrusting, though Zale could see he was no longer really trying.

"Are you alright?"

"Skip that, what's going on?"

Zale walked further into the room so the door would close behind him. He pulled out his sidearm and stood upon a disc, aiming the weapon at the glowing orbs.

As he pulled the first shot, he heard a call, "Hey, this range is for powers only!"

Zale ignored the voice, and continued to vent his frustration through the punching power of his pistol. When his clip was empty, he reloaded it and raised the weapon once more.

"The Council wants to put you in the Trials," he said softly. "It's ridiculous, but they're pushing your training ahead again. This time to the final stage."

"Why?"

"I don't know." Zale flinched, guilty for lying. Although it wasn't a total fib; he only had *some* idea of what was going on. "This would never have happened when I joined," he added tiredly. "This place has set rules. Now the whole thing has been just . . . " He trailed off, pulling the trigger again, firing off three perfect shots.

He could see Badrick watching him as he fired, and he felt

extremely awkward under the recruit's gaze.

But then he asked a question. A question Zale never wanted to answer.

He was probably just trying to distract himself, or maybe he wanted a little info from Zale's past in the hope of getting hints on what to expect.

"Zale . . . I've never actually asked, how did you get dragged into all of this? How did you find out you had Horas? How did this all happen to you?"

Zale didn't lower his gun. He didn't move whatsoever.

But at Badrick's prompting he couldn't help but cast his mind back.

Back to that day.

chapter
THIRTEEN

(Four and a Half Years Earlier)

The off-license owner threw open his door and screamed with rage at the fleeing kids, roaring all manner of threats as they disappeared down the London streets.

The older one cackled with glee as a bottle smashed right where they had been a moment before, missing them by seconds.

"You missed" he shouted, following it with some very rude profanities.

They continued to run, laughing excitedly, their adrenaline carrying them ever onwards. However, they did eventually stop, taking refuge in a dark alleyway. The older of the two lit a cigarette and puffed on its end with happiness.

The younger one watched with jealousy, but his companion

would never let him smoke. Charles always said he was too young.

Zale disagreed

He was fifteen already, he could smoke if he damn well wanted to. But Charles was adamant.

He was strange like that. He had no problems breaking the law, even hurting those who tried to stop him, but he had a contradictory regard for the 'sanctity of life'.

Zale found it a little obnoxious, someone hailing the beauty of life right after he'd smashed in the face of some random guy on the street.

Zale thought it illogical and stupid, and he hated Charles for his violence.

But the guy was his only friend in this violent, uncaring city. Zale had been in capital cities before; Rome, Dublin, Paris, Washington DC, but none had quite the same brutish . . . *je ne sais quoi* as London

Charles looked after him here. He wouldn't forget that.

His friend pulled out the multitude of crisps and chocolate bars they'd managed to steal, not to mention the vodka.

After all, that had been the objective.

"I gotta say it, buddy, you're one hell of a genius. Good work on getting the booze, chum." Charles forced open the bottle with his brute strength and took a massive swig.

"Shame you gave us away," Zale sighed. "Give us some." He reached for the bottle.

"Ah, ah, ah," Charles half sang. "You're too young and innocent for the destructive qualities of alcohol."

"For the love of God, so are you!" Zale shouted. "Seventeen is not the legal age. Now give us some before I hack your bank account."

"You wouldn't," Charles retorted, feigning hurt.

"Try me."

184

The older boy cackled and handed the bottle over. "Fine. Don't say I don't do anything for ya."

Zale took a huge swig.

He instantly regretted it.

He tried to spit it out and gag at the strength of it at the same time, which only served to force what he hadn't already swallowed further down. His throat burned like fire and his eyes watered so much they wet his cheeks.

"Breathe," laughed Charles, slapping him on the back as he doubled over and almost vomited. "Use those strapping lungs."

"It's the . . . nectar of Satan!" he coughed.

"Well, I never claimed it was ambrosia." Charles grinned and took back the bottle. He practically inhaled two grateful gulps. "*Pheeeew!* S'good stuff."

Zale leaned against the alley wall and watched Charles drink the vile poison, breathing heavily and wiping his mouth as his friend enjoyed himself.

It was raining when they'd entered the off-license and it hadn't eased up since, though they were protected in their small alley, the rain barely touching them here.

The cars on the road, which Zale could see at the wider end of the alleyway, were splashing water every which way. No pedestrian was safe on the uncaring streets.

From his hiding place, Zale could see the glow of the London Eye in the distance through the rainy haze. He gazed at it for a while, enjoying the blue light it emitted, standing out beautifully in the black of night.

London may have been a brutish city, but was also one of the most architecturally phenomenal. Though most people wouldn't have considered it up there with the greats, like Paris' Eiffel Tower, or Rome's Colosseum, Zale considered London's mass design the most beautiful.

He liked it here very much.

But even the shiny lights couldn't entertain Zale's ever active brain for too long, and he quickly turned back to Charles. "So what are we doing now?"

"I say we go joyriding," Charles muttered.

Without missing a beat.

It took Zale moment to properly comprehend what his friend just uttered. When he did, he blinked twice in surprise. "What?"

Charles gave him an excited grin. "I say we steal a motorbike and take it for a spin. I've never been on one before, except my bro's when I was a kid. I've always wanted to ride one again."

Zale crossed his arms and tutted loudly. He tried to give Charles a serious look, but was unable to as the rain had just changed its angle of descent and a few sharp droplets had just caught him in the eyes. "Dude, that's stupid. Actually, it's *insane.*"

Charles cracked up at that. His fits of laughter echoed out into the streets beyond the alleyway. "Dude, we just implemented an incredibly complex plot to steal vodka, crisps and chocolate bars and get away with it unnoticed, which *you* came up with. Instead of just robbing the store like normal hooligans, we did a Mission Impossible.

"And you think joyriding is a crazy idea? I think *you're* the insane one here. Besides I know for a fact you learned how to ride."

Zale rolled his eyes. "I regret ever telling you about Paris," he mumbled. "I needed to escape the police, what was I supposed to do?"

"Well, I wouldn't have remembered the story if not for the fact you learned how to ride in the space of five minutes." Charles grinned proudly, like a father congratulating his son for something impressive. "Little genius, like I always say. Now come on, we're doing this."

Zale had no choice but to follow as Charles led the way back onto the drenched roads. He didn't want to do this at all. Everything about the situation screamed warnings at him.

But he knew from past experience that Charles would leave him alone, lost in the middle of the city, if he refused to do as he did.

Zale had been alone in massive cities before. He was street savvy. But he'd never been in this part of London. He was in completely unfamiliar territory. It would be dangerous for him to be alone out here tonight.

To be honest, from the speed Charles had made his suggestion, Zale suspected he'd been planning this joyride all night. Charles was the one who'd suggested they come down to this part of the city, and Zale had a suspicion that he'd done it just to hang the threat of being alone in unfamiliar surroundings over him so he would have to agree to anything Charles would suggest.

He didn't want to spend another night living under a single newspaper, hiding in the grounds of Westminster Abbey or the cover of a sewer entrance next to the river or anything like that, scrounging and stealing for food during the day without Charles for help.

With abandonment his only other option, Zale reluctantly followed his friend and watched as he found a suitable candidate for their next stupid act.

Zale kept an eye out for onlookers—this area was thankfully devoid of people tonight—as Charles started on a bike, using his delinquent skills to get it going.

One of the few skills Zale had not picked up in his years was how to hotwire a bike, and so was thankful he wasn't eligible for this task. He already felt an overwhelming sense of dread as it was.

Something wasn't right.

This was going to end badly.

All of a sudden the bike exploded into life, the engine rattling throatily. Charles fist-pumped the air and gestured for Zale to take the throttle. "You're the one who knows how to drive this thing."

Zale reluctantly swung his leg over and mounted the vehicle. He tried to rev the engine, and was surprised, yet a little hopeful, when nothing happened.

"God damn it, the exhaust is . . . Hang on, my bro taught me how to fix this . . . Gimme two seconds."

Zale waited impatiently, casting nervous glances in every direction. If the owner of this bike came back now they'd both be in serious trouble.

Especially if Charles decided running was not his preferred solution.

"Aha!" he shouted triumphantly. "Rev it!"

Zale did as he was instructed. His stomach dropped as the engine roared loudly. Charles' cheers of victory were cut off by a humungous black cloud of fumes erupting from the exhaust. It engulfed his face completely, so that for a moment his head was obscured by the black.

He reared back, coughing violently.

"You alright?" Zale asked quickly.

"I'm . . . good!" Charles hacked back. He stumbled to his feet and mounted the bike, positioning himself behind Zale. "Hit it!"

With an ever growing feeling of impending doom in the pit of his stomach, Zale balanced the bike and struck a chord on the engine. The bike revved beautifully and, almost without warning, the wheels rotated. They shot forward so fast Zale almost lost control. They very nearly smacked straight into a wall, but he managed to twist it round in time so that they only skimmed the bricks before bouncing roughly onto the street.

Charles whooped with glee as Zale expertly swerved between cars, their angry drivers swearing at them as they rocketed past, nothing but a blur racing through the streets of London.

Within only ten minutes they were shooting past the Houses of Parliament. Charles threw his now empty vodka bottle as hard as he could and Zale glimpsed it smashing into the ancient walls of the building.

He was about to stop the bike and reprimand him for that, his anger at Charles' disregard for the history around them finally enough for him to stand up to the older boy.

But he never got a chance.

Without warning a sudden, sickening dizziness swept over him. His eyes blurred, his head rang and panic rose in his stomach.

But then it was gone—his vision cleared just in time for him to feel the bike give a lurch, leaving the road for a brief second as if a massive hand had just pulled them up into the air. When they hit the ground, a blinding flash seared Zale's eyes.

Everything went white.

Everything went silent.

Zale's heart raced. He couldn't see, there was no sound, no wind, no smells.

He almost cried out in panic. Surely, any moment, they would crash and get themselves killed.

What had happened to him?

It felt like it lasted an age, but in truth the white was only present for half a second. Despite this, Zale's panic managed to go through several harrowing stages, thanks to the human brain's ability to process vast levels of information in short amounts of time, before the white finally dissipated and his vision, along with everything else, returned.

Zale felt the cold air strike his skin again. Heard the roar of his bike.

But all was not well.

The smells were wrong. What he could see was *wrong*.

There were no exhaust fumes.

There were no other cars.

Zale had very little time to take everything in, but he noticed many things.

It was day.

There was no rain.

They were no longer in London.

Zale cried out and Charles whooped as he almost lost control of the bike, nearly crashing into some weird purple, glowing structure and coming very close to running down a startled teenager.

They missed him by inches and Zale heard him shout furiously at their departing backs. "Watch it, you idiots!"

He had no more time to process any more information.

Once again he went blind, the white returning and ruling his senses.

It lasted even less time this time around, but it was enough for Zale to finally lose control of the bike.

The shock of suddenly being back in London, in the dark and rain and gagging fumes of pollution, made him lose his footing on the vehicle. The shift in his weight forced the bike to the right, and they narrowly missed smashing into a group of black taxis.

Zale had just enough competence to direct them into a second alleyway before he lost it completely. He and Charles flipped head over heels, the motor skidding away into an isolated car park for residential owners and knocking over a group of city bins.

Disgusting piles of rubbish scattered over the ground. But that was the least of Zale's concerns.

He landed painfully, rolling across the tarmac, but luckily managed to get away with very little injury.

Charles was another matter.

He was very clearly drunk now, but it did nothing to numb the pain of his injured ankle, which was twisted at a horrendous angle.

"Holy crap!" Zale shouted.

"Aaaaaaaaargh!" was all Charles could say.

"Just be glad it wasn't your head!" Zale found himself shouting over him.

What the hell just happened!? Zale looked around for help, but they were alone. No one was around to offer them aid.

He took a second to check their surroundings, and instantly determined, from his time mapping the area of the city, they were three miles from where they should be. They were somehow somewhere completely different in the confines of the city, as if they'd teleported away.

They were back in parts he knew; he remembered there was a hospital nearby. If he could just get Charles there . . .

As if running on autopilot Zale felt his hand rummage into his pocket and produce the phone Charles had stolen for him a few months before.

He was halfway through dialling the emergency number when the phone was suddenly no longer in his hand. He heard it smash a few metres away with a loud clatter.

Zale fell backwards in an attempt to widen his range of sight and discern what happened, his usually high-powered brain barely able to process what had just occurred.

But then there was a menacing crunching sound, and a pair of shadowy figures walked into view, so stealthily, as though they'd come from the shadows themselves, materialising out of the darkness.

"Good evening, friends," one of the figures spoke.

He was shaking too much to get a proper fix on the newcomers, but Zale nevertheless tried to look at their faces, his instincts to learn everything he could about potential attackers for use as leverage later on naturally taking effect.

He felt fresh fear rise when he saw that their faces were obscured by strange masks.

No . . . Not masks . . . *Helmets*. In fact their entire bodies were covered with strange metal plating, armour like Zale had never seen before.

One was entirely white, the other black.

The white armoured figure was holding a huge, scary looking rifle Zale did not recognise.

And he'd seen *a lot* of weapons.

The other was holding a vicious, long, jagged knife in his right hand. The left was flexing, the fingers tightening and stretching slowly, purposefully, giving the owner a dangerous aura about him.

The skeletal-shaped helmet did not ease that aura.

"Who . . . who are you?" Zale stammered, scrambling to back away, dragging his legs across the ground.

Ordinarily he was quite composed when presented with dangerous people. Even now his mind was trying to work as it should; it had already assigned codenames to the pair to help him identify them quicker, Black and White.

But that first step in his usual process of surviving was all he could manage.

Right now, the fact that he was just a lost fifteen year old was all too clear.

The skeletal-headed figure chuckled darkly. "Your Hell," he hissed. With that he indicated to his white companion, who raised his gun and fired a single shot.

Zale screamed as the bullet ripped into Charles' chest. The older boy cried out in pain briefly, but ultimately fell silent as the expertly placed bullet took his life in a matter of seconds.

As his life left him, his body fell heavily to the ground.

He was still.

Black did not waste time; he took five huge strides towards

Zale and knelt down, pressing his dagger into his throat so hard and with such maliciousness it was almost as though he hated Zale personally.

"You will tell me the whereabouts of Daemnos!"

Zale choked with the pain of the blade sticking into the skin of his neck, but still managed to squeak, "I don't know what you mean!"

"You will help me locate Daemnos!"

Zale shuddered with fear, his legs banging out a beat on the tarmac, and his mouth opened and shut silently. He had no idea what to say, no idea how to answer the question.

But he never had to.

A loud bang interrupted the scene and, in the corner of his eye, Zale saw White fall to the ground, black liquid spattering from his head, a big hole in the metal of the helmet.

Black jumped, turning sharply and dropping his dagger in the process.

A second bang, and a bullet hit him in the stomach.

With a monstrous, inhuman snarl he scrambled to his feet and . . .

Zale's mouth dropped open as the black man's body appeared to shimmer. Right in front of his eyes, taking White's body with him, he disappeared.

Vanished.

An eerie silence followed, disturbed only by the sound of rain striking the tarmac. Blood was starting to dominate the area, pools from Charles' wound widening every second, too thick for the rain to water down.

From the shadows a third figure appeared. He was holding a similar rifle to the white man, practically the same in every way except for the iron sights attached to the top.

He too was wearing armour, *very* similar to Zale's two attackers.

Only this man wasn't clad in white.

Or black.

He was red.

The new arrival approached Zale with slow, steady steps. Zale wished he could see the man's face but he was also wearing a damn helmet.

He reached him, staring down at Zale's shuddering, exhausted body.

For a moment, that's all he did.

But then he reached down and grabbed Zale by the shirt, lifting him up and smashing him against the wall behind. He gasped aloud, pain shooting along his spine.

The red man brought his visor closer, and roared, "Who are you?"

"Zale!" was all he could manage in reply, his arms and legs shaking violently, half from pain, half terror.

"Do not lie to me!"

"I'm not lying, my name is Zale Hood!"

He could tell the red man didn't believe him.

Without warning he was thrown back to the ground. But he wasn't done with yet, and Zale's eyes widened as the red man unholstered a strange looking pistol. A second later agony shot through his leg as the weapon discharged, the bullet grazing his flesh.

His scream echoed, bouncing off the walls and out into the street beyond. He could hear people shouting in panic as a result.

But now everything was fading, and Zale, succumbing to exhaustion and shock, crashed into unconsciousness.

*

It was so dark.

There were no windows, and the walls were bare, devoid of any light fixtures.

The only illumination nearby was from some kind of phenomenon that was *completely* unnatural.

It was purple and blue, somewhat see-through, and shimmered as if it were alive.

It reminded Zale of Black as he'd 'shimmered', disappearing into nothing, and Zale often experienced nightmares of that night, unhelpfully fuelled by his surroundings.

He'd been in this room for what must have been several days now. Zale had no way of knowing for certain, but he'd slept a few times and eaten half a dozen meals that were always there when he woke.

Judging by the number of times sleep was managed and food was needed, it had to be two to three days since the . . . *incident.*

Zale began to feel like he'd never get out of here, and he was just starting to lose dissipated into nothing.

A light bulb he'd never noticed in the gloom flickered on, blinding him after so long isolated in the blackness.

Through the opening left behind walked a man in a crisp, red uniform.

Upon seeing his prisoner awake, the man gave a small smile. He studied Zale for a few brief seconds, watching as Zale slowly backed away, before heading for the bed and taking a seat on the hard mattress.

"Please, don't be worried," he said. "Greetings. My name is Sergeant Daniel Reynolds." Zale didn't respond, only stared, so Reynolds continued. "I apologise for the torture you were subjected to, but it was the only way for us to identify your demon, Horas. I also apologise for grazing your leg with a bullet . . . I thought you a genuine threat. Don't fret, our medical capabilities are advanced, there won't be a scar."

His mocking expression was pretty readable, Zale knew, but he didn't care. What this man just said made him sound like a psycho.

However, he didn't want to tell him that. This was the guy who shot him. He was probably very dangerous. Zale couldn't afford to rile him up.

What was more important was getting information.

And that started in one place.

Zale cleared his throat, and managed to utter in a hoarse, croaky voice, painfully dry after so long with only a rationed amount of water to drink, "Where am I?"

"You are in the prison of the Daemonium," Reynolds told him without hesitation. "I'm not going to beat about the bush, the men that attacked you were demons, one of them powerful enough to manifest on Earth without an Enthraller host, as well as summon a Singularis without the same necessity."

"What are you—" Zale began, but Reynolds unceremoniously cut him off.

"For time immemorial, demons have been getting trapped in the souls of humans as they are born. Literally ripped out of Hell and stuffed inside. Not all humans, obviously, but I'll be honest, sometimes it feels like they are in everyone. There's so many." Reynolds gave a small tired sigh, and rubbed his eyes.

"You're insane." Zale checked himself, but too late; he'd accidentally voiced his opinion. He braced himself for violence.

But Reynolds only gave a humourless laugh, his uniform creasing as he leaned forward and put his elbows on his knees. "I've read your file, Master Hood. I know all about you. So as it happens I know you're adept at figuring out who is lying and who isn't. You can see details in people's faces and body language, etcetera etcetera.

"So please don't play games with me. Don't ignore what your intelligence is telling you. I really can't be bothered with it. So truthfully, am I lying?"

Zale glared at him.

He briefly glanced at the exit, gauging whether or not he could make a break for it. Determining he'd never make it past Reynolds, he turned his attention back to the man and said, "No. But I never said you were. I said you were insane. You could easily believe what you're say—"

Reynolds didn't let him get any further. Without as much as the courtesy of a warning, he jumped up, reached forward and grabbed Zale by his shirt, yanking him out of his room.

Seconds later he was pressed against a wall, slamming into it roughly, next to another one of the shimmering anomalies.

A hulk of a shape shadowed him and he looked up, only to see a face that must have crawled straight from a nightmare.

He screamed and backed away as the monstrous owner of this hideous face battered the phenomenon keeping it in. Its spiked arms and shoulders gouged into everything nearby.

"This is a Kalik demon," Reynolds said with the air of someone describing a table. "A horrible thing, really." He watched it roar and hiss and throw its bulky arms around for a moment, biting his lip in thought. "Do you believe me now?"

Zale had no choice but to accept what Reynolds was telling him.

A long and terrible conversation followed. Zale learned all about the Daemonium, what its purpose was in the world.

What *his* purpose was in the world.

"Your demon, as I said, is named Horas. He is what I described earlier, a Singularis. He allows you to use electricity-based powers. You don't know it yet, Zale, but you are quite powerful. One of the most incredible Singularis Enthrallers we've ever seen."

The talks continued until they eventually arrived at the bottom line.

Zale had two options left.

Join, and become a supernatural warrior.

Or don't, and face eternal imprisonment.

No harm meant—Reynolds hammered into his head just how dangerous *all* of them were.

Far too dangerous to be allowed to wander around unchecked.

They had to control the demons. That was priority number one. But they also needed the monsters to succeed in that task.

It was a terrible truth, but that was the way it was.

At least that's what Reynolds told him, as well as an anecdote about him being imprisoned for two months before they trusted him to control his own Singularis demon.

"Every demon has to be controlled immediately," Reynolds sighed solemnly.

Zale didn't need much time to think on what his decision would be. What else could he do now?

"Yes," he muttered. "I mean, yes, I'm in. I've got no one left now."

"Excellent," Reynolds smiled, though, much to Zale's wariness, it disappeared a bit too quickly. "However . . . there is something . . . *specific* we need you to do."

"There is?"

"You told me the demon with the black armour wanted you to find someone called Daemnos," Reynolds murmured, rubbing his chin in thought.

"I said *something*."

"It's a someone, a demon. Do you remember the boy you joyrode past? The one you almost ran down."

Of course Zale did. He remembered as if it happened yesterday. He could perfectly picture the briefly terrified expression on the boy's face as he almost got taken out by their bike.

He could also recollect the furious rage that replaced the fear.

There was no way he was going to forget that guy for quite some time. How could he forget anything or anyone during that strange moment when everything went wrong?

He didn't speak. Only nodded.

"Good. Remember him." The Sergeant stretched, his body language suggesting he was dreading what he had to say next. "We've done some research. Studied the demonic energies. Even forced out the memories we could salvage from the residue of the white armoured demon. What . . . " He trailed off, sighing tiredly.

"Yeah?" Zale prompted him.

"The demon that killed your friend had the power to send himself, or someone else, to the future or past. This ability was limited. It only took effect for a few seconds at the most.

"It sounds like a pointless power, but you can do a lot in a few seconds, Hood. We don't know why, but they wanted you linked with the boy you almost killed, and sent you into the future to accomplish this.

"As you passed him your demons connected. Don't ask me why, we have *no idea*."

Zale could feel his eyebrow rising in thought. His mind was already whirring, as it had a tendency to. "What are you saying? This kid has a demon as well?"

"I'm saying the black armoured demon wanted you to find Daemnos, so sending you into the future must have been part of that, right? I don't know how he knew your demons would link, why this would work, or that it would work at all.

"I've never seen anything like this before. These things don't just happen. It's like a wire of energy connecting the two of you. It's very confusing."

"Why would us connecting mean I knew where Daemnos

would be? Did he think we'd share memories in some way? Why would he think this kid knew where Daemnos was?" Zale spat questions at a rapid speed, his brain working over-time.

Reynolds gave him a pleasantly startled look, as if pleased he was engaging in solving the problem so willingly, and responded, "I don't know. Daemnos hasn't ascended to Earth in so damn long. Any time he does there's a massive explosion of very unique energy. We haven't seen one of those in millennia. I think the last recorded sighting was eleven AD."

"Maybe this kid has a demon who knows Daemnos?" Zale suggested. "If this kid's demon has a way of linking with other demons, the black guy could have used any other Enthraller. Now I could have been random choice, but it would have been easier to use a willing participant.

"So maybe . . . maybe Horas can link with other demons, a power you didn't identify, and that's why he sent me to this kid so I could link up, so then through me the black bastard could find him, ergo find Daemnos."

Reynolds now grinned widely. "I'd read you were brilliant, Hood, but I never imagined how great. You came up with all that without knowing *any* of the actual facts besides what I told you."

Zale almost blushed with embarrassment. "It's just conjecture, and I put a bit together from what you told me, is all. But just assume anything supernatural is possible and numbers of possibilities present themselves. Limit yourself to what you know in situations where what you don't rules the board and you only limit what you'll find."

"Well, we can only guess at this point," Reynolds sighed. "You'll have to ask Horas when you can learn to talk to him. In the meantime, what we need from you is for you to remember the kid. When he comes here . . . and he *will* . . . I need you to become his partner. Keep an eye on him. I expect it'll be a few more years before his demon pushes him in a way that we have to intervene, or even straight towards us as most of them seem to do these days."

"Why don't you just get him right now? You said every demon has to be controlled immediately."

"No," Reynolds said quickly, shaking his head. "We don't want to interfere just yet. A demon is doing something big. If that black one wants Daemnos . . . Trust me, it's better if we stick to the shadows for now. He will come one day. Either he'll arrive or we'll be forced to pick him up.

"It'll be your job to train him and watch him. Feel free to become his friend, if you so desire. There's no problem with that."

"If I like him," Zale muttered, but otherwise saying, "Alright, I'll do it. But only because I'm interested in what is going on as well."

Reynolds smiled gratefully, and gave him a manly slap to the shoulder. "Thank you."

*

(Four and a Half Years Later)

Zale grinned at the back of the newcomer's head, amused at the aggression he was displaying. He could remember when *he'd* first arrived here. After the torture, and the pain and the imprisonment, he'd been exactly the same. They all had.

"I haven't joined you," the boy snapped. "I don't *want* to."

"Well, the other choices aren't exactly inviting," Zale laughed. He snapped to attention and offered his hand to him. "It's nice to meet you, though."

The boy—Badrick—glared at the hand for a while, giving it a wide berth. Eventually he seemed to decide there was no point in being rude, and he took it, shaking it firmly, and looking Zale right in the eye.

Badrick gasped in pain as Zale's hand suddenly tightened, and his mouth opened slightly as he felt the shock of recognition shoot through his brainwaves.

"Ow . . . " Badrick managed to utter through gasps of pain.

"Sorry!" Zale released him quickly and took a step back. There was an awkward silence, in which all he could do was stare.

Then he turned to Reynolds, treating him to an expression that displayed his feelings perfectly; a mix of anger and relief.

"So . . . he's finally here."

chapter
FOURTEEN

(Present Day)

"Zale?"

The sound of Badrick's concerned voice jolted Zale from his reverie, and he realised with embarrassment he'd been quiet for quite some time.

"Oh . . . sorry," he muttered, trying to get his thoughts back in order. He closed his eyes in an attempt to remember what Badrick asked him—it took him ten whole seconds, which was concerning. Eventually he was able to reply with, "Pretty much the same as you, to be honest. A church agent found me, hit me, got me here."

"Ah," Badrick sighed knowledgeably, his eyes glossing over. "That Hans dude I got whacked by was a fu—"

"Oh, I hate him as well!" Zale cried, unwittingly cutting

Badrick off. "Arrogant bastard." They both laughed for a moment, their tension alleviating, and the stress of the last few hours momentarily forgotten.

However, with the Trails now looming over Badrick like an unforgiving predator Zale knew they had to get back to his training, now more than ever.

"Alright, enough chatting. Keep practising. We have very little time until the Trials."

Badrick sighed dejectedly, but obeyed him nonetheless, facing the floating targets. He took only a moment's hesitation before resuming his fruitless arm thrusting.

Zale watched absently, taking note of the methods Badrick employed, the hand gestures, the positioning of his feet. Trying to see if his demon was influencing him to instinctively understand his powers as the damn hell-spawn was *supposed* to be doing.

Why was Vulrick so damn unhelpful?

Forgetting what he was supposed to be doing, Zale's mind went back to the day he joined the Daemonium, though this time he was able to keep a hold on some kind of reality, resisting the temptation to fall completely into the memories of the past.

Vulrick . . .

At least that explained why Black believed Badrick could find Daemnos; who better than his own servant?

But it didn't explain what Zale's purpose was. The ability to link to other demons was not unique to Horas; most demons, it turned out, could do it if pressed.

So why had Horas and Zale been chosen?

More bewildering, he also couldn't understand the link. He couldn't even see it, or feel it, which he should have been able to.

Zale still hadn't unearthed any answers to these questions, even after four years.

And knowing Badrick's demon was Vulrick also didn't explain

why the Daemonium was pushing Badrick so hard. What did they hope to accomplish by doing this? Had they discovered something else about the situation without telling him? Did it have something to do with the energy spike found on his partner?

Did they think Daemnos interfered, finally making an appearance after all these centuries? He wasn't aware of any energy spikes unique to the demon happening at all.

Zale wanted to ask them—nay, *order them*—to give him all the details. Or, at least enough that he could figure it out for himself, as he was always forced to do.

If people would just share things with him he could solve all the world's problems.

He smiled privately, thinking about what Carla would say if she knew he was being arrogantly confident again.

"Oh, for the love of—"

Badrick had reached the end of his tether, so frustrated with the lack of results that he actually stomped his foot on the metal floor, making an adorable clanging sound. Zale couldn't help but laugh.

"I'm glad someone finds it so funny," Badrick murmured darkly.

"I'm sorry, man," he chuckled. "I know it's hard, but you'll get there eventually—"

"How do you know that!?" Badrick cried. "I bet these powers don't even work. They're broken!" He threw his hands up in the air in defeat, stretching them to their limit above his head.

"Look, you'll be—"

Once again Zale was interrupted, though this time it wasn't because Badrick had spoken. As his fingers stretched to their full extent towards the ceiling, his hands glowed purple, and a blast of energy fired from Badrick's palm, smashing into the ceiling with the force of a rocket.

Badrick jumped so hard he fell back, right into Zale, knocking them both to the floor. They cried out in alarm as they tumbled over each other, with Badrick eventually coming to rest on top of Zale.

They grappled for a moment, Zale trying to push his partner off him and Badrick attempting to do the same.

Eventually they untangled their limbs and strained to their feet. Both of them stared at the ceiling, their eyes wide as they gawked at the smoking hole Badrick had just created.

"Broken, eh?" Zale laughed victoriously as people from the floor above gazed through the hole warily, a few even hefting weapons. "Vulrick has got one hell of a sense of humour."

"You think he did this?" Badrick glanced at his hands in wonder.

"I think he finally let you have one of his powers," Zale said. "Right when you'd resigned yourself to never getting them. Damn, how many powers does this guy have?"

"Five, by my count. The increased physical stuff, mind manipulation, fire throwing, grabbing me by the neck and throwing me during a battle, and now destructive purple light."

Zale whistled admiringly. "Damn, that looks like it'd hurt if you got hit by that. Jesus, look at that hole. It's awesome!" Zale was laughing gleefully. He grabbed Badrick by the shoulders and shook him roughly, excitedly. "We're finally getting somewhere. This is *wonderful!*"

"I don't think they'd agree," Badrick chattered as his teeth smashed together from Zale's manhandling. He pointed to the agents and soldiers giving them evil glares through the torn ceiling.

"Ah, screw 'em." Zale slapped him on the back. "Don't waste time, try it again. This time try and hit the targets and not the wall behind. We don't want to give the Apos an easier method of getting into the place."

The two weeks before the Trials passed painfully quickly. Badrick would have liked more time, but he ultimately had to accept it was a luxury he would not be afforded.

Zale spent every moment of every day with him, training, teaching, sparring. In his desperation, he even brought in Carla and, thankfully, under their combined tutelage, Badrick was able to learn a great deal.

By the end of the first week Badrick managed to *almost* grapple Zale to the floor, a feat most others couldn't even boast.

By the end of the second week he was still nowhere near beating Carla, though he couldn't say he was too disappointed with that. It was worth falling painfully to the floor just to have someone as incredibly hot as Carla on top of him.

Zale taught him advanced parkour techniques, and even introduced him to free running while *inside* his armour. He told Badrick that being able to jump a gap was all well and good, but if he couldn't do it with the added weight of his armour then he might as well put down his gun and give up now.

Badrick would watch in awe as Carla and Zale ran side by side over obstacle courses, pulling off flips and jumps he could never imagine being capable of. He gaped as they scaled the near sheer exterior wall of the Quarters Tower, all the way to the top, and traversed the trees outside the base without once touching the forest floor.

The whole time never taking off their armour or even being hindered by the added weight of their weapons.

The armour itself didn't add much weight to their persons—the supernatural metal was remarkably light—but it definitely made such movement more difficult, and Badrick was highly impressed with their ability to almost completely ignore the added nuisance. Their strength and tenacity was beyond admirable, and Badrick strove extra hard to be just as good as them.

And though he was nowhere near capable of the near superhuman feats they were, Badrick's heightened physical abilities gave him a gratifying advantage and enabled him to advance exponentially.

He could hardly believe it. Less than two months ago he was, shamefully, quite the terrible specimen of a human being. He wasn't strong, he wasn't bright, he wasn't incredible in any way.

Now he could match trainees with years on him in combat, run obstacle courses in minutes, and shoot his weapon with the skill of a pro.

Both Zale and Carla expressed their pride.

But the elation at how awesome he'd gotten couldn't last forever. Eventually, far too quickly, it was time, and the fun was over.

In no time at all there was only one day left until the Trials.

Badrick felt as sick as a dog.

With them being so close, there were several things that had to be organised. First of all was a meeting with all the chosen recruits and the representing officials, who would be two members of the Command Council that were selected to run the Trials this time around.

The first of the pair was a relatively old, gruff man, introduced as Agent Jonathon Carver. Badrick was wary of him immediately, simply because of the way he glowered at the recruits, as if he hated them all already. He looked like he'd enjoy nothing less than killing everyone in the room. His blue uniform looked crisper than everyone else's, and the way he held himself was very off-putting; the arrogance of pride in your authority.

The other representative, much to Badrick's great relief, was

Reynolds.

The soldier gave Badrick a comforting smile, a nod of greeting to his entourage—Carla and Zale—then treated the rest of the people present to the same kindness.

They were all gathered in the Council meeting room; the same room in which Badrick received his first mission all those weeks ago.

Remembering the Forsaken brought familiar thoughts of concern, though he quickly shook them away. The stress of the weeks since that day had beaten his worries out of his head, and he couldn't afford to think on them now.

Too much was at stake.

Although, they lingered at the back of his mind . . . distracting him . . . creating a hollow feeling in his chest . . .

He tried his best to ignore it. But he couldn't help but mentally berate himself; he'd gotten too excited about his new powers, and too nervous about the Trials that he'd stopped considering the most important things.

That scared him, and as a result his usual dramatic mentality started to pester him with worries about becoming just like everyone else. In a few years, was he going to be treating Forsaken with as little care as the rest of them?

He didn't want that. He had to *always* keep in mind what mattered. Having a demon may warp some people, but Badrick was totally determined to keep who he was. He would not let Vulrick warp *him*. Having a darkness inside you was *no excuse* for giving into it, no matter what the situation.

"Badrick, are you listening?"

He actually jerked in surprise when he realised the meeting had started, and he hadn't been paying any attention whatsoever.

Zale nudged him roughly, communicating that he had to start listening.

"Sorry, sir," he muttered, trying to ignore Stefan's cruel grin from the other end of the table.

"Something funny, Blackwood?" Reynolds snapped.

Stefan jumped amusingly. *"Nosirsorrysir,"* he squeaked pathetically.

Badrick would have laughed. But he couldn't. He was too busy worrying about Reynolds' colleague. The gruff Enthraller was glaring at him furiously, possibly livid that Badrick hadn't been listening. Or maybe he just didn't like him.

Whatever the reason, he eventually continued what he was explaining. *"As I was saying,* the Trials will consist of four tasks. The first is simply a written exam to test your knowledge to determine whether or not you've paid attention during your training. Something some of us *clearly haven't."* He gazed at Badrick, who shuddered heatedly as Stefan gave him another malicious smirk.

"The second," Reynolds continued, giving his colleague a vicious glare, "is a test of your control. This Trial *will* hurt. Essentially we will be hitting you, kicking you, making you angry. If you strike out, you fail immediately. Do you understand?

There was a chorus of *'Yessir'* from the recruits.

Jonathon took over once more. "The third Trial will be to test your grasp on your power. If you show us more than a modicum of control, you will pass. If you can't do that, you will fail. If you show no control whatsoever, you will fail."

"The fourth and final Trial is the most . . . challenging," Reynolds said softly.

Jonathon looked pleased with the worried looks that appeared on the recruits' faces. Apparently none of them imagined anything harder than what had already been described, just as much as Badrick.

"It is a duel between two recruits," Jonathon chuckled nastily.

"The goal is not to win," Reynolds informed them, "but to show us how well you fight with a weapon as dangerous to yourself as it is your enemy. With no training on how to use it."

"It will show us whether you can improvise, whether you can adapt, whether you have learned anything in your time here."

"If you *do* win the duel, it just grants you extra points."

A recruit, a Chinese girl who looked to be in her late twenties, immediately threw her hand into the air. "Sir, what happens if you lose the duel?"

The gruff Enthraller answered. "If you lose, but exhibit skill in adapting to the weapon you will undergo a month's training in its use, not to use it in the field but to gain control over it, and become a more competent warrior. However, if you lose the duel and show us nothing that impresses us, you will fail."

"The same goes for the winner, minus the extra training. Winning doesn't necessarily prove you are ready. You might just get lucky."

A chorus of dissent erupted in response, but Reynolds quickly silenced it with a ferocious roar of authority.

"Consider yourselves lucky," Jonathon hissed. "There were once five Trials, and the duel was a simple fight to the death—"

"It is no longer such," Reynolds interjected. "During your fight there will be Enthrallers nearby to ensure no one is seriously hurt. But for the love of God . . . don't kill each other."

"What was the fifth Trial, sirs?" Stefan asked them.

"An execution," was the cackling reply. "At the end you would prove your loyalty by executing a prisoner, Kalik, or some other dissident, with imprisonment awaiting those who refused."

Badrick felt his stomach take a violent turn, but was relieved to hear this was no longer the case. If he was called upon to kill someone to graduate, he would have definitely faltered.

He'd already killed a man, however involuntary it might have

211

been, and he never wanted to do it again.

This, he knew, would put him at odds with the Daemonium in the future.

These thoughts did nothing to calm him down.

"You will be paired," Reynolds told them, "at the end of the day."

"Your instructors will take you now for any final lessons you might be able to squeeze into your pathetic selves," said the other, "and to introduce you to the weapon we spoke of. But remember, you are not allowed to touch it. Not until tomorrow."

With that final order, they were dismissed. Badrick was surprised at how quickly the briefing ended, though not disappointed, and was hardly aware of where he was until they'd returned to the Main Hall.

Before they could go much further, a snarky voice whispered in his ear.

"Shame Mawr isn't here to see you fail in the Trials." Stefan's simper was doubly infuriating this time, and when Badrick looked into those nasty eyes he felt a white hot rage bubble up inside him. "But then again," Stefan continued shamelessly, "you could probably do much better than him—"

Stefan cried out as Badrick's fist met his face. There were shouts from Zale and Carla as they pulled Badrick away from his squirming enemy, and several other recruits either cheered them on, hoping for a fight, or backed away for fear of being dragged in.

"You're digging your own grave, Badrick!" Stefan shouted, scrambling to his feet. His nose was bloody, but Badrick barely noticed; his eyes were too busy spotting Stefan's hands going to the dagger at his side.

He tensed, bringing his hands up, ready to defend himself, remembering the training Zale had imparted upon him.

He hoped it was enough.

But before anything worse could happen there was an enraged shout from behind. "Enough!"

In a flash the dagger was back at his belt, and Stefan was looking around, an incensing look of innocence on his face. The call had come from Reynolds, who, along with his mean colleague, was striding up to them in fury.

It only took him two seconds to survey the scene and deduce what happened, and Badrick had a feeling the sergeant witnessed Stefan's willingness to use an actual weapon.

But before he could round on the bleeding teenager, the gruff man laughed gleefully and shouted, "I think we have the perfect pairing! Badrick, Stefan, you will be paired for the duel!"

Both Zale and Carla shrieked at the same time. "What!? NO!" They paired up on the Council Member, readying themselves to argue.

"No objections, please," he hissed menacingly before they could speak, his grin emphasising the fake politeness in his voice. "My decision is final."

Zale gave Reynolds a pleading look, and though the sergeant appeared as furious and anxious as he did, it looked like there was nothing he could do.

Carver treated Badrick to his most unsettling glare. "Bad start, Varner. Bad. Start."

With a sigh, Reynolds followed his clearly pleased fellow as he departed.

Zale watched them go with fury written all over his face.

Carla gripped his hand in an attempt to soothe him.

Meanwhile, Stefan was now invading Badrick's personal space. "I will kill you for that." He cracked his neck, and before Badrick's eyes the broken nose snapped back into place and healed. Stefan wiped away the blood. "Make no mistake. I *will* kill you . . . See you in the ring."

He gave all three of them a sneer, then turned and headed away to the Quarters Tower.

As he left, Badrick's unease intensified tenfold, and he began wondering exactly what was in store for him tomorrow.

By Stefan's vow, it didn't sound good.

chapter
FIFTEEN

Carla's worry was engulfing. It filled the room like a cloud.

Badrick didn't mind; he shared her unease.

"You don't . . ." she began, pausing for a moment. "You don't think he would really try, do you? He's not really capable of that . . . surely."

Zale shrugged dramatically, answering with, "Who knows? Does anyone really know with Stefan? I, for one, am in the dark. Who's his demon, for example? I've never actually been told."

"Me neither."

"He was going to stab Badrick earlier. We all saw it."

"Yeah, but surely it was just a hollow threat. Stefan is too cowardly."

"Maybe, but—"

"Do you actually think he'd kill Badrick right in front of the entire Daemonium?"

"In the duel, he could easily claim it to be an accident."

"He would never manage it. The guards would stop the killing blow before it landed."

"Stefan is at the seventh fissure. I know he's crap and has very little control, but I have a horrible feeling that he's hiding skills. Most Enthrallers here are no higher than six tears."

Badrick watched tensely as Zale paced the room with the speed of a cheetah, back and forth, back and forth. From her perch on an armchair—furniture that looked misplaced in the white-walled lab they'd found themselves in—Carla's left leg jerked wildly with nerves.

Unable to handle it, Badrick tried to distract himself by looking at all the weird stuff littering the big room.

Tables were positioned in organised places, leaving wide gaps for ease of movement. There were various bits of crap all over the place; strange inventions in the process of being constructed, disassembled weapons undergoing testing and, on the other side of a sterilisation chamber, a Kalik corpse.

Zale had brought them here to introduce him to the weapon they'd been told about, but so far hadn't done anything of the sort. All he'd done was rant.

As he raved about the Daemonium's stupidity, and Carla tried to keep him calm, Badrick did his best to distract his mind of it all, striding between the tables and studying every object intently.

One thing caught his interest more than anything else. He made a beeline for it, intrigued by the fact it looked so out of place in the lab.

It was a glass covering, sitting atop a small red pedestal on the very middle of a table, housing some kind of ancient looking piece of paper.

Tuning out his friends, he determined it to be an old scroll, weighed down by two paperweights and spread across a wooden lectern.

Badrick didn't want to risk dropping the glass covering, so he didn't touch it. He didn't need to remove it to see what was written on the page anyway, so he simply leaned in and studied the words etched into the browning material.

"Power of the thief, come to me—"

"Don't read that!"

Badrick almost knocked the glass from the table as he jumped in surprise. Luckily it rattled back into place, escaping the disturbance undamaged.

"What?" Badrick breathed, holding his chest.

"Sorry." Zale smiled apologetically. "Whoever left that in here is an idiot. Trust me, you don't want to read that parchment."

"Why? What is it?"

Carla stepped away from her chair and wandered up to it, giving the glass a tap. "It's a ritual."

"A ritual to steal a demon," Zale further explained.

Badrick rounded on him. "Steal a demon!?"

Zale gave him a sombre nod. "Read those words aloud with an Enthraller in mind and the power of the ritual takes effect. All that's needed after that is for the Enthraller to die, either by your hand or someone else's. His or her demon will then transfer to your soul."

"Think of the damage someone could do with that," Carla said. "You could collect demons, build power. Become unstoppable."

Badrick shook his head, disbelievingly. "But wouldn't that kill the guy who did it? Having two demons would be a huge strain. Having three would kill you, surely."

"Exactly," Carla laughed humourlessly. "So trust us, don't read it."

"Where did you get something like that!?"

"Just one of the many dangerous demonic artefacts we've confiscated over the centuries," said Zale. He placed his hand on Badrick's shoulder and edged him away from the table. "Come on, we've been distracted long enough."

"About time you realised," Carla tutted.

Zale made him stand close to the armchair before hurrying up to a different table that stood at the other end of the lab. He picked up something Badrick couldn't yet see, and wandered back over, fiddling with whatever it was.

"I finished the recent updates to the software last night when e're'body was in bed, so these new bad boys will be used in the duel tomorrow."

"Did you fix the short-outs?" Carla chuckled.

"Yeah, yeah, I fixed it. The output is stable now. Don't know why the version threes were doing it anyway. Mine wasn't."

"You mean, the one no one knows you have? The one you're not allowed to have?"

"Yes, that one."

Badrick sighed tiredly, irritated at the time this byplay was wasting. "What are you guys babbling on about?"

The proudest smile Badrick had ever seen Zale produce filled his face. With the look of a guy in love, he handed Badrick the item he had taken from the table.

He frowned confusedly; his partner had given him what was essentially a bladeless sword. It was quite ornate, with a large hand guard, a carved handle, as well as a pointed pommel . . . but not even a mention of a blade.

"What am I supposed to do with this?"

"Grip the handle tightly, and flick it twice," Zale told him, stealing Carla's seat.

"What will it do?"

"Trust us," Carla laughed. "Just do as he says."

"I will, I will," Badrick pushed back. He lifted it higher, giving it a wary look, but still didn't flick his wrist. "But what will it do?"

"Just clench the damn handle and flick your wrist already!"

With an irritated huff, Badrick tightened his hand as much as he possibly could and did as he was told.

"The wrist holding the sword, idiot," Carla sighed.

His face now red, he corrected himself.

He flicked it once, raised it again, and flicked it a second time in quick succession.

He instantly dropped it when a flash of blue light erupted before his eyes, shooting out of the handle. As it fell through the air, the light vanished, and the handle crashed to the floor with a clang.

"Dignified," Zale commented dryly. He bent down to pick it up. "I swear if you broke it I'll drop kick you out the window."

"What was that?" Badrick spoke over him, ignoring the jibe.

Zale merely rolled his eyes. He stood up again, and performed the same action, pointing it away from them.

Badrick jumped back as the light flashed again, a loud zapping sound vibrating the air particles. When he gave it another glance, he finally understood what he was looking at.

Out of the handle, a long, electric blue blade now extended.

"Whoa . . . " he found himself murmuring.

It was totally mesmerising. The blue was more vivid than anything he'd ever seen, and it shone with a glow that could only be described as otherworldly. Now and then tiny jolts of electricity would shoot along it, originating from the handle and travelling all the way to the razor sharp end.

"Cool, eh?" Carla smiled.

"What is it?" Badrick asked.

"Remember that I combined Enthraller's powers with

technology?" Zale questioned him. He nodded in reply, thinking back to the holograms and targets in the ranges.

"This is what happens when Zale combines his own power with tech," Carla explained.

"Well," he muttered, "it's not the only potential property it has, but I designed it for this purpose."

He quickly started to explain how it worked, pointing to the various parts of his design.

According to Zale, the blade was formed by positive and negative demonic electricity, working in tandem. On either side of the hand guard was a small light that glowed whenever the sword was activated. These were what Zale called the organs of the weapon.

The right hand light would produce positive electricity, shooting out a burst of Zale's power from the middle of the hand guard. The other side generated a negative burst, which would influence the positive energy into a near solid blade shape.

"*Near solid*," Zale emphasised. "As solid as you can get with something that isn't solid. Electricity isn't a physical object; you can pass your hand through it as if it were thin air. Though you would be electrocuted. Or, in this case, sliced open."

Zale showed Badrick how to deactivate the weapon; sliding his thumb down the handle slowly. The blade vanished, and he handed it back.

Badrick took a second turn, and this time managed to keep a hold. It had one hell of a kick when it activated, but Badrick actually liked that. It felt powerful in his hand, not to mention it looked damn cool.

"It has a failsafe," Zale said, "that deactivates it when you drop it so that it doesn't just burn through the world forever."

"What do you mean?" Badrick asked. He did this at the exact same moment that he tried to tap the blade on the table beside him.

His eyes widened when the blade simply sunk through, electricity sparking violently, the blade glowing brighter. He pulled it back and gaped at the burning gash he had just made in the previously perfect white tabletop.

"Didn't like that table anyway," Carla muttered behind him.

"That's what I mean," Zale laughed gleefully. He jumped over to study the gash in fascination. "Jesus, look at that hole! I don't yet know how far it can cut in one stroke, but the failsafe is to ensure that it doesn't harm anyone when dropped, and so it doesn't just sink into the earth."

"Good call," Badrick breathed. He quickly ran his thumb down the handle, deactivating the sword.

Safety first.

As Zale had already explained, the blade wasn't a physical object, so it simply passed through things like air. But it was so powerful that it affected them—very much *unlike* air—cutting them with the ease of a hot knife through butter at the slightest touch.

However, Zale delighted him with an interesting factoid; it couldn't cut through another one of its kind.

"Seriously?" Badrick questioned.

"Oh yeah, definitely."

"I don't even know why it can't," Carla piped up. "It makes no sense."

"It's magnetism, you fool," Zale chided her, though he was only playing. "But not in the sense that they're magnets, because they're not. But like magnets they have a positive and a negative attribute, thus creating their own energy spheres, which can melt through anything except another of its kind because, like magnets with the same sides, they repel."

"So *that's* what they meant," Badrick said quietly, barely

listening. He could actually feel his skin losing its colour as the realisation of what this new development meant for him. "A weapon as dangerous to me as it is to my enemy. One wrong move and it won't just bounce off my armour like a normal metal sword would."

"No, that thing is going to slice you right open."

He had to grip the table to ensure he didn't collapse to the floor; his legs had quite suddenly lost all function. He gave his friends a sickly look. "Why the hell do they use this?"

Zale grimaced, and held up a guilty hand. "Sorry, that's my fault. Like they said, back in ancient times the duel was a fight to the death. After that it was a regular duel, with the same rules as now."

"And then this idiot," Carla spoke, slapping Zale over the head as he sat back into the armchair, "decides to invent his sword. The higher ups discover it, confiscate it, then a few weeks later commission him to build twenty more. The really messed up Council members figured out a way to give the duel 'meaning' again, whatever that means."

"Ever since, last three years, we've all used these," said Zale.

Carla cackled delightedly, "You should have seen Zale's duel. There was no way the other guy was going to win, this idiot *invented* the weapon. The fight was over in three moves."

"Well . . . I don't like to brag . . . "

Badrick held up his hand before Zale could continue that sentence. He gave them a serious look. "Did you two make this place crap just in time for me to get here on purpose? Because it feels like you did. This weapon is insane!"

Over Zale's delighted chuckles, Carla took his hand and smiled reassuringly. "That is why we'll be training you tonight in its use."

He treated her to a very surprised expression. "But we're not supposed to know how to use it. *Heck*, I'm not even supposed to touch it." He quickly dropped the weapon back upon the table he'd sliced apart as though it were suddenly diseased.

"Yeah, well screw 'em and their stupid rules," Carla retorted aggressively. She fell back onto the arm of the chair, her body very close to Zale's. Badrick saw him turn his head, smile at the fact his eyes were directly level with her chest, and give him a private wink. Carla was oblivious to this; she was still shouting. "If they're going to dump you in this crap with this little training, their rules can go to Hell."

It took Zale a second to chip in. He only spoke when Carla looked around to see what was taking him so long and caught him leering. "I agree!" he concurred quickly.

Carla gave him a tap on his head. His hair flicked up briefly.

From there the conversation moved away from the swords. They wouldn't be able to get away with showing him how to use Zale's invention until the night shift, where they could sneak into a private room, so there was no point wasting the time remaining on the subject.

"Is there any last minute thing we can teach him?" Carla suggested. "Anything that can give him an advantage?"

"You mean like the whole damn curriculum?" Zale snorted aggressively, though his anger was not directed at her. "We've hardly scratched the surface. Badrick hasn't been here two months."

"I know, and we don't have a lot of time." Carla bit her lip in thought. "Is there anything that's *really* important to know before the Trials?"

Zale rubbed his lip with his thumb, presumably casting his mind back over the past five weeks, thinking on what they had covered. "What kinds of things have affected the Trials?" he asked. "What should he watch out for? I'm talking really obscure things. Stuff we wouldn't necessarily expect."

Carla thought for a moment.

But she never got a chance to speak.

This was because Zale had slapped his head and shouted, "Apparitions!"

"You haven't covered those yet?" Carla sighed, rubbing her eyes.

"Hey, let up!" Zale shot back. "I was going through the four year training program on schedule. We were only on the first lessons, me being silly enough to think we'd *have* the four years. Then we were too busy preparing Badrick for the Trials."

For the umpteenth time, an angry ramble about the Daemonium's attitude towards Badrick's training ensued, both Zale and Carla griping furiously about them. Badrick sighed tiredly; he was getting a little annoyed at all the distractions, and he quickly interrupted them with a cough. "Apparitions. You were saying?"

"Yes. Right, sorry." And with that, Zale dived into what was probably the last lesson Badrick would be lucky enough to get.

As he spoke, Carla sidled up closer to her old partner, and absently started playing with his hair. He didn't say anything about it—just kept speaking and allowed her to continue, as if he liked it.

This further enforced Badrick's belief that, if they weren't together, then they wanted to be, but were probably too scared to tell each other directly.

"Has your demon ever appeared to you?" Zale was now asking him, oblivious to Badrick's amusement at the pair of them.

He had absolutely zero clue how to answer this question. He barely understood what Zale was asking him. "I'm sorry, what?"

Zale rolled his eyes, but nevertheless explained himself. "An Enthraller's demon can '*appear*' to him or her. Basically, they enter your conscious mind and allow you to see and hear them as though they're right next to you, though no one else will."

"It's an apparition of their body," Carla stated.

"They usually appear to us clad in their own designs of our armours. Almost every demon does it now—I actually think we've told you this before."

"Don't forget," Carla continued anyway, "the Daemonium has been influencing demon lives for thousands of years. We've practically reshaped their culture."

"They do it for the sole purpose of communicating with us. Now have you ever experienced this?"

Badrick didn't have to think very hard on this at all, and he instantly said, "Yeah, when I was at the stupid therapist's. We were just talking and then all of a sudden Vulrick was standing right there, and he started talking to me, taking me right to the Main Hall."

Zale sat up a little straighter, almost dislodging Carla from her perch. "You teleported here? I don't remember seeing you. Did you see him, Carla?"

"It wasn't a teleport," Badrick spoke over them. "It was like a hallucination. Reynolds said it was part of Vulrick's plan to get me here, to keep us both safe."

"Here? To keep you *safe*?" Carla scoffed. "L-O-L!"

"That's a grade one vision," Zale mused, rubbing his chin. "Interesting."

"Grade one?" Getting sick of standing, Badrick dragged over a stool and plonked himself upon it. He was higher up than Zale now, but he didn't care; he was just glad to be seated once again. "There's different grades of visions?"

"Grade one is being shown an image of a place," Carla smiled. "Grade one is fun."

"Grade two is being shown a past event. And Grade Three—"

"Being shown a future event?" Badrick guessed.

Zale nodded in confirmation, leaning back in his chair once

more and allowing Carla to resume her hair twirling. Badrick pondered this new bit of information for a few minutes, rubbing his fingers together agitatedly.

Every day he learned something new; something weird, or cool, or just plain mental. Visions, fissures, powers.

Half the time he felt like he was in a comic book.

An evil comic book, of which the writer was an unforgiving bully.

"What are you chuckling at?"

Badrick was unaware he'd started smiling. He shook his head dismissively. "It's nothing." He uncurled the corners of his mouth and returned to the topic at hand. "How's this relevant to the Trials?"

"Vulrick is unpredictable," Zale explained. "I'm telling you so you know it can happen and won't be confused and distracted if he does it during the duel."

"Er . . . might he?"

Zale shrugged. "I don't think he'll sabotage you, but he might try to have some fun, or the demonic energy being thrown everywhere in the duel might attract him to watch with his own eyes."

Badrick nodded, musing on Zale's words, wondering if this truly was a risk. Even with the warning, if Vulrick appeared to him, would he have enough competence to be able to ignore him and focus on the duel?

"Are you done teaching him boring crap yet?" Carla asked, cutting through his thoughts. "You're dragging my day a bit."

"Be thankful," Zale rebuked her. "Tomorrow we won't have the chance for sitting around and having a pleasant chat. By his own admission, Stefan could very well be trying to kill Badrick tomorrow."

Carla sighed and nodded gently. She stroked Zale's forehead

lightly, watching with soft eyes as the strands fell across his forehead. "You're right, I'm sorry. What can we do to stop it?"

"We can't stop the Trials," he whispered. "We can't stop the duel."

"Can we go to Reynolds about Stefan?"

"Oh, I'm sure he already knows, but what can he do? Reynolds is respected, and when it comes down to it the Council is putty in his hands, but he is still just a sergeant. They won't listen to him on this.

"And I'm starting to lose my faith in the rest of them. Reynolds will be watching out, and the guards have always been vigilant. They'll probably stop Stefan if he tries anything. He's not exactly the greatest fighter, so I doubt he'd be able to sneak-attack Badrick without anyone seeing the signs ten moves before."

"He *is* very readable," Carla murmured.

"But he does have seven fissures. He could have tricks we don't know about." He paused, musing. "I don't trust anyone on this. No one will even listen to us."

"I don't think anyone would even believe us if we told them what Stefan said," groaned Carla. "Carver would brush us off, definitely."

"One day," Zale growled, "I will smack him. Always hated Carver."

"I'm sure you will," Carla chuckled, quite clearly humouring him.

"But we will practice with the sword when night falls," Zale continued without pause, "and you and I will be standing by in the stands. You don't have anything tomorrow, do you?"

"Cashed in some of my days off to help you with training. Have you forgotten already? What do you think I was doing with you yesterday?"

"You beauty." He kissed her on the cheek. "Be alert tomorrow,

Carla, even during their separate Trials. If Stefan tries anything—Actually, you know what . . . if *anyone* tries anything hit them with an energy ball. I don't care how hard."

"You don't got to tell me!" Carla exclaimed. "I'll leave 'em scorched."

Badrick raised his hand and clicked his fingers to get their attention. He'd let them talk between themselves for long enough and half wanted to ask them if they even remembered he was there.

But that would have been childish. The last few weeks were stressful on everyone present, not just him, and they were due some leniency. They'd been concentrating solely on him for *so* long.

"So is Vulrick supposed to be doing this appearing thing regularly?" he asked. "Because I don't ever see him." It was true; his demon had not made an appearance since the incident at Doctor Brian's office. Along with his inability to use his powers properly, learning that he was supposed to be seeing Vulrick upset him even further.

"Mine does," Carla told him, making him feel worse. "I can see Acro right now." She blew a kiss at the empty space to her left.

"Horas talks to me often as well. But it doesn't surprise me that Vulrick hasn't spoken to you since before you came here. The only reason I mentioned it is so that you know it could happen, and he doesn't distract you during an important moment, like the duel. Like I said."

"Well, it's not hard to see why it isn't surprising," Carla scoffed derisively. "Vulrick is most unhelpful. Badrick only managed an offensive power . . . what? Two weeks ago?"

"And I've barely been able to control it since," said Badrick dejectedly. He sighed, his shoulders sagging.

Zale kicked him on the shin to regain his attention. "I have faith it'll work in the duel," he said reassuringly—confidently—smiling like he knew something they didn't. "I just know it will. If Vulrick didn't want you to succeed, then he wouldn't want to be in you at all. You'd be a Forsaken."

Badrick was going to comment on this. Maybe even throw his hands up in the air and swear violently.

But he never got round to it, because he suddenly picked up on something Zale said that stopped him in his tracks. "Hold on . . . did you say 'in the duel'?"

Zale slapped his forehead so hard he left a red imprint on his face. Carla's laughs were so loud she almost fell from the chair again. "For someone so clever you're not half forgetful sometimes." She gave him a gentle nudge on the shoulder.

"What do you mean?" Badrick looked from her to him, then back to her.

"He forgot to tell you the use of powers are authorised in the duel," she cackled, grinning at her ex-partner.

"Oh come on!" That was not what Badrick wanted to hear. Stefan was at his seventh fissure; he probably had access to powers Badrick couldn't imagine even in his dizziest daydreams.

Plus, his cruelty . . . it would enhance his abilities. Badrick was a prime witness to this. Maliciousness had a nasty way of granting inspiration to those who possessed it so willingly.

He wasn't looking forward to seeing what Stefan had up his sleeve, as it was.

With this news his dread doubled in size.

"I'm so goddamn boned!" he said, almost shouting. "Stefan probably has loads of powers. His demon is a Singularis, as well."

Zale gave him a small. bewildered frown. "How do you know?"

"He's SpecOps."

Both Carla and his partner chuckled lightly, apparently sharing a joke between themselves that he was not privy to. When Badrick gave them a glare, the intensity of his expression enhanced by his never fading dread and panic, Zale coughed and apologised. "Not all SpecOps have Singularis, and vice versa. Acro is an Ordinarius but Carla was SpecOps before she transferred."

"And Reynolds' demon, Lora, is a Singularis, but he's army. So, truthfully, we don't know what Stefan's hell-spawn is."

Zale gave a wolf whistle, momentarily changing the conversation. "*Ooooh, Lora.*"

Carla rolled her eyes, but otherwise said, "She *is* a hot devil, isn't she?"

"That chest, man!" Zale laughed. "Do you remember when she took over Reynolds when he got hit by that rogue Enthraller? The one with the ability to power up other demons. That was a good day."

"I actually thought you were going to jump on her and drag her to your bedroom."

"Whaddya mean?" Zale asked indignantly.

"Your tongue was licking the floor."

"She was naked!" he cried, abandoning all pretence.

"And extremely hot, I know. Don't think I don't know what you get up to on your days off."

A less-than-innocent grin spread across his face, and he chuckled with delight. "Imagine how awkward that would have been. If Reynolds resumed control mid . . . you know . . . "

Carla fell into fits of laughter, and Badrick chuckled quietly along with them, actually thankful for the amusement. In truth, he needed all he could get right now otherwise he might just be sick.

He'd never been very panic-ridden in the past; even with his home life he'd stayed stubbornly silently seething.

But ever since that day at Doctor Brian's office his composure had been ruined.

They did nothing but chat and joke for a long time after that. There was nothing left for Zale to teach him—nothing of dire importance anyway. He couldn't even prepare Badrick for the written exam—according to both of them they changed the questions every time.

All that was required now—all they could do—was to wait for night and sneak into one of the training rooms with the sword for a few hours of illegal practice.

He was a little anxious about what would happen if they were caught, but it wasn't enough for him to cancel the night's plan. He needed this more than he cared about getting caught.

But until then they just hung out, desperately trying to enjoy themselves, Badrick using the calm atmosphere to keep himself pacified.

Alas, it could not last forever, and in no time at all Zale was standing up, announcing that it was time. "We have two hours," he said quietly, keeping his voice down. "Any longer and you'll be too tired for tomorrow." With one last reassuring pat on the shoulder, he led Badrick out of the lab, with Carla tracking close behind.

There they were.

He'd been looking for them all day.

To figure out what they were planning.

What they would do.

The three of them were coming out of the doors to Lab One now. They must have been in there the entire time.

He glared at them as they walked away, swore under his breath at the two males and leered lustfully at the girl.

When they disappeared from view, Stefan gazed down at the helmet he held in his hands, took in the bright yellow colouring, the uniquely shaped visor he'd designed himself, the camera strapped to the left side Stefan had fixed up so *He'd* always be able to look through stuff He'd missed.

He was watching Stefan now. The skeletal helmet was emotionless, but the scratched visor was facing him directly.

It unnerved Stefan.

And then He spoke, in a voice that was dark and cruel and frightening.

"Watch yourself tomorrow. I will *not* clean up your mess."

Stefan felt himself tremble.

chapter
SIXTEEN

They were all standing in a line, every one of the recruits signed up to the Trials that would dominate the next twenty four hours.

Though Badrick found it degrading, being herded around like cattle, he figured it was either just common practice, or maybe even an early attempt to test their anger control.

Or maybe he was just over-thinking everything.

Damn, this place is making me paranoid.

The first Trial was like being back in the confines of his school. Badrick never had the chance to take his GCSE exams and think about college—first he'd been held back a year, and then the Daemonium whisked him away forever, destroying any possible future in education—but this first Trial was *exactly* the same as his mock exams.

They were led to a back room Badrick had never seen or heard of before. A room where singular tables were set up in rows, with enough space between each one to afford the recruits privacy.

They were quickly ushered to their places, and thick examination papers were thrown unceremoniously at them.

Sergeant Reynolds was nowhere to be seen at that moment, and it appeared the Council member who would preside over this Trial was Mr Gruff-No-Fun-Bastard, as Carla had taken to calling him last night.

Remembering her fun sense of humour, and the laughs they'd had in the Lab, helped his nerves.

Aided him in placating the aggressive butterflies violently smashing around in his stomach.

The man himself was standing at the front of the room, roughly writing notes on a blackboard in large chalk letters. When he finally lowered his arm, Badrick could see he'd written the time they'd been given to finish the exam, as well as the grade needed to pass.

"You have two hours to achieve a minimum of fifty five out of sixty marks," Carver announced. He cast his disapproving gaze over them, his eyes lingering on Badrick longer than the rest.

Badrick glared back angrily.

What was this guy's problem?

He hoped Zale fulfilled his promise to smack him one day.

Carver tipped over an hourglass that sat in clear view at the front of the room, high enough for all of them to see the sand tumbling away their remaining available time.

At the same moment the sand began to fall, over a dozen exam papers were opened and the recruits began to fervently answer the questions. Having no other choice, Badrick did the same, opening the paper slowly, dreading what he would find inside.

"And just so you know," Carver spoke into the silence, "we

have demonic energy detectors set up in this room. If your demon tries to talk to you, or help you in any way during the test, and you don't inform us, we will know and you will be disqualified. Also if you use a power in the room, such as one that will help you pass the exam, which is also an offence, we will know."

With a shudder, Badrick stared at his paper with misty eyes.

The first page was simply an introductory section, detailing what he had to do, how he should answer each question.

It was extremely boring stuff.

But Badrick soon realised this exam was not promising boredom forever, and was going to be anything but easy.

It didn't matter that he was wholly unprepared for this; the exam was hard as nails, probably even for those who had years of preparation.

The first question, for example, was utterly mental:

Recite the chant it would require to trap
a demon in the Void between worlds.

"What . . . the . . . f . . . " Badrick glanced up to study the other recruits. They were all scratching away diligently, barely coming up for breath. "Great," he muttered, and skipped that question, saving it for later. Maybe if he found some easy ones he might be able to learn a little more from the wording, and answer the harder questions with less difficulty later.

However, it didn't quite work out like that.

Name the first eleven of the original Daemonium.

On a scale of one to ten, how likely is a Kalik incursion?

What is the Kalik Overlord?

What are the three grades of visions?

By a happy accident Badrick was able to answer this last one with ease. He wrote his response above the dotted lines provided with a smile, and took a moment to sit back and relax, enjoying his tiny victory.

Around him his fellow recruits never stopped, never faltered. Even Stefan looked to be completely entrapped in his exam paper.

Badrick may have felt happy at his little success, but he still had an hour and a half left to go, and many, many, many more questions to think about.

They were getting more and more insane.

His stress levels were rising, not to mention his embarrassment. He started praying something dramatic would happen, like a tidal wave—*anything* to get him out of this.

The further he got into the exam the more he wished a great deluge would wash him away, drowning him in the process, just so he wouldn't have to continue this wretched Trial.

In detail, describe the deciding factor in the Demonic Royal Family's ascent to power, and when it occurred.

What happens to the soul of a demon after the death of their Enthraller?

In detail, explain how a Forsaken comes into being.

What is the Apos combat mantra?

What was the Daemonium's founding vow?

What in the name of hell is this question?

Badrick shook his head roughly and stared wide eyed at his paper.

What. The. Hell. Was. That?

He'd been reading through the many evil questions with dread when, for no reason at all, he'd read this next one completely incorrectly.

It actually said, '*Detail what happened to the first eleven*,' and was very easy to read; the text wasn't faded, and it was simple-worded.

So why did he think it had said . . . *that?* It wasn't like—

This wasn't here before!

Badrick felt his head pang with pain and a small drop escaped his tear duct. He put his hand to his forehead, noticing that his temperature appeared to have shot up, and wiped away the tear, drying his face.

It took him a moment to realise his finger was now streaked with red.

And he realised it wasn't a tear at all, but a small drop of blood.

And then it started.

In a rush at first, a thousand deafening voices speaking all at the same moment—fast . . . loud.

Badrick almost screamed with the pain.

But then it slowed, the throbbing lessened, and the voices dissipated into silence.

And Badrick saw Vulrick standing in the corner.

He very nearly jumped in fright, knowing the demon's presence would be setting the alarms off at any moment, if they hadn't already.

But Vulrick appeared to laugh, his obscured head—which Badrick could actually see—leaning backwards and jerking, as if he found it all very amusing.

When Vulrick spoke, his voice echoed throughout the room as if he had a megaphone. It reverberated, bouncing off the walls multiple times in every direction. "They can't sense me, Badrick. Don't talk! Put your eyes to your paper."

Badrick hesitated for a moment, completely irresolute of what he should do.

However, he quickly did as he was told when he noticed Mr Gruff watching him carefully with squinted, suspicious eyes.

When his own were firmly set on the paper, Vulrick spoke again. "It took me four hours of concentration to enable mind reading for you," he whispered from the corner. "I cannot give you the answers to this *ridiculous* test. They would sense that. But I *can* give you this power. They won't be able to detect it. Use it. *I don't care if it's cheating!*" he hissed, hearing Badrick's thoughts straight away. "If you fail this I cannot prepare for what is to come. So use the power. *Now!*"

Vulrick disappeared, leaving Badrick on his own.

For a while he simply sat in his chair, his eyes glossed over, stunned into stillness.

He didn't want to cheat.

But . . . what choice did he have at this point?

Deciding that he really didn't have any other options, Badrick took several deep breaths, and, per the instincts afforded to him by the ability, sent his mind out to the other recruits.

One by one, he got the answers from them.

He did it slowly, carefully, worried that they would sense him lurking around in their skulls. If not, then their demon would, at least.

But he was cautious, and wrote the answers as best he could, trying to change the wording to minimise the chances of anyone deducing he cheated.

What the hell is this damn question?

There it was again.

Badrick now recognised this intrusive thought as someone's own internal voice. It was the first he'd heard, and though it had confused him at the time, after all this practice he now effortlessly zeroed in on the owner.

Stefan.

The person that Badrick hated most in the Daemonium was frantic, his mind a jumble of panic and paranoia. He was ranting inside his head, and when Badrick stole a glance over he could see sweat dripping from his face.

It wasn't here when I stole the test paper last week, so why is it here now?

Badrick's anger caused him to tut aloud, drawing the attention of the girl one table over. She glared at him, and roughly crossed out the mistake she'd just made because of his disturbance.

Sorry, he thought to himself, but didn't worry about it too much. She wouldn't lose any marks because of it, so she could shut up.

The news that Stefan was cheating didn't surprise him—it angered him, but didn't surprise him—but Badrick was still curious as to what Stefan meant.

Something had changed on the test? What was it?

Determined to discover what, Badrick focused solely on

Stefan's jumbled brainwaves and eventually, after having sifted through much of the crap, he heard a page number, and quickly scrambled to find it.

It didn't take him long after that to figure out what had Stefan so riled up.

Apparently, a question had been added.

Who is Daemnos?

This shouldn't be here! Why is it here? It can't be! Maybe they're onto him! What do we do?

Stefan's thoughts were getting chaotic now and he was starting to give Badrick a headache. He sounded panicked, and definitely like he was up to no good.

Badrick wanted to delve deeper into his mind, to read more of his internal shouts and get to the bottom of this *conjumbled* thought train.

But now his head was getting fuzzier, as if someone was rooting through his own mind. His vision started to get a little blurry, and his body ached.

In fact everything was starting to shake, like they were all in a giant vibrating machine.

Badrick bared his teeth and grabbed a hold of his forehead. His eyes felt like they were being smashed against the bridge of his nose.

He pinched it, closing his lids, once again very close to crying out in distress. He felt wetness escape his clenched eyelids, and opened them to see red splatter his exam paper.

That was it.

He couldn't do this anymore.

He had to get out.

Deciding enough was enough, Badrick went to raise his hand to get Carver's attention and be excused from the room.

And then a bell rang.

"OK, everybody stop, whether or not you've finished. Pray you have."

He looked up, and instantly the pain dissipated as if nothing had happened. The blurriness cleared, and his eyes stopped bleeding.

He rubbed his face roughly, feeling for wetness, and found none. He should have been covered in blood. By the end there he was practically crying the stuff.

Badrick stared up at the clock with disbelief.

It was telling him that their two hours had passed. The hourglass was finished, the sand done falling.

What?

Already?

Hadn't he just . . . Wasn't he . . .

Last thing Badrick knew he had an hour left and was getting the answers through sneaky, illegal mind-reading. No one had known he was cheating, and he wasn't going to tell them.

But he'd had plenty of time.

What happened? He couldn't remember where the time went. What had he been doing?

He tried to think.

He'd seen Vulrick.

Vulrick had given him the power.

He'd been taking down the answers, managing only a few short ones before . . .

Stefan's agitation pierced his consciousness.

And then . . . and then . . .

The bell rang.

That was it . . . it was all over.

"Time really flies," he muttered, closing his paper. He wasn't sure how well he'd done, but he didn't have much hope. He could only pray it was enough.

Though, as he stood up to leave the room, he couldn't help but feel like he was forgetting something.

*

The recruits had ten minutes before the next Trial. The two hour break was almost up, and Reynolds would be presiding. Jonathon was disappointed to miss out on this one; he always loved watching the recruits get angrier and angrier.

But it was his colleague's turn, and he had to grade these menial papers.

And so he had been for two damn hours, watching the clock vigilantly to see when the third Trial would start and his presence would once again be required.

He was so invested in watching the time he almost didn't notice when he reached that idiot kid's exam paper.

"Mr Varner," Jonathon chuckled. He'd watched Badrick struggle through the whole test with barely concealed amusement, and couldn't wait to see what the stupid child had written for his answers, if anything at all.

He opened the paper eagerly and prepared to stamp a huge, red zero next to the first answer.

But he had no choice but to give it a full mark.

It was correct.

The entire goddamn chant, word for exact word, written on the entire page, and the further into the paper he got, Jonathon realised Badrick had answered every question so far correctly as well.

But it was strange.

It was . . .

Jonathon had no way of explaining it.

Some of the answers were very formal, with somewhat shuddery handwriting, as though written by a person wracked with nerves.

But then, sometimes, Jonathon would find an answer that he would say, if he didn't know better, was written by a completely different person.

At times it just got very . . . *flamboyant.*

Take the question related to the first one, about the chant to trap demons in the Void. Jonathon flipped the pages, looking for it, his eyebrows gouging deep lines in his forehead.

Explain, in detail, why the chant to trap a demon in the Void is as it is.

A question written as confusingly as possible. He was sure the kid had to have written down something stupid.

But . . .

The chant, if translated from the demonic language, is long winded and unnecessarily pompous. One might conclude that this is because all demons are self-serving, but this is, in fact, false. In truth, the ritual was discovered to take a very specific amount of time to cast. It cannot take even a second longer, nor a second less. And so the right amount of words were devised.

In truth, the words are not what matter. The intent behind the chant, the power backing it up, what the chanter wants from the chant . . . that's what matters.

The words start the ritual, and the chanter's power moulds the energy into something that is desired. In theory, you could just shout 'I have a monkey that likes bananas' in their language and your power will do what is

required.
In theory.

Was the kid mocking him? It was chaotically written, the ramblings of a madman.

But the handwriting was neat.

Neater than neat, this paragraph had been written with *purpose*.

And he'd more or less gotten it right. The words *did not* matter in the banishment ritual; the desired effect was achieved by the power of the one performing the ritual. The words themselves were simply the ones widely accepted to be correct.

Forgetting the clearly mocking theory exposition, the kid answered correctly.

How did Varner know the answer?

It was impossible. *None* of the other recruits *ever* got this question right.

The sensors hadn't detected any cheating. Badrick never used a power, and his demon—Vulro . . . Vurack . . . Vulrick . . . whatever its stupid name was—had not helped him.

Jonathon glared at the test irately as his own demon, Jul'r, laughed at him whilst he flitted from question to question, finding nothing but correct answers.

Until he came to *the* question.

The one they'd put in only last night.

Just in case.

Who is Daemnos?

Jonathon was a tough man. In his day as a youth he'd been a strong agent, fighting his way through mission after mission, Jul'r granting him his Ordinarius powers and helping him along the way. He'd fought hundreds of otherworldly monsters.

He'd seen horrors in this world most could never imagine.

Not a lot scared him.

But as he read Badrick's answer, he felt the hairs on the back of his neck stand up and his body tremble in genuine fear.

You will find out. Very soon.

chapter
SEVENTEEN

Zale and Carla were watching from the viewing platforms as Badrick walked into the arena. They waved at him encouragingly, though it did nothing to ease his nerves.

Where he was now, this massive auditorium-like hall, was where the duels would take place, but he'd learned it was used for the two Trials that preceded it as well.

As Badrick took his place in the middle of the massive hall, with hundreds of agents, soldiers and SpecOps operatives watching his every move, an armoured Reynolds stepped up to him and placed a hand on his H-shaped pauldron. "Are you ready, Badrick?"

He gave the sergeant a nervous nod. Reynolds smiled, then shook his hand. He brought up his other limb and presented

Badrick with his helmet.

Badrick took it, taking a moment to study the olive green colouration fondly, remembering the day Zale had first given it to him.

That day felt like centuries ago.

Had it really only been five weeks since the Forsaken?

He sighed, breathing deeply, trying not to think too hard.

"We'll try not to bruise you too much," Reynolds told him.

Badrick could feel his arms shaking as he slid his helmet over his head and firmly fastened it. His heads-up display flashed into existence.

Figuring he'd prefer it, when they started smacking him about, if no one heard him cry out in pain, he discreetly set up a comm. link to Zale's helmet, hoping it would automatically pick up.

He saw the walking conduit frown and pull back his sleeve to reveal his port-pad. He tapped on it, then glanced at Badrick.

By the understanding expression that appeared on his face, Badrick deduced two things.

One; Zale's port-pad was linked to his helmet and so, because the armour was not in use, it had picked up the call.

Two; Zale understood exactly what Badrick was doing.

He felt the seal clamp tighter under his chin and around his neck, ensuring no sound would escape the helmet, meaning Zale answered the call.

However, in an apparent show of respect, Zale covered his port-pad back up with his sleeve and left his arm hanging by his side, keeping the call connected but giving Badrick his desired privacy,

He also suspected that Reynolds had seen what he'd done, his theory reinforced every time Reynolds smile widened when Badrick would only nod to his questions regarding his readiness.

"Ingenuity," he heard the sergeant chuckle.

Reynolds bowed to him, placed his own helmet on, and took three slow steps back.

And then, without any warning, the Trial began.

"Three, two, one!" a voice announced, quick as lightning.

People were immediately taunting him. Three agents threw rocks at his armour, striking his helmet and chestplate.

Reynolds darted forward and forced him to stand straighter, hitting him in the back of the legs with the butt of a sniper rifle.

"You think I'm your friend, Varner?" he roared aggressively. "I do what my job needs me to do. I am your sergeant. I am *not* your friend. Any kindness given to you is faked, to get the results we desire."

Abuse was thrown from every angle, every side. Different Enthrallers, agents, army—anyone the Daemonium could hire to put Badrick through this Trial.

And it wasn't playground stuff.

These guys knew things. They weren't just calling him names now.

No . . . Now they were getting personal.

His uncle, his parents, his entire family history.

"Of course your parent's deaths were your fault!"

"A demon doesn't protect anyone!"

"*You* killed your parents!"

"*You* started the fire!"

Badrick felt someone pistol-whip him on the back of the head, and though his helmet withstood the blow, it still sent shocks of pain throughout his skull. He fell, sprawling to the floor, his bones rattling inside his body.

"I have spent the last few months gagging," Reynolds sneered, bending down. "I have been waiting for this day for *soooo* long. Why do you think we put you in the Graduation Trials so quickly?

"Because we can't stand the sight of you. Nor the sound. Nor the smell. You are a disgrace. Having to be kind to you has been torture." Reynolds punched him on the visor, and Badrick's head bounced around painfully inside. "I am so glad I finally get to tell you how I feel."

The sergeant reached down and picked him up by the neck, gripping tightly. Badrick choked as his windpipe was mercilessly crushed.

He coughed as Reynolds kicked him back to the floor. He bounced and skidded along it, coming to a stop at the feet of a red soldier, who promptly kicked him on the head. The other Enthrallers wooed and cheered.

"You're lucky I'm not allowed to use my power in this Trial," Reynolds called, placing his foot on Badrick's chest and pressing down. There was a horrible grinding sound, and Badrick had the distinct sensation of being crushed inside a metal suit. "Otherwise I would speed-fist you until you were dead. It wouldn't take long, you are weak!"

At Reynolds prompting, the others continued their own verbal attacks.

"You are nothing!"

"Everybody hates you!"

"Die, you pathetic meat-sack!"

Someone kicked him in the ribs, purposefully missing the armour and hitting him in the under-suit, where there was no metal to protect him. An explosive agony ripped through Badrick's body and he screamed, unwilling to show pain by curling up on the floor, but unable to stop himself.

However, it made no difference—he could not get the relief of skin contact, his hands on his flesh, which would have helped him ignore the pain. The leather prevented this.

It was horrible. He'd never realised how confining his suit was.

Badrick started to hyperventilate, feeling trapped within his own protection.

"A child," Reynolds sighed, ignoring his obvious distress. "Your uncle was right. You are responsible for your parents' deaths, and you should have lived with the guilt all this time. You should die with that guilt. You uncle is a hero. He knew what had to be done."

And that . . .

That was the final straw.

Badrick's inhibitions, the ones he'd been keeping a hold on so tightly as they'd battered and bruised him, slipped from his fingers. His mouth opened, his teeth bared, and he roared, *"My uncle was a monster!"* He screamed so loudly he felt his vocal chords rip to shreds from the strain, and he was unable to suppress the cough that followed.

Luckily, nothing could penetrate his privacy seal, and the Enthrallers continued attacking him, unaware he'd shouted.

Badrick felt his rage grow white hot.

He'd spent *years* under the evil hands of that man, been accused of everything bad, been smacked, kicked, starved, and now these *pathetic excuses for people* were telling him *he* was the bad guy?

Those cruel . . . disgusting monsters!

Everything went red.

Badrick tried to stand up. He lifted his hand to push himself to his feet so that he could unload everything he had, and strike down everyone daring to even look at him funny.

He was going to *kill them all!*

He was nearly on his feet when he was forced back to the floor. He roared with unrepressed rage and fought against his oppressor, grabbing the red foot that held him down.

That was when he noticed it.

The foot was *dark* red.

It was not Reynolds, as he had originally thought.

It was bloody Vulrick.

The demon appeared to laugh, though Badrick could not truly tell because his face was hidden by that goddamn helmet!

Vulrick wagged a scolding finger at him and purred, "No . . . Fail, and I lose. Stay down, Badrick."

Badrick glared at him, hating him, wanting to strike him down for bringing him to this place. Vulrick only laughed again and shook his finger in his face once more.

Then he vanished and, as though Badrick had just been suctioned of all his anger, the teenager felt his body fall limp and his mind calm.

But he couldn't stop the pained tears falling down his face. With the vanishing of his anger, he was left with only an all consuming sense of despair and misery. The kind of sadness that could not be described. The kind that literally halted you in place as your brain aired nothing but mindless static.

He was done.

No more.

He just wanted it to end.

And then, out of nowhere at all, someone announced, "Time's up!"

It took Badrick a while to notice the cheers even though they were absolutely deafening. He was unceremoniously hoisted to his feet and passed among a massive group of whooping Enthrallers. They slapped him on the back and grasped his hands, shaking him with joy.

Badrick was numb to begin with, but eventually, when everyone finally stopped throwing him around, he was able to undo the seals on his helmet and slowly remove it.

He was instantly grabbed by Reynolds. For a moment they simply stared at each other.

Then the sergeant smiled with what looked like admiration,

and he grasped Badrick's hand tightly.

"You did well," he muttered, ruffling his hair boisterously. "Forgive me."

Badrick blinked in surprise, his body slightly angled as though he were about to fall. "It was so real," was all he could mutter. "It felt so . . . real."

"I've presided over five of the anger control Trials. I've had a lot of practice."

Reynolds shook his hand once more, and then nodded at a spot behind him. Badrick turned to see Zale and Carla clapping up on the viewing floor, whooping just like the rest, and he felt a smile tug at the corners of his lips.

At that moment Badrick felt the relief only the end of another Trial could bring.

Zale watched thoughtfully as Carla gently wiped away the wetness from Badrick's face. He looked very embarrassed but was managing a shaky smile as she gave him a kiss on the cheek.

"You alright?" Zale asked, slightly uncomfortable himself. Only once before in his life had he lost all composure, feeling as vulnerable and frightened as Badrick did now. Seeing his partner like this brought back those memories, the ones he hated above all others.

Whenever he got stuck on that day he usually felt the uncontrollable need to do something manly, something that made him feel strong and powerful. He would fight a Kalik, spar with and kick the arses of other Enthrallers or find a woman who he would *inspire* to forever remember him.

But right at that moment, he couldn't. Not unless Badrick didn't mind if he just took Carla right there and then and had his way with her in front of them all.

She might even go for it willingly. Just like him, she often said she loved it when other people heard her '*cavorting*'.

But probably not *right* now.

"Yes," Badrick muttered in answer to his question.

"I don't believe you," he chuckled, trying to make light of it. "I saw it, what happened. Vulrick stopped you, didn't he?"

"Zale, shhh!" Carla scolded, thumping him on the chest and glancing around anxiously. "He could get disqualified."

"I'm not telling anyone," he whispered. "Frankly, I'm thankful to the man . . . I mean, demon. Otherwise you would have failed. Am I right?"

Badrick didn't hesitate. He understood what had happened, and was making no effort to hide it from them. "With flying colours," he laughed.

"What was it?" Carla asked quietly. "The punches or . . . what they said . . . about . . . you know . . . "

"It just . . . struck a chord, you know?"

"Tell us," Zale quickly pushed him, not missing a beat.

"No, I don't thi—"

"A problem shared is a problem halved," Zale interrupted him. "Come on. Why did it affect you so much? None of it was true, so why did it matter?"

He glimpsed an angry scowl shoot his way, but it was gone before he could comment. It was replaced by a sigh, and Badrick ran his hands through his hair. "I've never told anyone . . . No one else knew, except my uncle, though I never actually told him myself. He knew from the police report."

"Knew what?"

"I was playing outside at our holiday home," he murmured. "I was daring destiny to see how high I could fly off my swing."

"Oh, we've all done that as kids," Carla said dismissively.

"But I failed to land properly and twisted my ankle. I'm lucky I didn't break it, but . . . " Badrick took a deep breath. "The story goes that my mum heard my cries of pain and was so desperate to reach her injured child that she left the stove on. That's what caused the fire. That's what killed them."

Zale couldn't help but frown at this, and he sneaked a glance at Carla, who shrugged confusedly. "But . . . it wasn't—"

"No," Badrick stopped him. "It isn't. What really happened was *I* killed them with my powers." He hesitated, taking a moment to glance back down at the arena, where Reynolds was conversing with Jonathon Carver. "But the swing is what I remember. To believe that I was responsible for so many years, only to *not* be told I wasn't, but I actually did it in a far more direct way . . . it hurts."

"But it wasn't your fault," Carla argued.

"We've all read the report," Zale stated. "No one is deluded enough to think you actually murdered them willingly. It wasn't you."

"Like the report matters!" Carla snapped. "It's obvious it wasn't your fault."

"Well, it was," Badrick growled angrily, temporarily forgetting himself. "My powers burned them in their house. And to be reminded of that, to be *judged* of that by . . . "

Zale did not miss the hesitation, the way Badrick's voice trailed off. He gave the recruit a sharp look and questioned, "By?"

Badrick closed his eyes. "By people like . . . *them*," he whispered.

And it hit Zale like a brick. Now he knew exactly what the problem was.

"I see," he whispered. "I'm sorry, Badrick."

Zale wanted to say something else, to try and tell him that the situation wasn't necessarily how he believed it to be.

That not everyone was inherently cruel.

But he never got the chance, because Badrick's name was once again announced and he was called to the arena for his third Trial.

His partner didn't look like he was ready for it in any form. His limbs were still shaking, and he was grinding his teeth, a look of anger and despair glittering in his eyes.

But as his name was called, something strange happened. Badrick appeared to be taken over by a neatly veiled fury, though Zale could see it in the way his hands now clenched tightly.

He glared down at the arena. In fact he looked downright livid that they'd been interrupted.

With a look of impatience, Badrick pushed past them and descended the steps, approaching Reynolds and Carver and stopping in front of them.

Zale saw Reynolds' concerned expression.

He knew something was up.

The sergeant reached towards Badrick and opened his mouth.

He never got a chance to speak either.

Just as he went to, Carver barged past him and announced to the hall, "A target dummy has been set up at the opposite end of the arena, as you can see." He indicated behind him, revealing to them the straw dummy standing a few feet away. "Mr Varner's task is to destroy the dummy, using only his offensive powers."

"The offensive powers of a demon are the most dangerous," Reynolds chipped in. He was still studying Badrick with disquiet, but now that Carver had spoken over him he had no choice but to join in the Trial, though he allowed himself a vicious glare at his colleague.

Zale had a sneaky feeling Carver would be paying for this later.

"The offensive powers are what we need to know you have control of," Carver continued, unaware of his fellow Council member's displeasure.

"So you want me to destroy that dummy?" Badrick asked

them.

Zale knew trouble was coming. Badrick sounded absolutely furious.

What was he going to do? He had to be careful. Carver could disqualify him at any moment if he continued snapping at them.

The situation got even worse when Badrick slapped Carver aside. At first, the agent grunted in discomfort and rounded on Badrick but in the end had no choice other than to flee when he saw what Badrick was doing. "The Trial has not started yet!" he shouted fruitlessly.

Badrick utterly ignored him. He took a step closer to the dummy and, without pause, slapped his hands together so hard the sound echoed throughout the stunned silence of the hall.

Purple light flashed in his hands, shining beautifully and dangerously all at the same time. The energy sparked and spat discharges at the ground, gouging deep burn marks in the concrete. With a roar of effort, Badrick opened his hands, palms forwards. The light exploded with the force of a bomb and rocketed towards the dummy with a deafening scream.

There was a violent crash and a blinding flash of light. Zale had to cover his eyes to protect them from the glare, and Carla buried her face in his shoulder to avoid being blinded herself.

When he was able to look back without fear of losing his vision, Zale was greeted with a sight of utter destruction.

The dummy was completely gone, its pieces scattered every which way, wood, straw and burlap stuck to any surface it had hit. With a hint of amusement he noticed Carver pulling a piece of sack off his face.

Beside him, Carla cackled with delight. "Now *that* was freakin' cool!" she shouted into the silence.

"If that had been a person . . . " Zale whispered. He gazed at Reynolds nervously, waiting to see what his reaction would be.

Carver, at least, looked absolutely furious. His face was creased with anger, his old eyes glinting dangerously.

Reynolds looked to be struggling with which reaction to choose; pride or disapproval.

"Is that good enough?" Zale heard Badrick snarl. "I've demonstrated my control. Am I done yet?"

"How did he do that?" Carla muttered in Zale's ear. "He's never been able to do it with such domination before."

"Nothing like a little bit of anger to help you gain control. The irony of emotions; they hold both the key to control, and the one to losing it. Emotions are more dangerous and more capable of anything than any other force in this world."

Down in the arena, Jonathon stomped his foot aggressively. "This is unacceptable. You put everyone in this room in danger."

"I had control, didn't I?"

The aged agent didn't know what to say. He gaped at Badrick for quite a while, his mouth opening and closing like a fish. Eventually, he managed to stutter out, "Our . . . our reports state you are a pyrokinetic. You have shown no such ability to use this power with competence. Either provide us with a demonstration of your control, or we will be forced to assume it could erupt at any time. You will fail this Trail."

Badrick actually laughed in his face. "My demon hasn't let me use that power yet," he hissed, menacing and livid. "But when he does, it will be mine. That will have to be good enough. I can't do it yet. You see, that's what happens when you throw someone who isn't ready into this crap.

"If it isn't good enough, you can throw me in the prison right now. I'm gone. I'm done. You know where to find me."

With that, he pushed Carver aside, nearly knocking him from his feet, and made his way back to the viewing stands, stomping up the stairs.

"You probably shouldn't have done that," Zale told him solemnly when he'd returned. "It looks to everyone that you're losing control of your rage from the previous Trial. They'll disqualify you."

"I don't care," Badrick snapped. He slammed his back into the wall and slid down to the floor, his armour gouging deep scratches as he fell. "These people are sick. I don't want to do this anymore."

Carla shared a sad look with Zale. She took a few steps closer so that she could plonk herself beside him, taking his hand in hers and smiling kindly.

With a heavy breath, Zale joined them, placing himself on the other side. "It gets to you, this place. I know. But we're not all bad."

Badrick chuckled humourlessly. "I know."

They sat there for a long time, hearing—but not watching—the other recruits undertake the second and third Trials. No one said a word the whole time.

They simply sat there, thinking to themselves.

chapter
EIGHTEEN

Another two hours passed before anyone drew near them in their small corner.

He approached from the staircase, appearing from below like a sombre father coming to check on his sulking children.

Badrick wasn't sure how he felt when he realised it was Reynolds, though his stomach did tense guiltily with the memory of what he did.

Now that his anger had subsided, only worry remained.

Upon spotting them on the floor, the sergeant moved to stand opposite, his back against the guard railing, nothing but the drop to the arena behind him.

Reynolds looked at the three of them in turn, lingering on Badrick for longer than the other two. "Do any of you want to tell me what's going on?" he asked quietly. When none of them answered, he turned his attention solely on Badrick. "Varner? An unasked question is knowledge wasted. What's up with you?"

Badrick sighed—he felt like he'd been doing that a lot lately—and let his helmet fall the floor. He'd been gently tossing it for fifty minutes, and letting it go felt wrong, but he figured it would just serve as a distraction right now.

"I don't know how I feel about this place," he whispered.

There it was. Finally out in the open. He'd told the truth of his feelings.

"You want to explain that?"

"I don't know what to say."

Badrick's eyebrows rose when Reynolds bent his legs and sat down opposite them. He gave Badrick's boot a playfully hard smack. "You do understand the second Trial was all manufactured, don't you? None of us meant any of what we said, and you passed the Trial. Very well."

Neither Zale nor Carla commented on the inaccuracy of that statement, and Badrick was extremely thankful for that.

Though it probably didn't matter; he already suspected Reynolds knew everything.

He puffed uncomfortably, pushing back his hair. Trying to be as gentle as he could, he whispered, "It's just . . . being judged like that . . . from people like you—sorry—people like *them* . . . it just . . . " He trailed off, not knowing what to say.

"People like them?"

Badrick fidgeted uncomfortably, and exclaimed louder than he intended to, "The people here are horrible. They're . . . disgusting!"

"I'm very sorry the showers have been broken this past week," Reynolds smiled. "They'll be fixed tomorrow."

"I don't—" Zale began, but Reynolds cut him off with an

impatient hand.

"Trying to relieve the obvious tension, Hood. Please continue, Badrick."

He sat up straighter and elaborated, no other choice but to, "All I've heard since I got here is crap I never thought I'd hear from people like us. The Forsaken I killed . . . he was a victim."

"Are you saying we shouldn't take out these threats?"

"He didn't choose to have a demon."

Reynolds scowled. "None of us did, Varner. What makes him so different?"

"He didn't choose to have a dick for a demon. His *soul*, Sarge. The demon ripped his soul apart. It's different because our demons don't do that. They work with us once we can control them."

"They still try to cause havoc."

"Not like that, they don't. But you're proving my point. Our demons are bad too. We could all end up in the same boat one day. At any moment, Vulrick, or Horas, or Acro might just decide they've had enough and attack from the inside. That would be our friends. Knowing that, why do we treat the Forsaken like animals?

"No one should be hurt like they are. But apparently it's not enough for them to suffer. All I hear is, *'Well done on killing the freak, Varner,'* and *'Congrats on killing the scumbag'.*

"Scumbag? Are you freakin' serious? The Forsaken aren't scumbags, they're victims. They don't choose to do what they do, they are tortured into it."

"Badrick," Reynolds breathed slowly, "if we don't deal with them they—"

"I'm not trying to take over the way this place works or anything," Badrick quickly stopped him. "I understand the need to keep people safe. I'm just saying, what's with all the racist-like behaviour? Why don't these arseholes try to be more understanding? You know how hard it is to have a demon. All of you. Just because yours is better, does that mean you get to bully the unfortunate ones?"

"I think what Badrick is trying to say," Zale interjected, "is that maybe the opinions of, well, *everyone* here are a little . . . distasteful."

"People make fun of mentally ill people all the time," Badrick said, refusing to stop now he'd started, until he'd said everything he needed to. "They call them schizo, and mental, and freak. But it's not their fault they are that way, and *anyone* could become just like them at any time. Something just went wrong, something they couldn't control.

"But that's *people*. When someone has depression everyone tells them to get over it. They don't understand what is wrong, that it's an illness, and they don't care. They harass and insult these unfortunate people without thought. But they're just *people*.

"We aren't just people! We have demons inside us. We're exposed to a bigger evil than anyone else. We should be making an effort just because of that to be better. We should be understanding. We should hold ceremonies for every Forsaken we kill, in memory of their . . . their . . . *unparalleled suffering!*

"But you don't. You all talk about them as if they're nothing. The demonically insane as well. It's disgusting, and I don't want to be a part of it. *I won't!* I've kept it in for too long. I'm sorry, Sarge, I just can't. I can't. I just can't."

Fully exhausted now, Badrick fell back into the welcome arms of Carla, breathing hard. She grabbed his hand comfortingly, and hugged him.

He hadn't spoken that much in weeks. He'd blurted out everything, all the big problems he'd had all this time.

Now all he could do was wait for the repercussions.

Reynolds was clicking his tongue, staring at Badrick sightlessly as he thought to himself.

"There's a point where it breaks," Zale whispered, a small smile playing at his lips, "and we can no longer take any more."

Reynolds eyed him with interest. "Who said that?" he inquired.

"Me," Zale smirked. "Pretty profound, don't you think?"

Reynolds hand went to his forehead, but Badrick could see an amused grin on his face. After a moment, he jerked his thumb at Badrick.

"What do you make of this?" he asked Zale. "By his own words, he thinks we're a higher class of people. That we're better, and therefore must act better, and not like the rest of normal humanity."

"I think he has a complete right to compare us to the rest of humanity," Zale stated. "All Enthrallers have similar experiences with these devils inside us, and we all run the risk of suffering what the people here detest and discriminate against. With these threats so close to home, you'd think our society would be too advanced for preconceived opinions that are not based on reason or actual experience."

"Badrick is right," Carla interjected. "We're not different, the Daemonium acts just as cruelly and thoughtlessly. We've proven that when old prejudices no longer matter, new ones crop up in their place. Truth be told, who're the real monsters here? I don't see the demons prejudicing anyone. Acro positively pities the demonically insane."

"And Lora wants to find a better way to help the Forsaken," Reynolds sighed. "Believe it or not."

Badrick cleared his throat; it had become filled with saliva after so much talking without breath. "I know the Forsaken have become animals," he murmured. "But they weren't always like that, and they didn't choose to be. I can't do anything to stop humanity from being disgusting. Racism, harassment, homophobia, religious extremists. They're all monsters. But . . . for the love of God, why are we? We shouldn't be the same. None of them deserve it; the Forsaken, the insane, the Apos—"

He knew as soon as he uttered the words that he'd hit a nerve. Reynolds face folded into a scowl and he almost spat back, "They attack us. They've killed hundreds of us."

"And you've killed hundreds of them," Badrick countered. "And the English killed thousands of French people. The Germans killed thousands of English people. The Americans slaughtered millions of Japanese civilians.

"But was it their choice, or did they do it because their leaders forced them? Our own country used to shoot their soldiers if they didn't follow orders. Can we be sure the Apos are any different? Do we know for sure they assault our guys out of choice? We can't possibly. But everyone brands every single one of them as terrorists.

"The Apos leaders get to new Enthrallers before you and poison their minds until their only future is a bloody, violent death, torn apart by the hands of our guys. But they were people before, and they are people after. Can we actually say we wouldn't be the same if we were found by the Apos first?"

"Alright, fine!" Reynolds cried, throwing his hands into the air in defeat. "We can't be sure it isn't like that."

"I'm not saying let them kill us," Badrick almost laughed. "I'm saying stop being so stupid, and stop confusing people with demons. We may be stuck with them, but that's no reason to act like them. There's a difference."

Once again, he'd drained himself.

Badrick had believed himself to be done the first time, but after the inputs from Zale and Carla, he'd thought of more to say.

He felt embarrassed. He never meant to spout out everything he had, like a fountain spewing, not water, but a torrent of rants.

A familiar sensation of sick filled his gut, and he pressed a hand against the leather lining his stomach. He expected nothing but the worst reprimanding he'd ever get from Reynolds, and he felt panic at having spoken at all.

But to his surprise Reynolds tilted his head back . . . and laughed. After several seconds of this he reached up and wiped away an amused tear.

Was the sergeant laughing at him? He knew he'd argued his opinion like an uncultured idiot, his words half jumbled into incoherent sentences, but there was no need to mock him . . .

Reynolds interrupted his indignation with a smack to the knee guard, saying as he did, "I never thought I'd hear such an intelligent argument from you, Varner."

Badrick didn't know what to say; this completely contradicted his opinions of himself, and he could do nothing but stare in confusion as Reynolds started, "You're right, things aren't pretty here. But what you have to understand, Badrick, is that we're not a higher race of people. We're just people; plain, dumb, boring people with only an ounce of interesting that doesn't even belong in our dimension.

"People are stupid, Badrick. People are sheep. We're not alpha males, we're not predators. We're herd animals, nothing more. We believe the first thing we're told by anyone who says it and live our lives as if it is fact.

"Mentally ill people *are* treated without care. Even the places we send our loved ones for help are practically prisons, and I've heard horrible stories of orderlies who treat their patients like criminals.

"They didn't choose to succumb to mental illness, but they're still judged as if they were behind it. It just isn't true, nature isn't controlled by people.

"And the difference between choice and nature doesn't end

there," Reynolds continued, clearly on a roll now. "We're born stupid, or we're born intelligent; we're born ill or we're born healthy; we're born brave or we're born cowardly. Nothing is truly a choice, yet our society is so obsessed with freedom that its forgotten that we have none."

Badrick squinted confusedly, not sure what Reynolds was trying to say. "What do you mean by that?" he asked.

"Everyone wants freedom," Reynolds began. "We want it so bad that humanity has unanimously decided, somewhere along the way, that *everything* is a choice. But it isn't. We make fun of unintelligent people, we make fun of ugly people . . . but it's all just genetics.

"Zale did not choose to have an IQ of . . . *ten billion*. Carla did not choose to be the most sought after girl in the Daemonium. *You* did not choose to have an abusive uncle. I didn't choose to be allergic to wheat gluten." Reynolds eyes saddened a little. "My father, God rest his blessed soul, did not choose to suffer from suicidal depression.

"We've all be insulted because of it. Zale is a nerd, Carla's too pretty to be intelligent, I'm weak, and you're a loser and a liar. Blah blah blah. And we've heard it from the people who are supposed to be our friends.

"That Forsaken did not choose to kill and maim and tear apart everyone it came across. It did it, but it did not choose that way of life. What we, as people, should learn is to judge by choice, not by nature.

"*That* is what has you upset. That we judge by nature, just like normal, petty humans when you believe, because of what we know and go through, we should have a higher level of understanding and care."

Badrick nodded vigorously. "And I don't want to be a part of that!" he shouted unwittingly.

"Badrick." Reynolds scrambled forward and placed both his hands on Badrick's pauldrons. "Remember what I told you after your first mission. Never lose sight of your morals. I knew you were thinking about this stuff. I could see it, though you refused to tell me at first.

"Just because you are one of us does not mean you are a part of the bad side. A Muslim is not automatically an extremist. A schizophrenic is not automatically dangerous. A Christian is not automatically discriminatory. You *can* belong to a group, belong with us, but you are only a part of what you despise if you adopt the same ideals. Do you understand?"

Badrick nodded, contemplating what he'd just been told.

He'd never considered that. Never thought he could be a willing part of the Daemonium and *not* be the same as the others.

Because Reynolds was right, as he always was. Badrick wasn't as angry at everyone for their behaviour as he was scared he would be too easily moulded to the same clay.

But Reynolds was telling him he didn't have to be.

Reynolds sat back down, smiling victoriously. He must have seen something on Badrick's face that told him he'd gotten through. "I gave you a long boring speech about the ways of regular people so you will understand this, Varner—we have evil in us, and I don't mean any of that fake, pathetic nonsense that murderer's claim to have. I mean *real* evil.

"Let's be honest, we're evil too. Maybe not inherently, maybe not by choice, but the majority of people have the capability for cruelty. Everyone has the potential to be evil, given the right circumstances. We're just flawed that way, and the people in this facility are no different.

"To make matters worse they all have an unparalleled breed of monster deep within their souls. I *agree* with you, Badrick, and I'm not making excuses, but their presence doesn't help our already naturally flawed human condition."

Badrick shook his head dejectedly, and muttered, "Do I really want to spend the rest of my life being a part of *that*? I know what you said but still . . . "

"You can't change the world, Badrick. You can't change hearts and minds, despite what the 'greatest' of men might tell you. Humans are too solidified in the belief of perfection that they've left no room for imperfection.

"And we're humans too. At the end of the day we're still just humans. Cruelty is to be expected."

"We manage not to be," Badrick hissed. "The others can too."

"But then again we *aren't* the rest of the world," Reynolds continued as if he hadn't spoken, his tone changing. Now he sounded more hopeful, less defeated about the subject. "And you're right. It's disgraceful, and if we don't change we run the risk of becoming those we fight against. Maybe that's your true purpose. To change this place for the better. Not to change hearts and minds, but to change souls. That is what our organisation deals in, after all."

Reynolds stretched his arms, and rose to his feet, gazing down at the three of them fondly. "You can start right now," he added.

Badrick's head shot up, and he gave the sergeant his most perplexed expression. Reynolds offered him his hand, and Badrick took it, allowing himself to be pulled to his feet. "Your final Trial starts in five minutes," Reynolds announced. "You've made it to the end."

Badrick's response was drowned out by Zale's victorious laugh. His partner thumped him on the shoulder, nearly pushing him into Reynolds from the force of it.

To be honest, he had no clue what to say. He was sure his behaviour in the third Trial would leave him disqualified, not to mention severely punished.

But it seemed he'd managed to do something good after all, even if he didn't know what.

"Just remember, Badrick," Reynolds whispered, "that sometimes what we do is necessary. We have to kill Forsaken otherwise entire towns could be slaughtered. We have to fight Apos to prevent them from unravelling all the good we've managed to accomplish.

"And we have to euthanize some of those unfortunate enough to fall into demonic madness. Sometimes it's just so bad there's no kindness in allowing them to continue suffering, alive on Earth.

"We have to do what's asked of us, as Enthrallers, and hope that one day we can make a real difference, and change the people, at their core, for the better. Against such despairing odds, what else can we really do?"

These words made an impact on Badrick, and he couldn't stop his brain from flipping over each and every one of Reynolds' points over and over again.

"What do you say, fool?" Zale laughed. "You up for changing souls?"

Badrick didn't hesitate. The conversation had carried on for so long his trepidation burnt out. He simply placed his helmet upon his head, and nodded his affirmation. "If that's the benefit of joining you bastards, then yes . . . I can do that."

He grasped the sergeant's hand, silently communicating his thanks for the understanding he'd been afforded.

It was a fresh feeling.

Badrick had never know it before.

"Any time," Reynolds smiled. "Now come on. Your final Trail awaits."

He gave all three a sharp salute, which they returned. His red uniform as crisp as ever, somehow untarnished by his sitting upon the floor, Reynolds turned his back on them and hurried down the steps leading to the arena.

"He's right, you know," Zale said. "All we have are good intentions, and we have to make the most of them."

"The road to Hell is paved with good intentions," Badrick chuckled humourlessly.

"And the road to Heaven is littered with the corpses of those who tried to build one," Zale snapped back.

Then he slapped Badrick's spine, hitting the back of his chestplate. "Come on. What we've been waiting for . . . It's here."

It was only now that Badrick remembered their previous worries from the other day. Everything that occurred today made him clean forget about Stefan and the threat they feared he posed, and he immediately felt his stomach drop as the memories returned to the forefront of his brain.

Stefan hadn't made a move all day.

This meant, if he was going to try anything, it would be right here, right now.

"Time to prepare," Carla sighed. "Let's get going."

They met Reynolds and Carver in the arena. The adults had already been joined by Stefan, who was staring at Badrick as he approached.

Badrick was glad he couldn't see that smug face right at that moment. There was no way he wanted to make eye contact with one of the worst of humanity right after all his concerns were eased.

Stefan was already holding a sword, the blade yet to be extended.

"Just keep calm," Zale was whispering as they approached. "Remember your training from last night. You have an advantage in this aspect at least."

"Don't bet on it," Badrick muttered back, quite suddenly remembering something from his first Trial. "Stefan's been cheating. He got a hold of the test paper before the Trial."

Neither Zale nor Carla questioned how he knew this, but they swore in unison, sharing angry looks and glaring at Badrick's yellow adversary.

Badrick felt it a little hypocritical, as he wasn't entirely innocent either.

And he hadn't even told them about the mind-reading yet.

Not that they'd care.

But still, he felt angered at Stefan's nerve as well.

"OK, you miserable idiots," Carver eventually grumbled. "You know the rules. Here you go, Mr Varner." He handed Badrick a sword, and Badrick took it, actually feeling a lot more confident with the weapon in his hand. "We will depart onto the viewing balconies, and when Sergeant Reynolds announces it so, you will begin the duel."

Zale gave him yet another reassuring smack on the pauldron, and Carla briefly gripped his hand.

Then they left him alone with only Stefan for company.

"Scared, Badrick?" the repulsive scumbag asked cockily.

"You'd like that."

Stefan laughed loudly, and closed the distance between them, bringing his visor so close to Badrick's that they clacked together. "I'm going to kill you today, Varner. Just watch me."

Zale felt Carla's hand grip his anxiously, and he held on to it tightly, doing his best to comfort her.

"Surely he wouldn't," she tried to argue one last time. "Not with everyone watching."

"I honestly don't know," Zale sighed. "I get some *very* bad vibes from him. Even Horas doesn't like him. Fears him, even. Not as a threat to his life, but as a threat to everyone in general."

"But he'd never manage what he's threatened." Zale didn't mind her voicing this idea for the umpteenth time. Carla wasn't stupid—far from it—so her continued denial about Stefan's intentions had nothing to do with a lack of intelligence. Just like him, she was simply scared. "If he tries, it doesn't matter if he succeeds or fails. He won't ever get away with it. He couldn't escape the facility."

"Can we really be sure?" Zale met her eyes, communicating his tension.

She sighed. "No."

"I didn't think so. And I don't trust anyone else to be fast enough to prevent it if the bastard does make an attempt."

"What are you going to do?"

Zale gave her a long, hard look, and he whispered so quietly she had to come in closer to hear him. "If things go badly . . . I may have to kill Stefan first."

chapter
NINETEEN

"Recruits!" Reynolds called out to the room so that everyone could hear his voice. Not that they needed much help; it bounced off the walls like a series of ping pong balls. "Extend your blades."

There was a rush of electricity as they both flicked their wrists twice and the swords flashed to life, the lights in the hand guards flickering on brightly.

"Recruits . . . prepare yourselves." Reynolds waited a few tentative seconds, pausing for dramatic effect, letting the apprehension build. Then he shouted with all his might, "Engage!"

Stefan immediately dropped his sword and brought his hands together. In his first display of offensive power with Zale as a witness, he focused a *huge* ball of green energy and flung it as aggressively as he could at the defenceless Badrick.

Zale was about to shout a warning, when Badrick suddenly dived to the right, rolling out of the missile's way with the grace of an expert, and landing on his feet. Without hesitating, he flicked his own hands towards Stefan and shot a power of his own—a small blast of purple light.

Unfortunately Stefan was able to dodge the responding attack.

And judging from Badrick's stillness, Zale could tell he was just as surprised at what he'd managed to pull off as everyone else.

"It's your demon, Badrick!" he bellowed over the din of the cheering Enthrallers. "He's helping you. Don't get distracted, keep going."

He watched Badrick tumble out of the path of a series of rapidly fired energy bolts. There was a tense moment when Zale thought he might have impaled himself on his own sword, and was relieved when his partner stumbled to his feet to reveal a burning hot, but small, scar on his green and white armour.

Badrick responded to Stefan's boldness by attempting to chop his opponent's weapon in half. He swung the blade of his sword down upon the abandoned weapon, aiming for the vulnerable handle.

But Stefan was too quick, and, using an obvious display of telekinesis, he summoned it back into his hand.

"Recruits are reminded this is *not* a fight to death!" Zale heard Reynolds bawl. "You are here to demonstrate your ability to handle the weapon. Badrick, you have already lost points for your self-inflicted armour damage. Stefan, you dropped the damn thing on purpose. *Now get back to it!*"

The fight continued, and though it was harrowingly tense, and made Zale want to cry out in alarm more than half the time, it definitely appeared Badrick possessed a better handle on the use of the sword than Stefan.

All that time sparring with him and Carla, not to mention the sneaky two hours they'd spent with the weapon the night before, was, thankfully, paying off handsomely.

But he also knew that winning the duel was not Stefan's true intention. As far as he was concerned, Stefan's behaviour so far proved exactly what he was worried about.

But he had to tread carefully. He couldn't just stop the fight mid-way; any distraction might give Stefan the opportunity to hurt Badrick for real.

All he could do was watch and pray that, if Stefan *did* try something, either he or Carla were fast enough to prevent it.

The duel raged on, both combatants engaging the other with determination. Badrick was displaying a half panicked ferocity, determined to beat Stefan and probably unable to clear his mind of the threat his enemy posed.

Stefan was fighting coolly, arrogance practically dripping from him as he swung his sword like an amateur. It literally pained Zale to see his invention being used so awfully, so ineptly, and he couldn't help frowning and cursing Stefan's name every single time he made a stupid move.

If only they'd had more time to sneak-train Badrick; with all the openings Stefan kept leaving he could have won this fight immediately if only he had more practice.

A particularly loud zap assaulted his senses as Badrick made a swing to knock Stefan's blade from his hand, with the other recruit only just managing to parry the attack.

He responded with a blast of green demonic energy. Zale whistled in admiration as Badrick brought his sword to bear and deflected it back at him. Stefan was thrown to the floor as his own power struck him right on the visor.

He roared furiously, jumping to his hands and feet and hissing, bouncing like some kind of mental gazelle. He threw himself towards Badrick, smashing his shoulder into his chest and knocking him back.

Somehow the green recruit managed to stay his feet, much to Stefan's fury.

And that was when he made his move.

Zale barely saw what he did, it was that sneaky.

Stefan stuck one of his hands behind his back. For anyone not looking out for suspicious behaviour, it would have looked like he was simply regaining his balance.

It was a cleverly disguised ploy, and if not for Zale noticing at the last second a grey object sliding towards Stefan, half invisible against the colour of the floor, the recruit might have gotten away with it.

It flew into his hand.

And with his enhanced sense of hearing, Zale heard the sound of a gun cocking.

Stefan darted forward, bolting closer to Badrick, twisting his body to the right. Zale saw Badrick bring his sword forward in a swing, expecting Stefan to attack him from the left—he had fallen for his enemy's feint.

Stefan took advantage of the opening Badrick just unwittingly gave him, bringing the pistol out into the open and shoving it violently into his throat.

It happened so fast.

But both Zale and Carla saw it; he was already building an electrical charge in his hand and Carla was in the process of lobbing the strongest energy ball she could muster.

Everything seemed to slow, as if their world was put into slow motion. Shouts of panic rang throughout the room as agents brought weapons forward, or began to leap over the railings in order to intervene.

None of them would make it in time.

Their only hope depended on Carla's attack, or Zale's own.

Or at least that's what he had thought.

As it turned out, no intervention was required at all.

The moment he saw what was cutting off his windpipe, spotted Stefan's finger tightening over the trigger, Badrick dropped his sword and slapped his left hand over Stefan's visor.

A blinding flash of red light forced everyone to cover their eyes, and Zale heard a scream of pain, not to mention an almighty crash.

When he was next capable of looking, Badrick was standing shakily, panting heavily, close to the edge of the arena.

Stefan was on his knees, laughing dramatically—his visor untarnished by what appeared to have been nothing more than a stunning power—as everyone else simply stared, too stunned to move.

Not one of them even considered Badrick would be able to fight off an attempt on his life.

Zale realised they had greatly underestimated the recruit.

Amidst the stillness, Stefan jumped to his feet and brought his hands together, rolling them over and over. More green flashed as the energy built up and up and up.

"You'll have to do better than that, Varner."

Stefan unleashed his attack. The demonic energy rocketed towards Badrick, the blast more violent than any Stefan had used before.

But Badrick did not attempt to dodge. He didn't even appear panicked.

He simply brought his hands together. As his palms met, the air around him seemed to warp, and right before Zale's very eyes a dome of white demonic energy surrounded his form.

Just in time too, as the missile crashed into the dome and exploded upon its surface.

When the eerie glow dissipated, Zale saw that it had done no damage whatsoever. Badrick's shield remained untarnished, and only dispelled at Badrick's compelling.

"Jesus!" Zale found himself exclaiming.

"What the hell?" Stefan shouted, apparently sharing in his bewilderment.

"I've never seen a power like that," Carla whispered, her voice laced with apprehension.

Badrick utilised everyone's stunned silence by staring at his hands. He didn't utter a word, didn't move another muscle.

He just gazed.

Zale *wished* he could see his partner's face. He would give anything to know what he was thinking. What was going through his mind right at this moment?

Stefan didn't know what to do either. He looked very uncomfortable, his body language practically screaming uncertainty.

Still, nobody spoke or moved.

It was as though time was standing still.

Badrick was the one to break the quiet. He raised his hand to the level of his eyes, summoned an electric blue energy in his palm, and then threw it at Stefan.

A huge electrical charge struck Stefan on the chest. Currents travelled across his armour and the Enthraller screamed, being thrown back even further. He crashed into the wall beyond, bouncing off it roughly.

"Holy hell!" Zale roared, his eyes widening, his pulse quickening rapidly, an unforgiving agitation settling into his chest. "But that's my power!"

And from twelve meters to his right, he heard a small whisper, barely audible above the shouts of the other Enthrallers. "He has the powers of other Singularis. But . . . that must mean . . . it *is* him."

Reynolds caught Zale watching him and quickly avoided his gaze.

Zale glared at him, instinctively knowing something major had just occurred and the sergeant was keeping it from him.

What the hell was going on?

Down in the arena, Badrick stepped up to the exhausted Stefan, crouching over his limp form. Stefan slowly sat up as best he could. He was breathing heavily, swearing under his breath.

He turned his gaze towards his defeater, and Zale just knew that he was glaring at him hatefully.

Even at this distance, Zale heard him say, "Go on then. Kill me. I know you want to."

Badrick recoiled away from him. "Do you really think I'd do that?" He slapped Stefan on the head. "I'm not like you."

He afforded him one last moment of eye contact—*visor contact*—before turning his back on the pathetic boy, and walking away.

Zale felt relief bloom inside him; at the very worst Badrick survived what they had correctly guessed as Stefan's intentions. At best he would have passed this Trial, and Stefan would be locked away forever for his crime.

He saw Badrick remove his helmet and cast his eyes over the stands, looking for them. Zale raised a hand to catch his attention. Badrick smiled, and waved back.

That was when it all went to Hell.

It started as a small electrical fizzle.

A tiny spark, but it grew quickly.

And Stefan roared, "How dare you turn your back on me!"

But it wasn't his voice that spoke. At least not *just* his; there was another voice in there, speaking at the same time, lacing Stefan's usually unimpressive tones with a growling, malicious resonance.

Badrick swivelled, eyeing his enemy with bewilderment. Every person present gaped in confusion.

Breaking the ensuing silence, Zale gasped, "I know that voice!"

Carla opened her mouth to question him, but she never got the opportunity. Before she could speak, Stefan exploded.

A white flash obliterated their vision, and every single person present was thrown backwards as if they'd been hit by a nuclear bomb. Zale smashed into the wall, rolling away and crying out in agony as his back flared with pain.

Carla fell on top of him, screaming in surprise.

Zale did his best to help her up. All around them the agents and soldiers of the Daemonium were scrambling painfully to their feet, either trying to see what happened or hurrying to the side of those wounded more severely by the blast.

But Zale didn't care about them.

His memory was going haywire, his thoughts casting back to the worst day of his life.

He recognised that voice.

"No! No, it can't be."

Ensuring Carla was uninjured—even in the direst situations he would never put anything before her—he dashed to the railings to gape down into the arena.

The first thing he noticed was Badrick stumbling to his feet. He was swaying so hard that he crashed back down to his knees before he'd even gotten fully erect, and didn't try again. He grabbed his head with both hands, trying to rid himself of the headache they now all shared.

Determining that Badrick was otherwise unharmed, Zale's eyes darted to the left, his eyelid twitching when he spotted what he expected he would.

Zale no longer got scared. It had been a long time since he last did.

Now he only got angry.

That was what he felt shooting through his tight muscles when saw *him*.

The black armoured demon.

He was standing where Stefan had once been, his skeletal helmet just as dark and menacing as Zale remembered.

He was breathing heavily, probably due to the strain of the sudden switch of his plane of existence. Transforming from nothing but energy and trading places with the original owner of the physical space he now occupied would have exhausted the demon.

Zale had read about explosive take-overs; when powerful Enthrallers let their rage get the better of them sometimes their demon would come to the fore, but all that emotion would be confusing the hell-spawn's mind.

Right now, the demon was tainted; he felt what Stefan felt.

That meant he shared Stefan's anger.

He'd be gunning for Badrick.

Before anybody could react, the demon harnessed his powers, creating a surge of energy that every Enthraller would have felt. The force of it made Zale lose his balance, it literally pushed him back. He stumbled to regain his footing.

Badrick was dragged across the floor towards Black, as if an invisible rope had lassoed his neck and was uncaringly yanking him along. The demon grasped his throat, lifting him up from the floor.

As Badrick choked, Black roared in his face, "I will kill you!"

Zale took that as his cue. His reflexes finally catching up, he fired as big a burst of electricity as he dared at the demon. The shock arced across the room, narrowly missing Badrick and striking the demon in the shoulder.

He instantly dropped his captive and stumbled back, roaring

savagely. His scratched visor scanned the stands until, finally, he found his attacker.

"Zale!" the dark voice crooned. "Long time no see."

The demon's visor warped, contorted, as if it was smiling savagely, delighted to see human meat he recognised. The sight of it made Zale's stomach churn.

His emotions did another flip when the black figure summoned Stefan's discarded sword to his hand, and activated it. It angered Zale to see his creation in the hands of such a monster.

Beside him, Carla quickly acknowledged his distress, recognised the new arrival from Zale's past descriptions, and brought her sidearm to bear, freeing it from its holster.

She pointed it at the demon and gave him a disgusted sneer.

The rest of the Daemonium followed suit.

Hundreds of guns were cocked and aimed down into the arena, powers were armed and held ready, demonic energy sizzling in their palms.

The demon took one look around, determined he was completely outmatched, then turned back to Zale.

They stared at each other for a few brief seconds.

At that moment his body shimmered, and the demon teleported to safety, escaping the threat of the Enthrallers.

Badrick was left alone in the arena, coughing, wheezing and panting in what must have been excruciation.

The grip of a demon was strong.

He was lucky to be alive.

With great effort, he forced himself to his feet and stared up at Zale.

Zale could only stare back.

chapter
TWENTY

Reynolds burst into the BCR, too impatient to wait for the automatic door and squeezing through before it fully opened.

Badrick, Zale and Carla were close behind.

They skidded to a halt before crashing into the tables. Badrick almost lost his footing and had to use a chair for support so he wouldn't tumble to the floor.

His neck was still very sore, and breathing was difficult, which meant exertion of any kind was agonising.

"We have a new priority one, people!" Reynolds hollered. He tapped ferociously on a keyboard, accessing the computer files of the BCR. Dozens of agents responded to his call, dashing to their own stations or hurrying up beside him to offer help.

Badrick attempted to shout over their loud, tense voices.

"Could someone please . . . tell me . . . who that was!"

Zale was the one to answer. "The black guy was a demon named Lucikefer," he said solemnly.

"*Lucikefer?*" Badrick parroted disbelievingly. "That's a name?"

"I don't think the Devil was going for the prize for best named demon baby," Carla inputted sarcastically.

"The Devil?"

"She isn't joking," Zale growled. "Lucikefer is the son of Satan."

"Are you serious!?" Badrick bawled, aghast. "I fought a guy who had the son of Satan in his soul? Why did no one tell me?"

This time Reynolds was the one to speak up. He raised his head over the agents crowding around his computer to address them. "We thought his demon was Teridae, a well known Singularis. That's what his demon told us. It's what our archives concurred."

"He must have been disguising himself," Zale announced, his fingers finding his chin and rubbing it apprehensively. "Not only that but there is no way Stefan only has seven fissures with someone as powerful as Lucikefer stuffed inside him. His soul must be fracturing under the strain. I would hazard a guess that he's harbouring nine, or maybe even ten."

"Jesus!" Carla exclaimed. "How is he even alive?"

"Lucikefer's been hiding from the Daemonium's sensors for a whole year," Zale mused. "He's part of the Demonic Royal Family, so it's not like that was hard for him."

"He's completely ignoring the rules of the fissures," Carla said. "Stefan should be dead."

Zale laughed humourlessly, and nodded concurringly. "Stefan should have exploded. You know what happens to people who don't have the room for source energy. The kid is probably already a corpse. Has been for some time. Lucikefer's presence is the only thing keeping him alive. Simple as that, he has the power. Reynolds, can we get Stefan's records?"

"Accessing them now."

Badrick was surprised at how quickly Reynolds did as Zale requested. However, he remembered, Zale *was* the most intelligent person in the building.

If he were Reynolds, in this situation, he would utilise every asset he had, no matter what that meant.

The sergeant wasn't stupid; he knew their best chance was letting Zale take the lead, because they couldn't just ignore this demon's sudden appearance.

The son of Satan! They had to do something about him.

Within moments Zale had a folder in his hands, and he was sifting through it at rapid speeds. As he read, his face dropped.

"Look at this past," he muttered quietly. "Abusive parents, bullied at school. Depression, anxiety, the works. His parents were killed by a demon, and his status as an Enthraller noticed by the agent that saved him from suffering the same death."

Zale lowered the folder and stared off into space.

"Zale," Carla said quietly, "you told me Lucikefer manifested on Earth in his own form when you first met him. How is he now suddenly in Stefan? Were you wrong?"

"No, I wasn't wrong," Zale said quickly. "Think about it, he's a Royal. He can probably completely ignore whatever force is pulling demons into humans. He wasn't shoved into Stefan at his birth; he *chose* to go into him later on." Zale made a puffing sound, his eyes wide. "That's some serious rule breaking. Stefan really *should* be dead."

"He's the son of the Devil," Carla said. "Are you really surprised he has enough mojo to ignore the rules of the universe?"

Zale suddenly made a loud 'AGH' sound and slapped his forehead. "He's a *Royal!* He can command other demons. Why bother jumping into a human for any other reason than to infiltrate the Daemonium? I bet he commanded that demon to kill Stefan's parents so that we'd find him and bring him here."

"But why Stefan?" Badrick asked. "What's so special about him?"

Zale gave him a look that suggested he should know the answer to this already. "Think about it," he said softly. "There you are, a beaten, bullied kid, wishing something—*anything*—would save you from this life. Along comes Lucikefer. Jumps into your soul. Tells you he can grant your wish. Tells you he is the son of the Devil. He's all powerful. Promises you power of your own, respect from everyone around you, fear from those who have hurt you. With his help, no one could ever do it again."

"As long as he played his part and joined the Daemonium," Carla finished. "He's the perfect candidate for a demon like Lucikefer. He would do anything to cash in on those promises."

"Stefan has felt inadequate all his life," Zale added thoughtfully. "A childhood like that will do that to you. That's why he's always been so aggressive. He wants to feel powerful, in charge, the top dog, but can't manage it on his own merits, so he takes out his own self hatred on other people." He growled, apparently at himself. "I should have seen this before."

"Instead of biggin' himself up," Badrick muttered, continuing the flow, "he stomps on people to reduce their worth."

He closed his eyes shamefully; he'd never once considered there was any reason other than his natural personality behind Stefan's behaviour.

How stupid he had been.

He should have known better.

"We have to find him," Badrick stated. "We can't let the son of Satan run around now that we know where he is." He stopped as he realised something. "*Do* we know where he is? Would he have

286

abandoned Stefan after this?"

Carla laughed aggressively. "No. I doubt even *he* has the ability to actually remove himself from an Enthraller once he jumps in. He has to wait it out or create a Forsaken just like the rest of them. Whatever he wants must be *really* important for him to trap himself like that."

"No kidding," quipped Zale.

"Well, we have to find them both!"

Reynolds turned to him, the agents dodging out of his way so he could sidle up to the three of them. "We are," he stated. "As soon as we find something, I promise I'll include you."

Badrick had no words. All he could do was nod and hope the Daemonium's best pulled out all the stops on this one.

Was there even anything *he* could do to help?

Unfortunately, he couldn't think of anything.

As the agents and soldiers panicked, fervently typing on their computers, doing their utmost to find Stefan and his Royal demon, Zale watched from the corner, deliberately separated so that he could concentrate.

Now and then Badrick would look over to him with a curious glance, clearly wondering what he was doing.

He didn't mind though. He was right to be curious.

But he didn't have to worry; Zale was utterly focused on the matter at hand. His mind hadn't taken its customary wander into other important matters since the duel. He was thinking only on this.

He was going through everything he knew, or hoped to know.

Was Lucikefer still trying to find Daemnos?

That was his goal four years ago. The purpose for which he had dragged Zale into this world of demons and death.

Lucikefer had an ulterior motive with his investment in Stefan. He was certain of it.

Zale had a feeling that wherever this Daemnos character was, he was most likely hiding out somewhere, using the same power as Lucikefer to avoid being dragged into a human soul.

If Daemnos was stuck in an Enthraller, then there'd be no reason Lucikefer would have any trouble tracking him down.

Zale spent years researching the Devil's son. Tried to find him and failed, like all others before. Wasted day after day obsessing over what happened to him and Charles.

He knew Lucikefer was childish and hated to lose. That was the one thing every single ancient text could agree upon. He was juvenile, self-indulgent, caring nothing for the lives of anyone else.

As with all the Royals, Lucikefer was obsessed with gaining power and destroying those who could stand up to him, even if they had no interest in doing so.

Daemnos would have to be powerful for him to take an interest.

And Lucikefer would only take interest in a murderous capacity.

Zale had no doubt that was Lucikefer's ultimate desire; to kill Daemnos and rid himself of the competition the other demon presented.

But what about the rest of it?

How did connecting Horas and Vulrick benefit Lucikefer? The oldest book in their archives listed Vulrick as subservient to an ancient power, known only as Daemnos—obviously the same—a demon of great evil and abilities.

But what was Horas' connection? It didn't feel right to say he was the first Enthraller the Royal had come across.

It just rang the large 'INCORRECT' bell in Zale's head.

Zale sighed, taking slow steady breaths, calming his racing

heart.

He was starting to second-guess himself. If he wasn't careful he would lose himself to third-guessing, and fourth-guessing, and he wouldn't get anywhere.

When he was sure he had slowed his heart rate, Zale began again.

What did he know?

Lucikefer wanted Daemnos.

The only reason he would show any interest in another demon would be to kill him or her.

Because? Lucikefer hated competition. He was an immature brat.

He couldn't find Daemnos. Even after all this time his quarry eluded him. Why else would he still be here?

He wouldn't bother keeping Stefan around if he'd succeeded, he would mutilate the poor boy into a Forsaken.

This obviously meant his mission was unfinished. But they'd been discovered now. Lucikefer's cover was blown. He no longer had the ability to slyly use the Daemonium to search for his prey.

And if this had happened, then Daemnos might even know about it.

There was only one course of action left to Lucikefer.

He would need a humungous surge of energy to attract the demon.

It didn't matter who they were, or what their logic told them; no demon, *especially* the super powerful ones, could resist a surge of demonic energy even if they couldn't absorb it. It simply attracted them, like flies to a light source.

This wasn't exactly an ideal course of action for Lucikefer to take. He ran the risk of attracting other demons, thereby possibly endangering his life and, at minimum, losing his chance to take out Daemnos with a sneak attack.

But there was no doubt in Zale's mind that this was the case.

However, what would this mean for them?

He grabbed his forehead; his skin was hot—burning in fact. He was overdoing it.

But he *just* needed to figure this last bit out.

There was something else, he could feel it. These events would include the Daemonium in a horrible, terrible way. He just had to figure out how.

He strained his mind, irritated at how long it was taking him.

Zale repeated the question in his mind, slowly.

What would this mean for them?

He arrived at the answer moments before everything went to Hell.

A shrill, whining, osculating alarm interrupted Badrick's train of thought. It was so ear-splitting he slammed his hands over his ears, dropping his helmet in the process.

Zale had vanished from the BCR. At the sound of the alarm he bolted out the door, returning a few minutes later, just as an agent slammed on the *shut-up* button and the alarm ceased.

"What the hell was that?" Reynolds exclaimed, his eyes exploring the Main Hall through the BCR window.

"Not good news," Zale told him. His eyes communicated just how bad it was, and Reynolds visibly tensed, waiting for the worst. "Lucikefer just came back. He broke into the lockdown storage."

"Oh God!" Reynolds slapped his hand over his forehead. "How did we not detect him? Please tell me he didn't take anything!"

"The crystals."

The sergeant swore loudly, uttering words so vulgar the like of which Badrick had never even heard before.

"What are these crystal things?" he asked quickly, intent on being kept in the loop.

Carla gave him his answer. "No one knows what they're really called, only what they do. When activated, they emit a hypersonic wave of demonic power. It's a bomb, Badrick. A bomb with a huge radius. It doesn't do any damage to real estate, but any living thing, be it people or animals or plants, is completely disintegrated."

"Everything except bone," Zale snarled.

"What the hell is he doing?" Badrick gasped. "What does he want those for?"

"How many did he take?" Reynolds asked soberly, his voice low, and deep.

"All three," Zale said. "Reynolds . . . I believe this is a move to locate Daemnos."

The sergeant did not reply for a while. He stared at the floor, his face blank. Badrick did not know what was going through that mind of his, but when Reynolds glanced at him and muttered, "I think it's time you told him, Zale," Badrick's stomach immediately dropped, and the sensation he often felt whenever he knew yet another 'grand revelation' was on its way stabbed at his gut.

Badrick turned his steely gaze onto his partner.

"Tell me what?" he hissed.

Stefan eyed the strangely shaped stones with a wary gaze. They were pretty big, white and purple in colour. Every five seconds they emitted a pulse that Stefan could sense using his natural energy radar.

He swapped his gaze over to Lucikefer—watched as the demon did nothing, remaining utterly motionless. Stefan had no idea what he was thinking.

And to make matters worse, he was stuck where the demon should have been. His body was gone; he was nothing but a wavelength now.

Just a soul, trapped in a demon's body.

It would wear off soon, he knew, but that didn't stop him hating it beyond everything else.

He'd gotten the hang of being the 'demon' in their relationship as Lucikefer had forced this upon him quite often. When he'd wanted to summon his 'pets' from Hell. When they subsequently met the Ordinarius in the caves.

When they killed Mawr.

Having his body stashed away for safe keeping so often, Stefan knew how to 'appear' to Lucikefer, just as the demons could do to their Enthrallers. It was nice, being at least able to pretend at having a body when he entered this state of existence.

It kept him calm against the all-crushing suffocation.

Stefan didn't understand why Lucikefer was doing this now. Why was he trying to lure Daemnos out when they could just go back to looking for him discreetly? They didn't need the Daemonium.

They both were too powerful.

No one could stop them.

However, their altercation with Badrick had left them both in a weakened state. The next time Lucikefer transformed back into energy and disappeared inside Stefan's soul he would not be able to force his way back out for quite some time. Stefan would have the reins.

Deciding it couldn't hurt to ask what Lucikefer was up to, Stefan cleared his throat—not that he needed to . . . he didn't have a throat—and said, "I thought you were waiting longer."

Lucikefer slowly turned to face him. It wasn't difficult to read the fury; his body language was literally roaring it at him, and he could hear it in the demon's thoughts.

"Thanks to your outburst," the demon snarled savagely, "I have been exposed. You have failed me, Stefan."

Stefan felt his own anger flare and he quickly retorted, "I fail no one, because I belong to no one. You need me!"

"I could use anyone. Now shut your human trap! You are nothing without me."

Stefan fell into a subdued silence, but he continued to glare at Lucikefer hatefully.

Nothing?

Is that what he thought?

In that case . . .

Stefan would show him.

He would show them all.

"These crystals will draw out Daemnos," Lucikefer muttered to himself. "My plan has to be accelerated. My cover is blown. I have no choice but to initiate a full-frontal assault." Without warning he reached out and grabbed Stefan by the throat, dragging him closer.

Stefan didn't bother contemplating the crazy demonic quantum physics applied to this situation—he'd gotten used to Lucikefer's power altering reality on various small scales during the last year.

Somehow he was choking, as though the demon really *did* have a hold of his neck.

"When these go off, and Daemnos comes crawling out of his hole, you will grant me control once more. Is that understood?"

The grip tightened when Stefan didn't answer.

"Yes!" he choked. "Of course."

"Good boy," Lucikefer breathed malevolently. He dropped Stefan and allowed him to stumble back.

Good boy, am I? he thought. *I'll show you.*

Lucikefer didn't know what he was thinking. The demon was underestimating him. He *always* underestimated him.

Just like everyone else.

Stefan had learned to block certain thoughts from the scrutiny of Lucikefer very quickly, only month after their combining.

No one else could do that.

He was far more capable than anyone gave him credit for.

I'll show you who's good.

Lucikefer wasn't listening anyway; he was once again talking to himself. "I'm coming for you, Daemnos," he panted, his tongue slithering grotesquely. "I'm going to kill you."

Zale spent the last ten minutes explaining everything he knew, understood, and could impart. The entire story was laid out for him, though Badrick had a hard time following.

In the end he had to break it down into very simple bullet points.

Lucikefer had his demon pal pushed Zale forward in time to find him, Badrick.

As they passed, their demons connected.

Why this happened, no one knew.

Lucikefer believed the link would help him find a demon called Daemnos.

However, the plan failed. The link did not work.

At least this was what they were able to guess.

Like Zale said, they really didn't know how this connection of energy functioned, or what it meant for the both of them.

The walking conduit then spent the next four years waiting for Badrick to arrive at the Daemonium.

"How did you know I would?" he asked them.

"We know Vulrick is connected to this Daemnos demon," Zale explained. "And I've studied up on the demon that did that to me. How his power worked wasn't simple at all. He would have constructed a function beforehand, rules for the way his power would have to work at that moment, like he was writing the code for computer software. He had to do this every time he used his power.

"He threw me at whoever Vulrick's Enthraller was, at whatever point in time your powers were really starting to reveal themselves. It was like a really bad locater ritual. I time travelled to a point in your future, not because the demon knew that was the right moment, or who you were, but because that was when our link would most likely establish strongest, and the power figured it out automatically.

"The fact *that* moment in time even existed meant you would be headed this way eventually. We wouldn't have been able to ignore you if your demon was coming to the fore, which Vulrick did, right when we predicted."

"That so confusing, Zale!" Badrick shouted at him. "Why did we even . . . *link?*"

"Again, I have no idea. I don't know what my part is in this."

A heated debate followed on why Zale had been chosen, the agents arguing among themselves. Badrick didn't really care about that; he had only two questions playing on his mind.

"Why didn't you tell me about this?" he said quietly, casting his eyes left and right, watching those closest in the room. He suddenly felt very suspicious of everyone present. "You knew about me for four years before I got here. Have you been watching me this entire time?"

For a moment no one said anything. Some even glanced away, as though shame-faced, unable to look him in the eye. "We had to watch you," Reynolds said in a near whisper. "For all we knew you posed a very serious threat."

"Why didn't you pick me up straight away?" he almost snapped.

"We didn't want to risk it," Zale told him. "The son of Satan, Badrick. Do you have any idea how dangerous it is to meddle with the Royals? The Daemonium has only ever done it once, and they came away from it in pieces. We didn't know what or who you were, or why you were so important to Lucikefer."

Badrick experienced a pulling sensation on his knuckles, and realised he had clenched his fists so tightly the skin over them was stretching painfully. He forced himself to relax, though he didn't take a deep breath.

He didn't want everyone to know just how incensed he really was.

But he couldn't stop himself from saying, "You were spying on me for years. You've all been lying to me."

"Think about what Lucikefer might have done if we'd chased you down immediately," Reynolds said quickly. "We worried he might be watching us. After I intervened the first time, there's no doubt he would have come to the conclusion that he had to. What if we went after you and, through us, he found you first? You were the one he wanted." Reynolds tilted his head and gave Badrick a piercing gaze. "What would you have preferred? One—we left you to your own devices, leaving you to the mercies of your demon, and all he could do to you. Two—we went after you and led Lucikefer straight to you. Three—we watch you, let you stay safe and alive for four years, and *didn't* lead the son of the Devil straight to you."

"I know which I'd prefer," Zale muttered.

Badrick glowered at them. He was still angry, though he couldn't deny the logic behind what they were saying.

It was difficult. He hadn't spent a lot of time letting logic direct his life.

Emotions had ruled him for a long time, and they were *very* different to intelligence.

But despite his inability to argue his point against theirs, he still looked up and muttered, "You could have gotten to me first and saved me from everything that has happened since."

"The first time was pure luck," Reynolds argued. "Lucikefer panicked, he was ambushed. It was *luck*. You being affected by that power surge was unfortunate timing, but at least it got you to us safely, without us having to pick you up. It couldn't have happened better. Remember that, would you?"

The hesitation, not to mention the tone of voice he used when mentioning the energy which enabled Vulrick to kill his uncle, did not pass Badrick unnoticed.

He frowned at the sergeant, confused. If Badrick hadn't known better, Reynolds had almost said something entirely different and only just caught himself.

The resulting tone had been very similar to the one Badrick himself used when telling a lie.

What did that mean?

Much to his irritation, he didn't get to question it, because Carla suddenly shouted, "Badrick, look, we're sorry, all right? But it was for the best. Now can you *please* put it past you? We have a very dangerous situation to deal with. We need to start scanning for those crystals."

Reynolds immediately scoffed, "Do you think I've been doing nothing for twenty minutes? We're already in the process of scanning. Although it would help if we knew where to look."

"Focus on the UK," Zale said. "That's where he's likely to be."

"Why?"

"Both the two people he used to try to find Daemnos were in England. That says to me that he must believe Daemnos is focused on this country, or at least the land mass. So that's where Lucikefer and the crystals will be."

Reynolds nodded, and swiftly turned to make the alterations to the scan.

Deciding Carla was right and he should at the very least put the issue of the Daemonium's deceit aside for the time being, Badrick cleared his mind and said, "Can we use this connection thing to find him?"

Zale shot his suggestion down instantly. "We think its only purpose was for me to be able to sense where you were. The time travel guy sends me to you, wherever you are, I then lead Lucikefer to you, and Vulrick leads him to Daemnos."

"It doesn't even work in *that* way," Carla laughed. "It's pointless."

"How *does* it work, then?" Badrick exasperated. "The whole thing is mental. Past Zale links with future Badrick, then returned to the past. Does that mean the connection didn't actually begin until my point in time? How do you know that isn't why the connection didn't work? Because it had to wait four years to work."

"No, Badrick, that's not what happened. I linked to your future self, but when I returned to the right time the connection established in the present day. We've been linked for four years."

"But . . . *how does that work!?*" Badrick half screamed. "That doesn't make any sense. If I travel to the future and shoot you in the leg, that doesn't mean it occurs in the past too."

"This isn't an episode of Doctor Who," Zale laughed dourly. "It's terrifying, super powerful, reality bending demonic power. He created a connection between our demons' souls. Souls are pure power, Badrick. They transcend the logic of time. The link may have been forged in the future, but one of its points came from the past. The link manifested in the timeline of the earliest point."

Badrick nearly spat at him, he was so confused now. His mind was no longer trying to understand, it had simply shut down.

There was no way he was going to comprehend Zale's

explanation at this moment, so to keep the conversation moving along he simply went back to the most important topic of discussion. "How the hell are we going to fight Lucikefer when he is capable of that?" he sighed. "Can we even?"

Reynolds chuckled dryly from behind his computer. "Exactly. Isn't that just a bitch?"

"But how—Holy crap!"

Zale gave him a curious eye. "What?"

Badrick closed his eyes in an attempt to stabilise himself; his world was flipping like crazy right now.

This was worse than anything that happened beforehand.

"I remember you," he gasped. "You drove past me the *same* day the church guy kidnapped me. You and your friend." He reopened his lids and gawked at his partner. "I can't believe it, I remember you."

Reynolds stopped Zale from replying.

He suddenly shouted, "We've got him!" He tilted his head, correcting himself. "Well, not *him*, but we have the crystals. They're positioned in a triangle around London." His gaze found them. "He's going to blow up the city. Just to lure out Daemnos."

His eyes flicked to Badrick, and he stared at him for a moment, as though scrutinising him. It made Badrick feel extremely uncomfortable.

"Then that is our priority," Zale announced. "Sergeant, requesting permission to take Badrick out and turn off those explosives." The sergeant gave him a long, hard look. For a long time he didn't say anything. "Reynolds," Zale whispered, "something is going on. We're important, or Badrick is at least." He paused for a moment, then murmured, "I heard what you said, Sarge. I know what you meant. You understand what I'm saying."

Reynolds looked angry for a brief second.

But then, to Badrick's utter amazement, he mumbled,

"Granted. But take your armour. The panic of the population at the sight of you is the least of our worries. You need to be suited up."

Zale nodded, and gave his old friend a sharp, proper salute.

Reynolds returned it, and allowed the three of them to dash away.

As they ran through the Main Hall, up the ramps and across the walkways, Badrick called after Zale's departing back. "Us? Why us? What can we do? This is a job for the other agents. *All* the agents! They can't risk it, just sending us out!"

"This has something to do with us, Badrick!" Zale called over his shoulder. "Lucikefer connected the two of us together. We're important. This is between us now. Trust me, Badrick, we can do this."

"But Lucikefer . . ."

"I asked Reynolds permission to deal with the crystals, not Lucikefer. The Daemonium will deal with him, don't you worry. Are you with me?"

Badrick did not feel very confident about that; in fact he felt very much that Zale had not considered the minutiae of his plan.

As they rushed through the Quarters Tower and as he watched his partner strap on his armour, he had the nauseating feeling that everything was going to go very wrong.

But what could he do about it? Zale was one of the best agents in the damn place. He *knew* that, he'd seen it firsthand. Reynolds wouldn't let a random guy out on a mission as dire as this.

He trusted Zale.

Zale was worth that trust.

Badrick had to remember that. Hell, half the time his confidence relied on it.

"Yes," he finally announced, resolute in his decision. "I'll help."

"Faster on the replies there, Badrick" Zale muttered. "That took you ages."

"I'm coming with you," Carla said.

"No!" he heard Zale nearly shout behind him. "I don't want you to come."

"Why not!?" Carla roared angrily.

"It's too dangerous."

"Zale, we fought and killed over a dozen Kalik on our own, and we were only two years into our training. After another two years of improvement, I don't think your concern is very justified. I can handle myself. I can handle you too. You really think I need you to protect me?"

"Carla," Zale whispered. "Lucikefer is doing this because of me. If he'd chosen *anyone* else he might have found Badrick sooner. He would have succeeded."

"It isn't a bad thing that he failed," she scolded him.

"But it *is* because of me. I failed him, and he had to resort to a new plan." He hesitated, and Badrick glimpsed him pulling her into a tight hug. "I won't put you in danger for me. Please, if you care for me at all . . . don't come."

Carla didn't say anything.

Badrick expected her to argue some more. Deny his request. Call him an idiot, at least.

But, to his astonishment, she bit her lip worriedly and nodded her agreement, hugging him back and burying her face in his neck.

His request accepted, Zale reached over and picked up his helmet. Badrick noticed the visor had been fixed sometime since their last outing. The newly untarnished gold sparked and turned electric blue as it covered his face.

"We'll be careful," Zale promised, stroking her cheek one last time. "See you soon?"

She smiled sadly. "See you soon."

With that, he turned his attention to Badrick. "Better get your helmet on," he said. "We're going out."

Reynolds barely even looked up as the door to the BCR swished open and what looked like half the Command Council burst in, shouting angrily, looking around, demanding the location of 'Sergeant Daniel Reynolds'.

He half smiled at the sight of Jonathon Carver among them.

When the idiots *finally* noticed he was sitting right there, they immediately charged at him, crowding his workspace, their bodies creating a suffocating wall between him and the rest of the BCR.

They were shouting at him now.

"What the hell do you think you're playing at, Reynolds?"

"You sent Zale and Badrick out to recover the crystals?"

"What kind of fool are you?"

"This kind of disregarding behaviour is unacceptable."

"Disregarding? It's downright stupid."

"You are not an agent."

"You do not send out agents without *our* authority, especially a pair of untrained kids."

They may have been bombarding him with a thousand accusations, insults and a great level of disrespect, but, in the past, what he had accomplished garnered him a lot of what they were refusing him right now.

And it amused him that when he held up his hand to silence them . . . they did so.

He took a moment to show them exactly what he thought of them at that moment, communicating with his eyes and body language. He rose from his seat menacingly, radiating so much fury that many backed away as he drew to their eye level.

He waited for his frightening presence to really hammer their attitude down before speaking, and when he finally did, not one interrupted him. "None of you deserve the prestige you have *'earned'*. You do not force me to do things you don't want to do, then talk to me like this. The next one who does will find their skull caved in within the week. Do you understand me?"

No one replied. But some did nod agitatedly.

"You have used me as a mouthpiece for weeks. Your conniving, and scheming, and conspiring has put me in a very difficult position, and you were all too cowardly to face Badrick and Zale yourselves.

"You have put Varner through so much since he arrived. I understand the need for it. *I do.* But you are yellow, weak-willed cowards. Look at all he has achieved *despite* your pressure. The same goes for Zale.

"That kid is one of the most powerful Enthrallers I have ever seen. The most intelligent person the world has probably ever seen. The sheer skill . . . it's almost beyond godlike. If *anyone* can take care of those crystals, it's Zale. It's time you accepted that, and stopped treating him like a child.

"We all saw what Badrick managed in the arena. You *all* know what it means. There was no external manipulation. There was no burst of demonic energy. It was Badrick.

"You must all be very proud of yourselves. You were right. Or at least that's what you're saying. Most of you are lying; you really didn't know either way. Half of you failed to catch up to what the rest of us were even thinking.

"You probably don't even understand the reason we didn't tell Badrick immediately after the duel."

An American Council Member snapped, "What are you talking about, Reynolds!?"

With an irritable huff, he explained, "We would have told Badrick the truth, if not for the fact Lucikefer never realised the kid was his target all along, the one he sent Zale to. Make that information public, and the Devil's son figures it all out. We could never put him in that kind of danger.

"At the very least, you understand that, on the matter of the crystals, we have nothing to worry about. Now . . . I suggest we focus on Lucikefer. He is still a massive threat, even after Badrick and Zale defuse the crystals. Can you all keep your mouths shut and focus on the real problem?"

There was a series of furious, but subservient nods. The only one who didn't was Carver, which only served to amuse Reynolds.

Who cared about Carver anyway? He was useless; a politician. Not a warrior, despite what he told people.

One of the Council broke through the ranks of her fellows and put her hands on Reynolds' desk.

"But what do you suggest we do," she asked, "with Badrick and Zale's mission?"

Reynolds smiled gently, and whispered, "We trust. They can do this."

chapter
TWENTY ONE

A collection of startled teenage girls in skimpy outfits and boys wearing way too many tasteless hoodies scrambled out of the way as Zale drove the motorbike up a thick sign propped up on a pile of bricks, using this little corner of the nearby construction site as a makeshift ramp in order to bypass the traffic jam they'd encountered.

Badrick yelped as he almost flew straight off the back of it, and gasped as his crotch was nearly crushed upon landing.

Terrified pedestrians jumped out of their way. Those fortunate enough to not be in their path pointed and shouted in alarm at the two heavily armoured guys nearly mowing down whole roads of people.

"Zale, you're gonna bring the police down on us!" Badrick

roared over the din of the engine.

"Screw the police!" he hollered back, swerving expertly between cars. "We don't have time to waste."

Something flashed on Badrick's heads-up display; he glimpsed the numbers update and realised they were coming close to the first crystal. "Zale!" he called.

"I see it!"

He tilted the bike so that they spun ninety degrees at a nauseating rate. Badrick gulped, worried he was about to vomit. Bikes were not designed for the way Zale drove.

Their vehicle rocketed down a tiny, distressingly thin road, and twenty seconds later he was almost thrown from his perch as Zale brought the bike to a sudden stop. Badrick's single-rifle, which was slung over his back, swung up and hit him on the back of his helmet, causing him to moan in irritation.

Zale dismounted and hurried away, heading for a rubbish skip.

With the strength four years training at the Daemonium had granted him, he forced it aside with relative ease, revealing the purplish crystal they came for.

It was large, as high as Badrick's stomach, with jagged edges like an amethyst stone, both white and purple in colour. It emitted a purple light, the glow pulsating, and its core was throbbing with unnatural energy.

As he approached it, Badrick got the distinct impression of a timer ticking down.

Zale was crouched over the crystal, his hands hovering just above. He didn't speak for quite a bit, though Badrick guessed his eyes might have been closed.

When he did stand up, he didn't seem happy. "It's been set for a timed detonation," he said. "There's about an hour and a half left. I reckon they all have about the same time."

Badrick didn't understand that. "Why leave it so long?"

"So Lucikefer can make it clear of the blast wave," Zale explained. "This thing vaporises demons too. Not even the highest Royal could withstand its power."

"Who the hell would make something like this?" He jumped as Zale grabbed his wrist—he'd been reaching for the crystal, determined to try and sense what Zale could.

"Do *not* touch," Zale whispered, his voice distant, as though he was deep in his own thoughts.

"Why not?"

Zale took his time replying. His hand went to the chin of his helmet, rubbing it as though he was touching his own skin. "Lucikefer *needed* to get into the Daemonium," he muttered, and Badrick recognised the familiar tones of Zale deducting. There was something off here, and on an intelligence level Zale seemed to sense that.

Now he was just trying to make sense of it in his head.

"OK?" Badrick prompted him when he didn't continue.

"These crystals were not part of his original plan. If all he wanted was to get explosives to draw Daemnos out, he would have done this a year ago when Stefan was inducted into the recruitment program.

"No, he needed information. But I bet it was deeper than that. He needed a backup plan in case everything failed. If Daemnos is more powerful than him, and Lucikefer *does* want to kill him, then the subtle, ambush approach is far more likely to succeed.

"This must be his fallback plan. An outright attack. But it's so badly thought out. Or . . . is that just how he wants it to appear."

When he fell silent, Badrick once again prompted him. "What are you thinking, Zale?"

"Lucikefer can't be that stupid. He *knew* he would trip the alarms when he grabbed the crystals, and he knew we would be able to find them. This plan is bad . . . we can stop this . . . If I were Lucikefer I'd hide an extra detail in here . . . something to stop us . . . No. To kill us. We can't do anything if we're dead."

He turned back to the crystal, his hand hovering over it once more. "He's boosted it, the bastard."

"What do you mean, Zale? What's he done? Can't you disarm it?"

An angry chuckle sounded from beneath Zale's helmet, and he reached up to tear it off. His steely gaze made the hairs on Badrick's neck stand up.

He knew what Zale had to say next was going to be bad.

"Like I said, we found this really easily. The power is too much to be disguised. This is a bad plan. Except it isn't. Lucikefer is powerful. He's dumped his own demonic energy inside the crystal."

"What does that mean for us?" Badrick enquired, dreading the answer.

"It's the only thing he can do to stop us disarming them. He's surged them with his own power. Now the only way to stop the thing is to drain the crystal of all demonic energy. I've seen this done before, but never on such a large scale. His energy will push us out every time we try to disarm the device. The only way to stop that is to pull Lucikefer's crap out of there, but the problem is his power will have mixed with the crystal's."

At that very moment, Badrick actually figured it out himself.

"The only way to pull Lucikefer's energy out is to drain the crystal's power too," he finished. "OK, so how do we do that?"

Zale smiled without humour, and whispered, "It's not that simple. The only way to drain demonic energy is to use a conduit. That conduit has to be an Enthraller. We have to pull the energy out and absorb it." Zale closed his eyes in defeat. "It's a basic ability of all Enthrallers, like sensing demonic energy, but not only would trying that on the crystal kill anyone who attempted it, but we wouldn't even be able to take out all the power, there's *so much*. And then when we died, what we took would all siphon back in, meaning we won't even be able to bravely sacrifice a hundred Enthrallers to the cause."

His piercing blue gaze bored into Badrick's eyes, and he sighed in defeat, something Badrick had never heard him do.

"Lucikefer has prevented us from disarming the crystals. We can't stop the explosions."

Stefan roared in agony as he was forced to exist on the physical plane once again. His skin, freshly summoned back, itched like crazy, his skull felt like it was going to fracture, and he could barely stand upright.

But stand he did, refusing to give Lucikefer the satisfaction of seeing him in pain.

The demon was back where he belonged inside his soul, and nothing but a vision in Stefan's view.

"Remember, Blackwood," Lucikefer crowed, obviously grinning beneath his helmet. "You will give me control when Daemnos emerges, or I will shred your soul and you will become a Forsaken. When you are dead, I will drag you back to Hell with me. Do you understand?"

Stefan tried to sneer back. These were empty threats. According to the demon, Stefan couldn't fight Daemnos without his help.

His threats meant nothing; if they lost then Lucikefer would die too.

But it didn't matter.

When Daemnos revealed his presence, Stefan would show Lucikefer exactly what he was capable of.

"Your grenades will explode soon," he laughed. "We'd better

get to cover."

"Then *get* us to cover!" Lucikefer roared, pushing the holographic representation of his body so close to Stefan's that he fancied he could actually smell the rotten hell-spawn breath.

Stefan eyed him with anger. He wanted to tell him to get lost, but in the end did as he was told.

With three massive bombs about to blow, it would've been be stupid not to.

Badrick winced as Zale kicked the skip with all the force he had. Hollering with rage, he swivelled and threw a huge electrical blast into the building that sheltered them from the rest of the city. It continued to strike the bricks, shattering windows and splintering window sills.

"Zale, calm down!"

The blast stopped but the noise only quietened at first. Only after all the bricks had fallen to the ground did silence return.

Badrick's partner was breathing hard, his chestplate rising and falling with every pant. The look on his face was heartbreaking. Even with his fast brainpower, he couldn't think of a way to bypass Lucikefer's meddling.

He truly thought they were finished.

As he fell to the ground and cursed, Badrick stepped closer to the crystal, inspecting its jagged features.

"What do you think?"

Badrick jumped at the sound of the voice. He swivelled, knowing he'd find Vulrick behind him.

"I think we're screwed," he replied.

Zale looked up, noticed he was talking to what would have looked like thin air to him, and smiled crudely. "*Now* he talks to you."

Vulrick ignored him. "Those crystals are very powerful. But they are a demonic creation. They lack a very complex, very human element." His voice was different—far softer than it had ever been, his manic personality lessened in the face of this deadly threat.

"What—"

"Passion," Vulrick laughed. "No *feeling* went into the creation of these. There's something to be said for the human condition. Why do you think we demons can do nothing to your souls? Why we can't break out of them. We can only corrupt them, or attempt to destroy them.

"Think about that. Think about what that might mean. Bravery, sadness, happiness . . . no demon can defeat that. Badrick . . . don't you think it's time you stopped letting people tell you what you can and can't do?"

He vanished before Badrick could question him, disappearing into nothingness. He cursed the demon's name, balling up a fist.

But only half-heartedly, as he didn't really need to ask Vulrick anything

He understood what the demon meant.

And he was right.

Everyone was always hinting at him that he wasn't able to do things, that he wasn't ready. Control Vulrick, use his powers, complete the Trials and become a proper Daemonium operative.

Badrick was always telling himself the same thing. Not once had he ever looked back on his life and seen accomplishment, only failure and disappointment.

It was ridiculous that it took a *demon* to tell him how it truly was. Badrick should have acknowledged himself for what he was long before this. He should have had the confidence to give himself praise.

What the world didn't understand was he had been fighting

greater battles than this for as long as he could remember. His uncle, his anger—that all encompassing, heart-hurting rage—he'd been surviving both for most of his life.

Instead of believing himself to be useless, it was time for him to acknowledge what kind of effort that took.

It took heart.

It took bravery.

That took powerful emotion. Logic and intelligence couldn't defend against the kind of life he'd had, you had to possess a strong will that could fight against the illogical nature of human emotions.

Badrick understood, right then, what Vulrick was telling him.

He was capable of so much more. The life he endured had shaped him. His soul was deeper and more complex than most. He was worth more than he'd believed.

He was better than he'd believed.

Look at what he'd done in the arena. All the power he harnessed with ease. Look at what he'd managed to accomplish.

Three fissures at once and he'd survived with no lasting injury. Something never before done in recorded history.

Badrick didn't need much more convincing. He was ready.

Zale's eyes widened when he raised his hand, his fingers twitching nervously.

"Badrick?" he whispered. "What are you doing?"

"Something brave," Badrick said. "Something stupid."

His partner jumped to his feet in a hurry when he heard that. He rushed over, trying to grab his hand away. Badrick pushed him off, saying, "Don't. We have to try."

"We're not trying that! It won't work. Worse, you'll die!"

A nervous laugh escaped Badrick's mouth. As he stepped forward, something his father used to say echoed in his brain, rattling around and forcing him to say it aloud, "*Qui onques rien n'enprist rien n'achieva."*

Badrick smiled even thought Zale couldn't see it.

And he said, "Nothing ventured, nothing gained."

Badrick slammed his hand upon the crystal.

Zale was thrown from his feet, smashing into his bike. He and his vehicle rolled over each other. Thankfully he was uninjured; the strength of his demonic armour made sure of that.

The scream that burst from Badrick's mouth deafened even himself. He shrieked so loudly his vocal chords stung.

And even after they could no longer stand it, he continued to roar in furious agony, the forces pressed against him not allowing any respite.

The crystal surged and sparked. Purple light erupted from it, striking the buildings explosively. More bricks fell to the ground, which only threw them back up as it was ripped apart by the light. Tarmac and glass swirled around them, kept aloft and spinning by a demonic force of pure malevolence.

Pretty soon they were surrounded, and the local area utterly devastated.

Badrick's body was trapped. He couldn't move. His hand was fixed to the crystal, which now had cracks lining it, its structure failing beneath the power crashing through and around its form.

Badrick's soul was alight with demonic energy. It was tearing, shredding, coming apart. His body felt like it was going to explode.

And then a voice whispered in his ear, "You are brave, Badrick—strong—stronger than most . . . But not enough. I think you need a helping hand."

Something soft touched his right arm, and Badrick realised he was making skin on skin contact with someone. He strained to look, and saw a hand gripping his limb; his armour and under-suit were shredded and destroyed from the power thrashing at him, the flesh on his arm completely exposed.

The owner of the appendage smiled to him kindly, warmly, and Badrick's eyes shot open in shock. "Dad!?" he gasped.

His father, standing there, completely whole as if nothing ever happened, nodded to the space to his left.

Badrick turned to find the only other person he'd ever cared as much for in his life.

"Hi, baby," his mother sighed sweetly. Her hand caressed his visor. "You are so brave."

"You're everything we ever wanted you to be," his father grinned proudly.

"Let us help you, sweetheart. Let us give you the strength we weren't there to give before."

She put her hand on his left pauldron. His father did the same on his right.

With a white flash, they vanished. Where they'd stood, only white, shimmering orbs of light remained.

These orbs blinked twice, then floated closer, phasing through his chest and disappearing into his body.

Everything grew clear. His mind, brutally torn at by the crystal's power only moments before, became lucid, whole again. With a metallic clang, the armour he'd lost reappeared from nothingness. The under-suit 'healed' like it was his skin, and his arm was once again clad in metal.

His soul exploded with light, and he roared, the only thing he could do to prevent himself going mad with such energy flowing through his body.

The souls of his parents protected him, boosted his own power, and gave him what he needed to survive.

He no longer felt the need to scream. It no longer hurt.

His hair whipped in the gusts, his armour shone, as if reflecting the light around him, and his eyes flashed with purple energy, obscuring everything, his irises, whites, the pupils.

Badrick pressed his hand harder against the crystal, glaring at it hatefully, imagining all the damage it could do and how determined he was to prevent it.

Everything went white.

And a symbol appeared in his field of vision.

With a crash, the crystal shattered into a billion pieces. Badrick's hand clutched at nothing as the forces cascading around them settled and quickly vanished.

The bricks, tarmac and glass fell back to Earth, the regular, human force of gravity finally given back its rule over the world.

Badrick stumbled, losing the strength in his legs and falling on his back with a metallic thud. As he lay there, breathing hard, Vulrick materialised over him.

After a moment's silence, he offered Badrick his hand and helped him to his feet.

"Summoning the souls of the long dead has never been easy," Vulrick sighed. "But, sometimes, even the strongest needs the help of the ones they have loved and lost. Now hurry up; there's two more crystals to destroy."

Once again, he vanished, leaving Badrick with an utterly, completely, *entirely* bewildered Zale Hood.

His partner rose to his feet and stumbled over, gazing at him like his very being was an impossibility, as if he were an anomaly. Moments after he got within striking distance, he jumped back, shouting, "Holy crap! Feel that radiation!"

"What are you talking about?"

Zale ignored his question. "How did you survive that? No one can survive that."

Badrick shook his head. If he was completely honest with himself, he wasn't sure either. All he could do was tell Zale what happened while he held the crystal.

But it would have to wait. The sounds of sirens pierced the air, and Badrick finally became aware of the screams ringing loudly around them.

Zale shoved his helmet over his head, and yanked on Badrick's arm, dragging him to his bike. He righted it, kicked it into life, and before Badrick knew it they were rocketing away.

When they reached a quieter road, Badrick told him what he knew as they sped across the tarmac. Zale listened raptly, never interrupting.

When Badrick was finished, he puffed air and said, "It doesn't surprise me that your parents were able to give you strength. Our emotions are power. Their deaths were premature, the emotion behind their loss, how you felt because of it and all the horror that came after . . . imagine the raw power that would generate."

"I can," Badrick sighed.

"You're lucky you're not dead. Even with your parents, it shouldn't have worked." Zale seemed to glare at him in the side mirror, though for some reason he felt like it wasn't directed at him per say. "Vulrick is a lot more powerful than he's been letting on. He's stronger than Horas. Stronger than Acro. Maybe even more than Lucikefer."

Badrick didn't like the way that blue visor appeared to be eyeing him. It was very reminiscent of the way Reynolds studied him before they'd left. "What is it?" he snapped, suspicion tickling his consciousness. What was everyone looking at?

"You need to know," Zale said, "you ripped open three more fissures." He didn't allow Badrick a moment to think about this; he dived right into rambling. "This defies all logic. Doing it once—mental. Doing it twice—impossible. Unprecedented. You're nowhere near prepared for the seventh fissure but absorbing all that energy would have required you to make room for it, so your soul ripped as needed. Your body—Dude, your body has to be freaking out. How do you feel right now?"

Badrick didn't answer at first. At Zale's words his stomach had gurgled and a pained sick sensation overtook him. He couldn't speak, he was stunned into silence.

Another three fissures?

Was Zale yanking his chain?

No. He wouldn't. Not at a time like this.

He tried his best to swallow, his now tightening throat constricting his breathing painfully. Once he'd managed to force it to sooth, he found he was able to speak once more.

Finding his voice, he uttered untruthfully, "I feel fine." In reality he was aching all over.

But he wasn't about to tell Zale that.

Not when there were still two more crystals to drain.

If Zale knew he had even a little pang he would be even less likely to accept the plan Badrick was now inventing for the rest of the problem.

As it turned out, Zale utterly refused to allow him to even attempt another crystal. He shot him down before Badrick could even load up the coordinates on his HUD.

"Zale, don't argue with me!" Badrick roared in response. "We don't have any other choice."

"Everything is a choice, and I'm not letting you kill yourself!"

Zale snapped back aggressively. "When we get to the second crystal we'll find another way."

It didn't take them long to find it; the readings transmitted to their helmets from the BCR scanners led them outside the city, to a farmer's field in the middle of nowhere.

Badrick didn't give Zale a chance to stop him. Before the bike even stopped moving, he leapt from it, charging as fast as he could towards the crystal, which was situated at the far end of the field.

What other choice did he really have? As far as they knew, he was the only one who could survive draining the crystals of power.

"Badrick, you can't do this!" Back at the bike, Zale dismounted and sprinted after him.

"The hell I can't!" Badrick shouted over his shoulder.

"Badrick, stop and think about this for just one minute!"

"Done thinking, more doing!"

He heard Zale grumble something unintelligible, but didn't stop to find out what it was. He almost ran headfirst into the makeshift bomb, he was racing so fast.

Regaining his footing quickly, Badrick thrust his hand at the crystal, slamming his palm against it.

"Badrick!" Zale's terrified cry rang out from afar.

The effect was far more instantaneous this time around; the crystal cracked down its right side and light spewed out, illuminating the grass with a brilliant purple glow. A massive wave of power smacked Badrick in the chest and demonic energy surged around him, ripping the grass from the mud and throwing rocks every which way.

He shrieked as he felt his body shudder in agony, and he almost buckled under the pressure.

The crystal exploded and Badrick was thrown from his feet, coming to rest on top of Zale. They grunted as they fell to the dirt and rolled through the long grass.

Wishing he didn't have to go through this again, Badrick clenched his eyes against the pain of a familiar, yet unwelcome sight.

When his vision cleared, he became aware of Zale attempting to yank him to his feet, but failing.

"Badrick, you can't keep this up. You're going to kill yourself. Do you hear me? Your body is dying."

"No . . . " Badrick panted. "I'm fine."

That was a grand lie, and he was painfully aware of how unconvincing he sounded. His breathing was laboured, made more difficult by the pain in his chest and the shaking of his limbs.

He sat up, trying not to vibrate like a mobile phone.

"Badrick, don't lie to me. I felt it. You opened the eighth fissure. No one's ever survived that. If you try to stop the third crystal you'll rip open another one, or another two, or three. That *will* kill you!"

"Zale," Badrick snapped unintentionally, "don't you understand yet? I'm not stopping. I can't. You said it yourself; no one can survive what I'm doing. But I *am*. Somehow I can survive it. I'm the only thing we have that can stop this.

"You've done your bit. You've earned your keep. You figured everything out and saved our arses multiple times. Now it's my turn. I'm taking the last crystal down, no matter what."

It was impossible to read Zale without seeing his face. His body, at least, was tense, his limbs static, unmoving.

"You don't have to do this," he said softly.

"Yes," Badrick sighed. "Yes, I do."

He wasn't sure if he was brave or stupid; he just understood he had a responsibility. It was true, he was fear-stricken about dying . . . but knowing all those who would suffer if he stopped . . . that, by Zale's own words, there was probably no one else who could do this . . . it gave Badrick a bravery (or stupidity) unlike anything he'd ever experienced before.

It gave him a sense of duty.

Zale gave him a reluctant nod, communicating his disagreement, but also his resignation. "Why are you so stubborn?" he half chuckled.

Badrick shrugged. "I just know I can succeed. If we can do something to help, we shouldn't not do it."

"I'm sure that's a quote somewhere, and I'm certain you just butchered it." Zale pulled him to his feet. Badrick swayed precariously; his body was weaker than he'd realised. "Are you able to walk?"

"I'll manage."

Despite his confidence, his friend had to help him to the bike. They mounted it together and sped away in search of the final deadly crystal.

chapter
TWENTY TWO

Lucikefer's plans lay in ruins. He needed all the crystals to generate the amount of power it would take to attract a demon as powerful as Zale believed Daemnos to be.

But the blast from the last crystal would still kill thousands.

Tens of thousands.

Maybe even millions.

Badrick didn't know how far the crystal could reach, how much of London would be engulfed in its blast. But that didn't matter, because they wouldn't allow it.

The bike shuddered to a stop—frankly Badrick was surprised it had lasted this long against the two explosions that had pummelled it. As the engine died, he got the worrying feeling that it was the last time it would ever run.

But he couldn't focus on the loss of such a beautiful machine. His helmet was flashing red now, his timer screaming at him, beeping uncaringly into his already ringing ears.

With only seconds left, Badrick threw himself at the crystal.

His hand made contact, and the draining of energy began.

Badrick expected his chest to implode; the pain shooting through his heart was so unbearable. He staggered away as the crystal shattered and the energy that exploded from it died away.

Zale, once again having been thrown to his back, jumped up and caught him as he fell, ensuring he did not lose his footing.

"It happened again," Badrick breathed with exhaustion.

"Fissure nine," Zale confirmed. "Again, the first ever."

"Did I do it? Did I stop the explosions?"

"You did, man. You did. You can rest now."

Badrick shook his head and pushed Zale's hands away. He had to stand on his own two feet. The fate of the world probably depended on it.

"No, I can't," he said resolutely. "There's one more target."

There were no flies on Zale; he knew *exactly* what Badrick was talking about. "Don't you dare! Lucikefer is not our problem. The Daemonium will deal with him and Stefan. Now, come on home with me. I reckon all the girls will sex the hell out of you for this."

Though that was quite an enticing thought, Badrick declined.

"Zale, you said it yourself. Lucikefer is the son of Satan. He's too powerful. The Daemonium is out of its league."

"And, what, you're better than them?" Zale scoffed, though it was only due to his concern. Badrick knew he meant no disrespect.

"Not what I'm saying." He clutched his chest as an especially painful twang struck his heart. Gulping in air, he started again. "The Daemonium is going to kill Stefan and Lucikefer, if they can. But I have to try talking to him first."

"You can't reason with Lucikefer, he's a demon!"

"Not him. Stefan!" Zale fell into stunned silence, so Badrick continued, "I know, Zale. I know what it's like to be Stefan. I *was* him. Aggressive, hateful, inadequate. I've lived his life. I could have ended up just like him. He's not evil, Zale, he's angry. There's a difference. Anger such as he's feeling can lead a person to terrible things.

"I have to try and talk to him. If I can find it in myself to be caring towards others, despite everything, so can he."

Zale didn't agree. "I don't believe he's capable of listening to you. I don't think he's even worth saving. What intrinsic value does his life have any more?"

"Everyone has a value, Zale, even the demons. With our help, Stefan can start his life anew."

"Badrick, he's a walking corpse. You do realise this, right? Take Lucikefer out of him and he dies."

"We don't have to separate them. Stefan can learn to control the monster inside him, just like us."

Badrick wasn't lying. He truly believed if he could just talk to Stefan, then maybe he could prevent everything.

No one had to die.

Zale regarded his partner with the manner of an impressed father. Though, one who wanted to tell his son *not* to sacrifice himself for the good of the many.

But how could he possibly refuse Badrick?

Not that he would listen to Zale, even if he did.

Besides . . . Badrick was the only one who could fight Lucikefer and win.

He'd known it the second his partner touched that first crystal.

Everything had been clear to him in that moment.

There was no one else on the planet, or in Hell, that could stop Lucikefer once and for all. He was the *biggest* threat alive. A hostile Royal was such bad news it wasn't even funny.

Nothing was too much to sacrifice now.

That was the *only* reason he decided to agree to Badrick's plan.

Although, he suspected his partner's motivation was less because he understood Stefan's hardships, and more because he always seemed afraid of becoming what he despised.

Since Stefan did exactly that, the recruit was a little too close to home for Badrick to ignore.

But that wasn't what was of importance. Not at that moment. Badrick had his mind made up, and Zale knew he wasn't capable of making the stubborn bastard change it.

So, in the end, he nodded reluctantly.

"I'm doing it alone," Badrick added. "If he sees you he won't be as receptive. You have to stay back."

That was harder to agree to, but eventually he did so, throwing his hands in the air with frustration.

How was he going to explain this to Carla?

Or to Reynolds?

Badrick smiled at his partner, thanking him for his understanding.

It was certainly refreshing; that was all he'd ever wanted from anyone. He grasped Zale's hand firmly, putting all his strength into the gesture.

"I have to do this, man," he told him. "I *can* do this."

"I already agreed," Zale spat at him. "When you get back, I'll tell you why. Idiot," he added under his breath, but Badrick knew it was light-hearted.

He laughed, and let go of his hand.

He didn't say any more. There was no time to waste. Neither Lucikefer nor the Daemonium would wait for them to finish brotherly handshakes, and Badrick was determined to get there first.

He stepped aside to allow himself some breathing room, something he knew was necessary for what he was about to do.

He was at nine fissures. Not only was that an unprecedented number, but it meant a *crap-load* of demonic radiation was leaking into his soul and body, powering him like a battery and filling him with supernatural abilities and knowledge.

He could feel it all rushing through his veins and flooding his mind, giving him what he needed.

Sensing Stefan's power signature would be the only way to find him. Badrick's natural ability to sense demonic energy was greatly enhanced now, far more than any other Enthraller. Whereas they could only sense energy at close range, reading its strength, levels, amount, Badrick could scan a wide area.

As it happened, luck was on his side.

Stefan was only half an hour away, somewhere in the West, heading towards London.

It surprised Badrick. He should have been further away than that, standing beyond the blast radius. Lucikefer must have told him to come back once he sensed his crystals had been depowered.

That would have infuriated him greatly after all the effort he put into stopping that very thing from happening.

His target located, Badrick opened his eyes, having closed them in order to concentrate. "I have him." Zale only nodded in reply. "You promise you won't interfere?" Again, a nod.

Badrick was certain his plan required his partner's absence. Stefan needed a kindred spirit, an understanding soul, one that not only understood, but had also experienced, the same pain. Zale's presence would just aggravate Stefan, blinding him to Badrick's help, and rendering his plan fruitless.

With their bike out of commission, Badrick would have to walk. He cast his eyes over the tree line through which he would pass to get to Stefan. The idea of trotting through the woods, a slow and tiring method of travelling, gave him the horrible sensation of walking to his execution.

Because, if he was honest with himself, that was what it was.

He'd already exhausted his body to its limits. He could feel his heart pounding, every beat a struggle. It was in its last throes. He'd pushed himself too far.

It didn't matter how much power Vulrick had, Badrick was still only human. He had the same weaknesses and failings as every other Enthraller.

He was past the point of no return now.

Badrick didn't know how he felt about that. It should have scared him to death.

He should have been blind with panic.

As it was, he only felt strangely calm.

There was a mission to accomplish. A soul to save. He had a purpose.

And if he couldn't save Stefan . . . if Stefan refused to be saved, as Badrick knew he might . . . then he would have to stop the guy.

This knowledge kept his mind strangely tranquil. He couldn't afford to freak out like he always did.

People were depending on it.

Whether or not he was egotistical about his importance, he didn't know. All that mattered to him was that he was doing his best to act altruistically.

Against such danger, what else could he do?

His mind made up, he glanced one last time at Zale, knowing this would be the final time they were together.

Zale knew it too. How could he not? Maybe that was why he was being so agreeable; granting a dying man's final wish.

"Say bye to Carla for me," he said. "And thanks for everything. You too, Zale."

"Shut up!" Zale snapped in response. "I'll see you later."

Badrick smiled, and nodded. "Later."

Zale watched his partner turn his back and stagger away. Badrick was very weak at this point. He was barely able to stand.

If reasoning failed and a fight broke out, everything rested on one thing; Badrick wouldn't survive the fight on his own . . . he would need some help.

Help that only an infuriatingly deceptive demon could provide.

He just hoped *Vulrick* was still in a helping mood.

The walk didn't take long. Ten or so minutes after he hit the tree line, Badrick sensed Stefan stop. The yellow-armoured recruit was no longer moving towards him.

Badrick knew he'd been detected, and now his quarry was awaiting his arrival.

Well, Badrick thought, *best not keep him waiting*.

When he broke through the opposite side of the woods, he

emerged into a vast, flat open area. Most of the English countryside was like this; a never ending series of fields, segmented into squares by lines of bushes, as well as the odd forest.

So he wasn't astounded when his eyes were treated to the beautiful sight of the plain green grass, which swayed softly in the gentle breeze, alleviating the harshness of the sharp bushes that surrounded this segment.

Badrick had noted a few weeks before that summer started at some point and he was pleasantly grateful that the sun was shining brightly. He hadn't even realised it when they'd left the Daemonium; he'd been too preoccupied with the threat of the crystals looming over them.

Badrick smiled tenderly. If he was going to sacrifice himself, he was glad he could do it under such fine weather.

Stefan was easy to spot, his armour a tarnish on the beautiful scenery. Badrick wasted no time approaching him. He walked as fast as his ravaged body would allow, pushing ever onwards despite the protests of his limbs.

Soon enough, he was within earshot, just far enough away to talk, and Stefan was already speaking. "Mr Varner," he chuckled, his tones so malicious Badrick was filled with fresh surprise that anyone could be so cruel, despite having spent his life around such people. "How pleasurable it is for you to join me."

Badrick had to remind himself that this was all because of Lucikefer. Stefan was not the enemy; he was a *victim*.

Of course he was. Badrick knew because he had come so close to being the same.

He ran the risk every day of allowing his anger and hatred to dominate him. How could he judge when he was just as corruptible?

It was horrible, the influence a monster such as Lucikefer had over weaker-willed people.

Badrick allowed himself a sad smile at the thought of the demon. "You even sound like him," he muttered.

"What was that?" Stefan snapped, taking a step forward.

Badrick winced at his aggression. "You sound like Lucikefer. He's had such an influence on you that you sound the same."

Stefan threw his head back and laughed a mocking, dramatic guffaw. "You've got that all wrong. I don't sound like him, he sounds like me."

"Arrogance is pointless right now, Stefan."

"It's not arrogance, you moron. That's what happens. Demons undergo many changes when they are absorbed by humans. One of the biggest is that their voices change. They adopt your same tone. When they speak, they will sound like their Enthraller, if their Enthraller's voice was put through a voice changer to sound all growly and monster-like. It's happens to them all."

Badrick frowned; he couldn't say he'd ever heard himself in Vulrick. "I didn't know that," he muttered.

"Of course you didn't" Stefan exasperated. "You're a novice. Worse than that, you know nothing. Letting you into the Trials was an insult." He sighed tiredly. "Though at least now I've finally figured out why they did it."

"What are you talking about?"

Stefan didn't answer him; he continued to talk to himself, addressing him, but not looking, as though Badrick wasn't even there. "Though you've blindsided both Lucikefer and me. Disarming those crystals took power. Power that only one person could have harnessed. We didn't think it was you."

"What are you talking about?" Badrick snapped. He quickly checked himself, taking a deep breath. Shouting was painful, not to mention detrimental to his goal.

"Are you serious?" Stefan cackled. "You don't know? How

could you *not know?* How could you possibly disarm the *dru'dar* and not realise you . . . You're a fool."

Badrick didn't question what the dru'dar was. He could tell from the context Stefan meant the crystals. He also didn't wonder how Stefan knew their name when no one else did; Lucikefer was a Royal. He probably knew everything, and had shared that information with his Enthraller.

"Explain," Badrick sighed. "Please."

"No doubt Zale figured it out ages ago. His powers of deduction *are* good, I hate to say. But I can't deny it any longer. He's too clever. I will have to deal with him after I've dealt with you."

Badrick's temper rose a little too high than he was able to hold, and he found himself snapping, "Explain what you mean right now!"

Stefan focused back on him and, with a derisive snigger, he shouted, "You're Daemnos, Badrick!"

Badrick's mind went numb. He forgot about his pain as he stared at Stefan disbelievingly. "You're wrong," he muttered. "I'm human."

Stefan moved his head in such a way that suggested he'd just rolled his eyes. "I don't mean *you* specifically, you idiot. Your demon is Daemnos. Have you not learned yet that you and your demon are one in the same when he's inside your soul? You are him, he is you."

"My demon is Vulrick," Badrick argued.

"Oh, yeah," Stefan sneered sarcastically, "because *Vulrick* could absorb that much power *and* keep you alive as he does it. Only the most powerful demons can alter physics and biology and quantum mechanics and grant their Enthrallers impossible capabilities.

"Only a Royal can do that. Daemnos is a Royal. Vulrick is

nothing but his servant."

Badrick felt a tiny surge in his body, and instinctively knew his demon had just materialised behind him. He whirled on the spot, rounding on him angrily. "Is this true!?"

"More or less," was the cryptic answer, his manic way of speaking back in all its glory.

"I can't believe it!" Badrick roared. "You lied to me. Just like everyone else."

Vulrick—*Daemnos*—sighed tiredly with the manner of someone explaining the reasons for his actions to an idiot child. "I needed to hide. I think you can understand why."

Badrick didn't want to admit it. Just once he would have liked be to angry with someone without understanding that they were justified in their actions.

But—yet again—he just couldn't.

Daemnos had known Lucikefer was after him.

If you fail this I cannot prepare for what is to come. That was what he said during the first Trial.

And then, during the other three, he'd sneakily granted more and more of his power and aid, the sole reason Badrick passed his exams at all.

In the duel Badrick had been capable of *such* things. Power he had never experienced before. He hadn't understood why it was so easy during the fight.

But now he could comprehend it. Not just that, he could figure everything out.

Daemnos took over Badrick, using the time to kill his uncle, and therefore alerting the Daemonium to their readiness to be picked up.

Because of Lucikefer's actions with Zale and the link, Daemnos knew all along that the Daemonium was suspicious of Badrick.

To ensure Lucikefer didn't find them if he was attracted to the burst of energy created by the takeover, he caused Badrick to display that special, psychotic behaviour, making Doctor Brian initiate those top secret executive orders.

Hans realised the source of energy the Daemonium was tracking had just walked into his safe house, and took Badrick hostage for the agents.

As opposed to simply leading Badrick to the Daemonium, which would have enabled Lucikefer to witness their arrival earlier than he wanted, Daemnos manipulated him into being arrested and thrown into captivity, away from prying eyes.

Knowing what the Daemonium would do if they suspected someone housed a Royal, or was affiliated with one, he waited until they presented him with a opportune time—which he knew the predictable humans would—one where it would be most beneficial to him to reveal Badrick's power.

When he was presented with such a moment, at the Forsaken's cave, Daemnos pushed Badrick to open three fissures at once, inciting jealousy in a demon who he knew was just childish enough to care.

Consequentially, Stefan introduced himself to Badrick instead of observing from afar, unwittingly revealing himself to Daemnos, who, with his vast power, could see Lucikefer standing next to him.

Lucikefer had the power to do the same, but unlike the petulant Devilson, Daemnos didn't constantly appear next to Badrick. He kept quiet and invisible, unless needed.

Why had it taken Daemnos four hours to enable his mind-reading?

Because he'd been forced to focus a whole ton of energy into staying invisible when appearing in front of Stefan and Lucikefer during the Trials.

All of this scheming eventually created a rivalry between Badrick and Stefan. Daemnos knew Badrick was awful at keeping his emotions to himself with a personality such as his. Of course he did; he was in Badrick's head.

His conniving paid off; they were paired up in the duel.

He knew Stefan would eventually try to kill Badrick. Daemnos understood perfectly the kind of person Lucikefer preyed upon.

Daemnos then provided Badrick with power, so much that he would foil Stefan's plans of murder and infuriate him, making him vulnerable to an explosive take-over and revealing Lucikefer to the Daemonium.

And then he could sit back and watch as the Royal's plan unravelled beneath him, keeping himself hidden from everyone, disguised as Vulrick the entire time so that Lucikefer wouldn't see him coming.

Badrick could see it all his head.

Every step of the complex scheme in vivid detail.

It was a vicious plan, the intelligence behind it on par with even Zale.

Daemnos was a clever demon.

"Do you see now?" Daemnos crowed, his tone suggesting he was grinning widely behind his visor. "Aren't you proud you lucked out with your demon? You got the best one."

"Are you done talking to your girlfriend!?" Stefan roared suddenly.

Badrick jumped and turned his attention back to his fellow recruit. "I'm sorry, Stefan. It's a bit of a surprise to hear it. Especially from you."

"What does that mean?" Stefan snarled.

Badrick shook his head despairingly and put aside the Daemnos matter in favour of the direr situation. "It doesn't mean anything, Stefan. Nothing I say to you will ever *mean* anything ever again."

". . . What does *that* mean?"

Badrick laughed, and almost fell to his knees because of it. He wished he could wipe his mouth; he was starting to lose control of his body, his working parts no longer obeying him. But he couldn't summon the energy to remove his helmet.

He was running out of time. He needed to get this done. His body could fail at any moment, and the Daemonium would surely be closing in soon.

"Stefan," he started, "I read your file. I know what you've been through."

"You know nothing about me!" Stefan immediately hollered back.

"*Yes, I do.* I've lived your life. I know what it's like." Badrick took a step forward, reaching his arm towards him in a pleading gesture, indicating for him to just listen for five minutes. "My uncle very nearly killed me once, he beat me so hard. He accused me of killing my parents. He made me feel responsible.

"I wanted to kill him for a long time. And I would have, if I wasn't so timid. That is the *only* thing that stopped me. I wasn't bold enough. But I learned that I had done the right thing, not fighting back.

"I understand, Stefan, it is so easy to be angry, to take it all out on everybody. Hatred is a terrible thing. It infects every other emotion, and no memory stays safe from it. You begin to attribute everything with that lonely feeling."

Stefan scoffed and tilted his head sardonically. "What drivel," he muttered.

"Stefan, it doesn't have to be this way. You don't have to prove your worth to anyone. You aren't alone in this." Badrick took another step forward, determined for Stefan to listen to him. "I'm going to tell you something," he sighed. "Something you don't want to hear. Something that is too difficult to hear. You'd rather I never said it so you don't have to face how you feel. You can stay inside your angry shell, and never think about it

"But you have to hear it. From experience, I know you do. Because I have to stay hopeful. I refuse to let you fall into this dark hole. You don't deserve it."

"What are you—"

"I forgive you, Stefan," Badrick interrupted him. "I forgive you."

"Shut up!" Stefan bawled, clenching his fists. "Shut up. You don't get to say that to me. Don't you dare say that!"

"Stefan, its alri—"

"I said, shut up! Listen to me now. We want to kill Daemnos. Daemnos is inside you. Do you even understand what that means?"

Badrick didn't answer him. He tried once more to penetrate the veil of anger that was filling Stefan's heart. "Stefan, listen to me, it—"

"I said, *do you understand?*"

Knowing he was only infuriating him further, bolstering Stefan's belief that he was inadequate by not answering his question, and therefore just making everything worse, Badrick retreated, and sighed. "I understand."

He reached up and painfully pulled his single-rifle from his person, letting it fall to the grass. The sound of its dull thud seemed strangely reminiscent of how his stomach felt at that precise moment.

"I hope you've made peace with your God," Stefan sneered. "I don't know if you're religious. Seems stupid not to be when you have a demon inside your soul. Pretty solid proof of the afterlife's existence, if you ask me.

"But you can't stop me. Not as you are. Look at you, you can barely stand. You're too weak."

"I get a burst of strength every time I open a new fissure," Badrick stated—which was true; it was how he'd made it this far. "I can use it to get some energy and make it last long enough to fight you."

Stefan instantly bawled at him, laughing in his face. "You're going to open the tenth fissure? Are you kidding me? That's a death sentence, Varner. You don't have the guts. You're still the scared, scrabbling child you were when you first joined the Daemonium."

Badrick felt a terrible emptiness in his stomach as he replied with, "If you don't listen to me, I will stop you."

"I'm one with Lucikefer now. It's too late for your help. I will show *everyone*, including the both of you, just what *I* can do."

Badrick got the impression that Lucikefer just shouted at his Enthraller, because Stefan whirled to his right and roared, "Shut it!"

Badrick utilised the distraction to turn to his own demon. He studied the dark red features of Daemnos' armour, the menacing helmet, the unique visor. "Can I do it?"

Daemnos whistled with delight. "You're the Enthraller of Daemnos," he said conceitedly. "Of course you can open a fissure at will."

"Will it be enough?"

"We'll see."

Badrick decided it would have to be. He turned back to the furious yellow recruit and called out to him. "I'm sorry, Stefan. I'm really, really sorry. I tried to help you. But you're too dangerous to allow to go free, and I don't know when the Daemonium will get here.

"I have to stop you."

And with that, he reached inside himself, located his soul,

grabbed it with metaphysical hands . . . and tore it open.

The power surge was immense.

So large the earth shook. Rocks broke through the dirt and shot into the sky, coming back down like meteors. The trees behind him threw themselves to the ground as if hit by a nuclear bomb; damn near the entire woods was flattened.

A furious rumbling was echoing across the land.

Badrick's eyes were tightly closed against the pain shooting through his body as his soul convulsed and spat power at him. His heart did the same, but with blood.

He felt a rib snap, and screamed with fresh pain.

When he was next able to open his eyes, he realised he was kneeling on the grass, his body arched backwards and his hands stretched towards the sky like a dramatic comic book character.

He was surrounded by an orb of brilliant orange light, energy swirling within it, quivering, pulsing, changing. He couldn't see Stefan—the orb wasn't transparent—but he could sense the recruit's surprise, his paralysing shock at what Badrick was doing.

The distress of it became too much again, and Badrick clenched his eyes, falling to the grass, his visor splattering with dirt. The ground was wet; the forces involved were mutilating the area, rocks and dirt and moisture from deep beneath the earth were being pulled to the surface.

This was beyond powerful.

This was damn near godlike.

And Badrick couldn't handle it.

His vision went white, his mind blank.

And the last fissure he knew he'd ever tear finished opening, leaving him with a total of ten. The symbol he saw was larger than the ones that came before. More detailed, thicker, colourful in his mind, but still black with an orange glow, just like the rest.

The noise ceased. The rumbling stopped. Everything settled.

But it didn't change the fact that Badrick had utterly destroyed the local area. If this field belonged to anyone, they were going to be *so* angry.

The energy dissipated quite quickly, leaving only sparks of residual power floating around. Stefan was staring in his direction, frozen still, clearly shocked and a little afraid.

It took Badrick quite a long time to realise he was no longer lying on his front. With a start, he stared around.

He was standing, and not where he was supposed to be.

Forgetting that, he realised with a jolt that he couldn't feel his body anymore.

The pain was gone, along with any and all other sensations. He stared at his hands in confusion and panic. They were right there in front of him, but feel them he could not.

His armour was gone—he was dressed in regular clothes.

What the hell was this?

Stefan's frightened gasp helped him understand. *"Daemnos!"*

His head shot up. When he saw Daemnos standing where he should have been, his head bowed, his body slumped, he realised what had happened.

He was nothing but a soul, a vision appearing to his demon.

Daemnos had taken over.

This was his fight now.

"You planned this," he said angrily. Nevertheless he also muttered encouragingly, "Kick Lucikefer's arse."

Without warning, Daemnos' head ignited, fire exploding with a rush of air. The flames surrounded his whole head, but were thin enough that his visor was easily visible. He stretched, righting himself and spreading his arms out to his sides. "Ahhhh!" the demon bellowed happily. "It's good to get out." He relaxed his body and turned his attention to Stefan. "I wish to fight Lucikefer. Unveil him."

Stefan took a contravening step forward, clenching his fists angrily. "*No!*" he screamed. "This is *my* fight. I'll kill you myself."

And then Badrick heard a third voice. A voice that sounded a little like Stefan, but definitely wasn't at the same time. A voice he'd heard for the first time only a few hours before. "Stefan, don't be a fool. Let me take over!"

With a start, he realised he could see Lucikefer's visage, appearing to Stefan like Badrick was appearing to Daemnos.

This was something he knew to be impossible.

But Badrick had done all manner of impossible things today. What was one more?

Daemnos was laughing again, and he vibrated on the spot with barely concealed pleasure. "This is gonna be easy.

"This is going to be *fun*."

chapter
TWENTY THREE

Stefan darted forward, pulling a pistol from a holster on his side. He fired three bullets, which had zero effect on his target.

The rounds bounced off Daemnos' powerful form. When Stefan was close enough, the demon grabbed the weapon from his hands and punched him on the visor. The acrylic glass cracked and Stefan fell to the ground.

He was only stunned for a moment, quickly jumping up and reaching for his other side, producing something Badrick hadn't counted on.

He flicked his wrist twice and a brilliant electric blue blade extended from the handle Lucikefer stole from the Daemonium.

Zale was going to be pissed when he found out he still had it.

Daemnos didn't appear to be worried in the slightest. He

simply raised his hands; they glowed red and he swung them crazily as Stefan began to flail the weapon in his direction.

The blade bounced off his fingers as though they were made of metal.

The sword couldn't melt through them. Badrick had to take a moment to really think about what that meant. The power Daemnos was using was *insane*.

Stefan really didn't stand a chance.

Heck, even if Lucikefer was allowed to drive, Daemnos would still destroy them.

The son of Satan didn't agree however. He was shouting at Stefan as the recruit swung wildly, chaotically, trying to pierce his enemy with the stolen blade. "Stefan! Let me fight this battle. You cannot win this. You'll kill us both!"

"Never!" Stefan roared back. "This is my fight. I'll kill him myself."

"Your arrogance will be the death of both of us!"

Catching the young Enthraller off guard, Daemnos grabbed the hand holding the sword and twisted. Stefan screamed as the bones cracked and he lost his grip on the weapon. The blade fizzled out of existence before it hit the dirt.

Daemnos pulled Stefan in close so that their helmets banged together. "Say hi to my nephew in there for me!"

With barely contained fury, Lucikefer roared "I will kill you!" just as Daemnos kicked Stefan away. He rolled along the grass painfully, coming to rest on his back.

He scrambled to his feet, getting further enraged by Daemnos' manic, derisive laughing.

It was a simple tactic Daemnos was utilising, and Stefan was falling for it hook, line and sinker.

The demon didn't need to do this; he could have killed Stefan simply enough without the need for games. But he was enjoying this fight.

He wanted to see just how angry and stupid he could make the kid get.

Stefan charged a green blast of energy in his hand and lobbed it at Daemnos.

A white dome deflected it; a tactic Badrick used himself in the arena. The shield vanished, and Daemnos responded in kind with a humungous laser-like blast of red power.

Stefan only just managed to dive out of the way.

He was barely back on his feet before Daemnos had rushed up to him, running with supernatural speed, and smashed him in the chest with a balled up fist. Stefan stumbled, though somehow managing to withstand the blow.

Daemnos awarded his tenacity and strength with a new blast of energy, which hit him squarely on the stomach. He fell to his knees, gripping his torso in agony.

Daemnos gripped him by the neck and yanked him to his feet. He drew back his fist—

Stefan's hand flashed to his leg; he pulled out a knife that had been concealed inside his boot and sunk it into Daemnos' neck.

The red Royal choked and dropped him, stumbling backwards, his hand gripping the dagger's handle.

He yanked it out. A torrent of black blood gushed from the wound, and Daemnos had to slap his palm over it to stem the flow.

In front of Badrick's eyes, the wound flashed orange and instantly healed.

Daemnos laughed victoriously when he'd finally stopped choking blood.

And in Stefan's own voice, he said, "You'll have to do better than that." Parroting his foe from the battle in the arena.

This further infuriated the boy.

But it didn't matter. There was nothing he could do before Daemnos struck him with a blast of electricity that threw the Enthraller's limp form through the air, flying like a ragdoll until he came to a crashing stop on the ground.

Stefan was screaming profanities at an impressive rate. He tried to jump to his feet, but ultimately failed.

He glanced up, breathing hard . . .

Only to find that Daemnos had disappeared.

His head darted left and right in a panic, trying to determine where the demon went.

Badrick knew. He'd seen it happen while Stefan's face was in the dirt.

Daemnos had gone invisible, his body vanishing impossibly. Badrick could no longer actually see him, but he could sense where he was.

Directly behind Stefan, and it didn't take the demon long to punish the kid for his inability to match his power.

He kicked Stefan in the head, knocking his helmet clean off. It rolled away, and Stefan screamed as he was struck again, this time in the abdomen.

He looked to be at the end of his strength, and he definitely knew it. In an attempt to run, Stefan's body shimmered and he teleported away.

Badrick sensed a burst of energy and looked up, seeing the tiny speck that was Stefan, floating high in the air, as far away from Daemnos as he could manage.

It wasn't enough.

A grinding noise assaulted Badrick's ears and he watched as Daemnos, too, relocated, joining Stefan in the air. He grabbed a hold of the Enthraller's shoulders, taking the time to break one of his arms, before using all his strength to catapult him back to Earth.

Stefan fell like a meteor. When he hit the ground there was a violent explosion of dirt and rocks.

The only thing that saved him from death was Lucikefer's presence in his soul.

It wouldn't have mattered anyway. He was done. He was spent.

And Badrick sensed Daemnos heading in for the kill.

He glanced around desperately as Daemnos fell gracefully and landed on his feet, chuckling with the manner of someone having a good time with a group of friends.

There was no one else around. Nobody at all.

Not a soul who could stop this happening.

Would it even matter if there was anyone nearby? Was there another power equal to Daemnos who could prevent what was to come?

The Daemonium *still* hadn't gotten here. Badrick had no doubt they were on their way, but maybe they'd waited until all the crystals were disarmed.

That would have meant they'd left only an hour ago.

It would be a long time before they got here.

Badrick could do nothing. There was no way he could stop Daemnos from killing Stefan. He could feel the demon's determination invading his own consciousness.

Badrick had failed.

Stefan was lost.

He tried to find solace in the fact that Lucikefer would die too, thanks to Stefan's refusal of his demands to take over.

In a way, Stefan had saved them. It would have been a far worse fight if Lucikefer was one of the combatants.

With Stefan, this fight had been over before it started.

Daemnos' gravelly voice punctured his consciousness, and he diverted his attention back to the scene unravelling before him. Stefan was trying to stand again, but he was unable.

There was no way he was going to get back up.

"Oh, this has gone on long enough," Daemnos was saying. "I'm going to kill you."

With that he raised his hands to the sky, laughing menacingly. He shouted words in a language Badrick didn't understand, but through his connection to Daemnos he recognised the origins.

As the demon continued chanting in the archaic language of his birthplace, Stefan glanced up as well. His eyes widened with terror when he spotted what Badrick already knew to be heading his way.

A barrage of energy blasts was travelling towards him at incredible speeds, falling from the sky like meteors.

Stefan screamed as the first one hit him.

The cry died out as the rest obliterated the area.

Stefan's body was utterly destroyed.

Badrick felt his stomach drop, knowing that it was finally all over.

When Daemnos was sure his victim was completely dead, he lowered his hands and the barrage stopped.

For a moment there was only silence.

Then the demon turned to him and chuckled. "This was fun, Badrick. We must do it again sometime."

Badrick's skin began to itch, and with a trembling cry of pain, he felt his body forced back into the physical plane. Daemnos returned to where he belonged, and Badrick's feet hit solid ground, a sensation he hadn't realised he'd missed until it returned.

For a long while all he could do was stand there.

He could sense his body ready to shoot pain through every nook and cranny the *moment* he moved.

But he couldn't stay on his feet forever; his body was done.

Within seconds of realising it was about to happen, his legs gave way and he fell to the grass.

More bones were broken that he originally realised. Blood seeped from dozens of tears in his skin, filling the inside of his suit. For a brief moment he was worried he'd drown in his own gore.

But he knew in his heart he would be gone long before that happened, if that was even probable. He tried to move, but instantly decided against it. There was nothing to be done. All he could do now was wait for the darkness.

A voice pierced his consciousness, and he suddenly became aware of a second person in the clearing.

A familiar electric blue visor appeared in his field of vision, and he felt a happy smile tug at his mouth.

"Zale," he groaned gladly, coughing violently because of it. Zale held his head aloft and allowed him to clear his throat of blood. "Where . . . where did you come from?"

"I was watching," Zale said sombrely. "That was one hell of a fight. Blasts, forcefields, invisibility. That was the whole *shebang*."

Badrick laughed, quickly regretting it. "It was, wasn't it?"

Zale studied him for a moment, examining the tears in his under-suit that Badrick hadn't even realised were there until he felt Zale's fingers against his skin.

His partner sighed. "Badrick . . . you've exhausted yourself. Ten fissures . . . it's broken you beyond repair. You have . . . seconds left."

Badrick didn't need to hear it from him. "I know," he voiced his thoughts. "It's alright . . . We stopped Lucikefer."

"It's not alright!" Zale retorted. "This *isn't* right. Who am I going to brag to about all the girls I get?"

"Ever the joker," Badrick sighed. Though he was grateful; he preferred the idea of going out amused.

"Don't you dare!" Zale exclaimed. "Carla will kill you if you die."

"She needs you, not me," Badrick said. "Do me a favour, you idiot. Both of you. Stop pretending." He started coughing again, and had to wait until it subsided. "Everyone already knows what you want."

He could feel time running out, so he coughed and tried to speak faster. "Listen . . . You guys have shown . . . shown me a life where I actually had purpose. Thank you, Zale.

"But it's time to let me go."

He sounded braver than he felt.

In reality he was terrified. There was no way to know what would happen when he lost consciousness.

But he didn't want to upset Zale.

He didn't want his partner to return to Carla with the memory of him freaking out.

So, despite his terror, he simply sighed and said, "We did what we had to do. Later . . . buddy."

Darkness began to crawl over his thoughts. It scratched at his mind, deleting memories, personality . . . everything that made him who he was . . . erased.

He saw Zale smacking the dirt in fury as his eyes closed.

And for the final time the all consuming blackness devoured him.

chapter
TWENTY FOUR

Zale didn't leave Badrick's side for many hours after his passing. He sat there, studying his dead partner.

He didn't even feel angry anymore. Or even sad.

He felt resigned.

He'd lost another friend.

Another one to the evil of Lucikefer.

He wanted to be happy the son of a bitch was dead.

But he didn't even have *that* luxury.

As he sat there, he went over everything that had happened. Mused on what could have been different, what he might have done differently.

Maybe if he hadn't been clever enough to realise Vulrick was actually Daemnos, then it would have changed the outcome. He would never have allowed Badrick to go on his own.

What killed his ability to feel the most was that he now understood Lucikefer's plan entirely. Knowing he'd gotten it wrong all these years just spiralled him into a pit of numbness.

Everything that happened today clicked it all into place for him.

Lucikefer *knew* Daemnos was in an Enthraller, but he didn't know who he was—Daemnos had been disguised.

The time travelling trick hadn't been to find someone who knew where Daemnos was hiding, it was to find Daemnos' Enthraller.

They'd never realised this because the bastard ascended to Badrick in secret, somehow masking the unique energy he was supposed to generate upon arriving on Earth.

The functions of the time travelling power meant that Zale had been sent to the correct Enthraller, whoever he was, and then Lucikefer would find Daemnos that way.

After his failure to get anything out of Zale, who was nothing more than the first candidate he came across, Daemnos remained unfound and Badrick safe.

Lucikefer never realised Badrick was his quarry, because he thought Vulrick was his demon, having never heard the Daemonium Council talking in secret about how Badrick had been the result of his efforts four years before.

If he had, Lucikefer would have realised Vulrick was a fake, and actually Daemnos in disguise.

Sighing, Zale put his hands on his face—or at least he tried to; his helmet prevented him from making contact.

He was going to remove it . . .

But then he felt a power surge.

A tiny flicker.

Off to his right.

Zale jumped up and glanced over.

He instantly knew what the energy meant.

Someone had survived.

And it hadn't been Badrick.

A white hot rage the likes of which he'd never felt before consumed his consciousness. Zale bared his teeth like some kind of animal.

The desire—nay, it was a *need*—to kill the one running away like the coward he was was all consuming. It engulfed him like smoke, darkening his soul and corrupting his mind.

He should have been worried.

This was not normal.

But right then he didn't care.

He hissed dangerously, whispering, "This isn't over."

He took a step forward, pushing his demonic senses out into the world, detecting where the coward had fled.

As he did so he caught his reflection in a puddle of water that had surfaced due to Badrick's overwhelming power.

The water was clear, and he could see himself without difficulty.

There was something very wrong.

Again, he didn't care.

He should have been terrified.

He wasn't.

Zale glared at his reflection, almost enjoying what looked back at him. It was a simple thing. Something most would never consider. But he knew it meant something.

It meant he was powerful.

Unstoppable.

The Zale that looked back at him was not the Zale he remembered.

He looked aggressive, dangerous, volatile.

And most of all . . .

His visor was no longer blue.

It was black.

And some final words:

As this book is self published and I lack the advertising and marketing budget of more traditionally published books, my main form of advertising comes from you guys (the readers).

So please, if you liked, loved, hated, despised or felt/thought anything about this book at all, leave me a review and let me and others know what you thought.

For more immediate updates on new releases and works in progress you can follow me on:

http://www.facebook.com/JavscoBooks

or

http://www.wattpad.com/user/Josh_Brookes

CONTINUE THE SERIES:

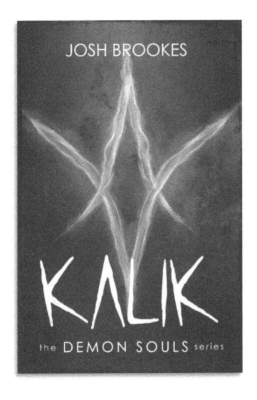

JOSH BROOKES

KALIK

the DEMON SOULS series

Overcome with rage, Zale abandons the Daemonium to pursue revenge against Lucikefer.

However, the threat of the Royal is overshadowed by the emergence of a far darker and more powerful force.

With an army under their command, this new darkness begins a reign of terror only the Daemonium can stop.

Daemnos was just the beginning . . .